Physics and Metaphysics

Physics and Philosophy

Physics and Metaphysics
Theories of Space and Time

Jennifer Trusted

London and New York

First published 1991
by Routledge
11 New Fetter Lane, London EC4P 4EE

Simultaneously published in the USA and Canada
by Routledge
a division of Routledge, Chapman and Hall, Inc.
29 West 35th Street, New York, NY 10001

© 1991 Jennifer Trusted

Typeset in 10/12 pt Times by
Redwood Press Limited, Wiltshire,
Printed in Great Britain by
Redwood Press Limited

British Library Cataloguing in Publication Data
Trusted, Jennifer
  Physics and metaphysics.
  1. Science
  I. Title
  500

  ISBN 0–415–05948–8

Library of Congress Cataloging in Publication Data
Trusted, Jennifer.
  Physics and metaphysics: theories of space and time /
Jennifer Trusted.
     p. cm.
  Includes bibliographical references and index.
  ISBN 0–415–05948–8
  1. Space and time—History.   2. Philosophy and
science—History.   3. Religion and science—History.
  4. Metaphysics—History.
  I. Title.
BD632.T78   1991
113—dc20   90–46821   CIP

Contents

Acknowledgements

I first became interested in the relation between science and meta-physics when teaching the two 'Science and Belief' courses AMST283 and A381 for the Open University and I am particularly grateful to the members of the course teams and for the interesting extracts that they compiled for the Anthologies associated with those courses. In addition I should like to thank Professor D. J. O'Connor for advice on background reading and Dr. W. G. V. Rosser for help in discussions about relativity theory and for lending me papers and books on this subject and on the development of Einstein's ideas. I should also like to thank Mr Martin Davies for kindly reading through the manuscript and for invaluable suggestions as to explication and style.

Jennifer Trusted
Exeter
September 1990

Preface
What is metaphysics?

As used by Aristotle the word 'metaphysics' meant 'beyond physics', that is beyond the scope of physical science. The various senses in which the word is used today all carry something of Aristotle's meaning in that they all imply theories, presuppositions or beliefs that cannot be established by direct scientific inquiry and appeal to sense experience. However it does not follow that because this is so metaphysics is irrelevant or unimportant to science. In this book I hope to show that metaphysical theories are not only not irrelevant, they are absolutely essential to scientific inquiry.

To maintain this view it is necessary to offer a brief indication of the significance that the word 'metaphysics' has for us today. The account given below does not purport to be exhaustive but it does show the range of meanings that bear on my thesis. In my text the references to metaphysics and metaphysical theories may be regarded as references to different aspects of metaphysics under one of three headings which I shall call speculative conjecture, basic presupposition and mystical belief. The distinction between the three is somewhat arbitrary for there can be no strict demarcation. Thus though speculative conjectures may become empirical theories they may also acquire the status of fundamental presuppositions; mystical beliefs may come to be dismissed as nonsense but they too may be accepted as fundamental presuppositions. Nevertheless classification can be helpful in assessing the different roles of metaphysical theories.

The first aspect, speculative conjecture, might be called the Popperian aspect. Popper argues that speculative conjectures about the world are metaphysical theories if they cannot satisfy his test of falsifiability.[1] He hold that this test provides the criterion of demarcation between empirical scientific theories and metaphysical theories. However he is at pains to stress that these metaphysical theories are not meaningless or nonsensical; they can be *genuine conjectures –*

highly informative guesses about the world'.[2] Democritus' atomic theory that matter is composed of minute indivisible particles and Descartes's theory of matter as a continuum may both be regarded as Popperian conjectures. Neither theory can be refuted (or indeed verified) by appeal to observation but they were genuine conjectures as to the physical nature of the world and both have directly stimulated scientific inquiry. We shall encounter other conjectures of this sort: for example Copernicus's conjecture that the cosmos was too large for stellar parallax to be detected[3] and Newton's theory of inertial motion, i.e. that change of velocity demands an applied force.[4] The former is no longer a metaphysical theory because it has been established on the basis of observation; the latter can be taken as a methodological rule but it is also a fundamental presupposition of classical physics.

This brings us to the second aspect, metaphysical theories as basic presuppositions about the nature of the world. Some of these presuppositions are so fundamental that we do not seriously question them: for example that there are physical objects and that there are causal relations. These are what Russell has called *instinctive beliefs*.[5] However not all fundamental presuppositions arise instinctively. For example Newton's law of inertia (referred to above) and Einstein's definition of *simultaneity*[6] were the result of much thought and have been carefully formulated.

Fundamental presuppositions are necessary to provide a framework whereby we interpret our sense experiences and give factual descriptions of the world. Theory *precedes* facts and it is important to appreciate that what we call facts are not the raw data delivered to the senses; facts emerge as a result of complex, though largely unconscious, organization of that data. As Whewell said 'A Fact is a combination of our Thoughts with Things'[7] and 'In a Fact, the Ideas are applied so readily and familiarly and incorporated with the sensations so entirely, that we do not see *them* we see *through* them.'[8] We have to depend on some presuppositions in order to *establish* empirical facts and to describe the world around us in terms of objects and events.[9]

All facts emerge from theories, and this is the point where we approach the third aspect of metaphysics, the mystical beliefs which do not purport to offer physical descriptions but which claim to show a greater reality beyond sense experience. Examples are: that there is an ultimate purpose in the construction of the universe and in natural events, that the material world is but a pale shadow of an ultimate non-material reality, that matter is the ultimate reality, a that there is life after death; that events are predetermined, that human beings are free to choose their course of action. Religious beliefs in the existence of a personal or impersonal God or gods are also examples of this kind of metaphysical belief.

It is this third aspect of metaphysics which predominates in claims that metaphysics can lead to transcendental truths and it is this aspect which positivists and logical positivists find especially suspect. More than a century earlier it had been dismissed by Hume; of metaphysics he said 'Commit it then to the flames: for it can contain nothing but sophistry and illusion.'[10]

I suggest that mystical metaphysical (including religious) beliefs are not so nonsensical and useless as Hume and the positivists have claimed. This is partly because it is not possible to detach them entirely from speculative theories and physical presuppositions, but also because, as my text will show, mystical and religious beliefs have clearly motivated and inspired many of those who have sought to understand and to explain the physical world. All science presupposes some metaphysical system of beliefs, and mystical beliefs have been an important part of most systems.

In this book we shall be considering the relation between scientific inquiry and all three aspects of metaphysics in Western Europe from mid-eleventh to mid-twentieth century. Much of the early chapters will be devoted to the influence of the Christian religion; in later chapters there is more emphasis on the importance of philosophical presuppositions. However the influence of religion, and of the Christian Church in particular, should not be underrated even in times near to our own. There is more to the relation between religious faith and scientific inquiry than the apparently contingent fact that many scientists have been motivated by their religion and that some Christian clergy have been scientists. Certain fundamental tenets of Christian doctrine support presuppositions that have been, and still are, of prime importance for science. Thus the mystical belief that an omnipotent God created the world and maintains the smooth running of the cosmos supports the presupposition that there is an orderly succession of events which may be accounted for in terms of causal laws; the belief that God is infinitely good supports the further belief that He would not deceive mankind and this supports the presupposition that human sense experiences can give reliable information about the created world; the belief that God created Man in His own image supports the further belief that human beings are capable of reasoning from sense experience and are capable of discovering the causal laws ordained by God.

Indeed some writers have gone further than this: in his book *The Road to Science and the Ways to God*, Stanley L. Jaki argues that the historical facts show that Christian theism has been essential for the development of modern science. He points out that there were the beginnings of scientific inquiry and imaginative speculation in Ancient Greece, in China and in India but that science, as we now conceive it, did not develop. Others cited by Jaki, such as Whitehead in *Science and the Modern World* and Needham in *Science and Civilisation in China*, have suggested that at least some form of theistic belief was necessary because there had to be an assurance of the existence of a rational Lawgiver or Creator who had made a world that was understandable. Today our beliefs about rational cosmic design, about order in nature and about the status of causal relations may be complex and hedged with qualifications. They are not necessarily dependent on religious faith, let alone Christianity. But we have to accept that in earlier times, perhaps even into the twentieth century, the dependence of science on belief in a rational and consistent God has to be seriously assessed.

I very strongly advise readers to study the numerous quotations, and especially those of early philosophers. For when we try to understand the ideas and purposes of those who lived so long ago we are inevitably affected by subsequent ideas and events and what is presented is therefore inevitably distorted. At least direct study of their writings involves only one distorting medium (the reader), whereas study of contemporary comments involves a double distortion. I have tried to present views fairly but by reading quotations readers will be in a position to criticize my interpretations and perhaps come closer to the truth. We all need to bear Hartley's words in mind:

The past is a foreign country; they do things differently there.[11]

1 The ordered cosmos

Primitive religion and primitive science

From very early times human beings must have been aware of cycles of events and would have had expectations based on past experiences. But they would also have appreciated that often their expectations were not fulfilled. Hence beliefs in orderly sequences in the world about them were modified by beliefs that the course of nature was subject to the wishes and decrees of capricious and possibly malevolent spirits, so that explanations of the unusual or the unexpected presupposed their intervention. But though the spirits were thought to have superhuman powers they were credited with human appetites and emotions and therefore they might be influenced by entreaty and by flattery: with suitable propitiation ceremonies mankind might hope to have some control, albeit indirect control, over events. Thus early ideas about the world and primitive attempts to influence the course of nature were intimately involved with religion and with religious rites. Even the much more sophisticated theories and practices of Ancient Egypt, Babylon, India, China and Ancient Greece and Ancient Rome were profoundly influenced by religion, and in all countries ultimate explanations of events were in terms of the desires and purposes of the gods.

Today we do not base our scientific explanations on appeals to divine plans and purposes. Our attitude to the roles of metaphysical and religious beliefs has changed, and for many of us these beliefs are thought to be not only irrelevant but dangerous. They are regarded as impediments to the scientific search for objective knowledge of nature.

In this book we shall be considering whether that view is justified. We shall study the influence of religion and metaphysics on methods of inquiry and on the interpretation of observation. We shall also see how scientifc theories (natural philosophy) have, in their turn, influenced metaphysical assumptions and religious beliefs. We may conclude that objective facts, interpretative theories, metaphysical assumptions and religious faith are too closely connected to be separated, and that explanations of natural events depend as much on appeal to metaphysical beliefs as they did for our ancestors.

Primarily we shall be concerned with speculations about the nature and origin of the cosmos (cosmology and cosmogony) and the development of theories of motion, of force and of energy. We begin with the Middle Ages because, although there was what we now call scientific inquiry long before that time, much work had been lost to Western Europe and what was effectively a fresh start had to be made. The rebirth of learning, stimulated by the re-emergence of classical texts, began in about AD 1000; it has been called 'the Little Renaissance'.

The Little Renaissance was largely a result of the introduction of Arab writings into Western Europe. The Arabs had surged westward, across North Africa and into Spain in the eighth century but the work of Arabian scholars, including Arabian transcriptions of many classical texts, remained inaccessible until their armies were halted and were no longer regarded as a threat to Christendom. By the twelfth century the situation was stable and Christian priests, monks and friars were free to travel to Spain and to Sicily where they were able to study the texts and to translate them into Latin.

Christian scholasticism

A cornucopia of manuscripts awaited the scholars. There was an abundance of material, but it was largely disorganized; the riches of Ancient Greece and Arabia were amassed haphazardly and in uncatalogued collections. In order to be assimilated they had first to be translated and then sorted and classified. Attempts to date the texts had to be made; the inevitable errors of hand copying (the printing press was still to come) had to be detected as errors; inconsistencies within texts and between texts had to be discussed. The priests then had to assess the rediscovered pagan manuscripts in the light of their own Holy Scriptures and the writings of the Church Fathers (the Patristic writings). These were held to be inspired by God so, if the newly discovered philosophies were sound, they would inevitably be in accord with the Scriptures and the Patristic writings. Hence it is not surprising that careful study of texts, diligent annotation of sources and detailed discussion of interpretations were held to be of major importance.

The aim was to establish a reputable body of material, reputable because documented and authenticated, which would serve as an authoritative source of knowledge. To us reliance on 'authority', and *a fortiori* the authority of ancient sages, seems to be the very antithesis of philosophical speculation and scientific inquiry. Yet we must admit that any investigation has to be based on a reliable body of accepted facts and theories. The early Schoolmen had no base apart from the Scriptures and the Patristic writings, and therefore they had to use these to judge the new material. Once established, the new texts could themselves become 'authorities', and the source of definitive statements that might be used as premisses in logical arguments.

As we shall see the Schoolmen greatly valued deductive logic for they appreciated that conclusions derived from valid logical arguments would necessarily have the same standing as the authoritative premisses from which they were deduced. It was the Schoolmen's strict adherence to texts and to deduction, their very pedantry, that eventually was to lead to the firm belief that human beings were capable of understanding the world and of finding rational explanations of the course of events.

But that conviction was to come later, for in medieval times a mere mortal presuming to aspire to full understanding of God's creation would have been held guilty of a deadly sin, the sin of pride. As compared with God's powers, human capacities were thought to be insignificant. It was held that ultimate truths about the world God had created could not be discovered by the unaided human mind; if any were known they would have been vouchsafed to Man through divine revelation. It was for this reason that medieval scholars held the truths of faith to be far superior to the truths of reason though, since both came from God (the former directly, the latter indirectly), they could not contradict each other. The Schoolmen held that knowledge of the natural world, what we should now call 'scientific knowledge' but which they termed 'natural philosophy' was part of Christian philosophy and was not to be separated from it.

Natural philosophy as part of Christian philosophy

The early Church Fathers had been suspicious of inquiry into the natural world. St Basil (330–79) had said:

> Grand phenomena do not strike us the less when we have discovered something of their wonderful mechanism . . . let us prefer the simplicity of faith to the demonstrations of reason.[1]

and St Augustine (354–430), though taking an interest in natural philosophy, regarded it as totally subservient to religion and to faith:

> For the Christian, it is enough to believe that the cause of all created things, whether in heaven or on earth, whether visible or invisible, is nothing other than the goodness of the Creator, who is the one and true God.[2]

However, the Fathers did concede that Christian teaching was about the world as well as about salvation; God had created the world and study of the world might lead to a deeper reverence for God's Creation and to a fuller understanding of the Scriptures. There was, therefore, a subsidiary place for natural philosophy; if studied wisely it might serve as the handmaiden of theology. St Bonaventura (*c.* 1217–74) followed St Augustine in stressing that empirical knowledge was not to be pursued for its own sake but in order to stengthen faith and to honour God. As Grant says:

> the study of nature and its laws was not an end in itself, pursued merely for the sake of knowledge; it had to serve the higher need of religion and theology. Under these circumstances the secular sciences could hardly avoid the status of handmaidens.[3]

The universities

The earliest universities were founded in the Middle Ages; they were established in order to maintain the scholastic religious tradition and all university teachers were in Holy Orders. Some of the universities were Church foundations in which the students and masters formed a closed corporation under a Chancellor, as at Pisa, at Oxford and at Cambridge; there were also civic universities in which students elected a rector who governed them, as at Bologna; and there were state universities founded by a monarch (with papal approval) as at Naples. Everywhere instruction was in Latin.

Not surprisingly, theology was considered to be the queen of subjects reigning over the seven liberal arts: grammar, dialectic and rhetoric (the trivium) and geometry, arithmetic, astronomy and music (the quadrivium). Music meant study of a half-mystical doctrine of numbers, related to Pythagorean philosophy; geometry consisted of the Euclidean axioms and common notions followed by a series of theorems; arithmetic and astronomy were valued chiefly because they showed how to establish the date of Easter. These last two subjects were effectively one for astronomy was primarily a mathematical discipline and mathematicians were also astronomers. Arithmetical calculations were very complicated because Roman numerals were used; our present decimal notation was not introduced until the fourteenth century and it was not generally adopted until the seventeenth century.

Students looked to their mentors for guidance; guidance as to what to read and guidance in interpreting the 'authorities' who were held to be the source of all truth obtainable through human effort. One could pray for divine revelation but it would be impious to doubt the authorities or to seek to advance beyond their teaching. The authorities had demonstrated that the entire cosmos had been created in full perfection and therefore would not develop or change. Hence the universe was seen as being essentially static, subject only to harmonious cycles of events. True there was some confusion on earth due to Man's free will and his moral weakness, and because of the less conscious strivings of lower forms of life, moreover God might very occasionally intervene by performing a miracle. But such confusion and the rare miraculous intervention were superficial. God had fashioned the cosmos out of chaos and the frame of nature would remain essentially unchanged until the Day of judgement. However, though the philosophy of the Schoolmen was unsympathetic to critical inquiry, their view of God as perfect and unchanging and of His Creation as perfect and orderly, encouraged explanation in terms of regularities rather than in terms of divine caprice.

We need to bear in mind that the new learning was the concern of a tiny élite. Almost the only literate people were priests and only a small proportion of them devoted themselves to reading ancient texts and discussing interpretations of the Fathers and the Scriptures. These scholars, the Schoolmen, were very conscious of their position; they tended to regard the majority of mankind as beings incapable of intellectual pursuits who must remain irredeemably ignorant.

Because knowledge was confined to a select few it was, in one sense, arcane and closed. But in another sense, because there was much logical analysis, it was open, much more open than it was to become in the fifteenth and sixteenth centuries. Basic premisses were not criticized but arguments were. Funkenstein says:

> Medieval schoolmen, at least since the thirteenth century, were intoxicated by the idea of strict proofs, and their knowledge was an open one within the confines of those permitted to participate in its administration; it was, so to say, open horizontally, but closed vertically.[4]

The respect for logic

The Schoolmen were devoted to deductive logic which, for them, was syllogistic reasoning. A syllogism consists of three statements: two that constitute the premisses, and a third that is the conclusion. All the statements affirm or deny the attribution of individuals or groups to classes. If the syllogism is valid the attribution made in the conclusion will follow necessarily from the attributions made in the premisses. For example:

All men are mortal	Major premiss
Socrates is a man	Minor premiss
....	
Socrates is mortal	Conclusion

This is a valid syllogism and therefore the conclusion follows necessarily from the premisses.

But not all syllogisms are valid; for example:

All men are mortal	Major premiss
All animals are mortal	Minor premiss
....	
All men are animals	Conclusion

Of course we accept this conclusion as true but it does *not* follow from the premisses and therefore it is not *established by* the premisses. A valid argument *must* lead to a true conclusion if its premisses are true but an invalid argument may lead to a true or to a false conclusion. As Aristotle (382–322 BC) had stressed centuries before, it is important to distinguish validity from truth. Medieval scholars greatly admired Aristotle's exposition and they used his analysis to construct a code for different types of syllogisms and to classify valid and invalid syllogisms.

Yet Aristotle's writings had not been unreservedly welcomed when they were first rediscovered. In the tenth, eleventh and twelfth centuries the Church establishment considered them dangerous because they appeared to deny the individual immortality of human souls. This interpretation was confirmed by the Muslim philosopher Averroes (1126–98), and those scholars who debated Aristotelian philosophy in the universities (for example Peter Abelard (1079–1144)) were regarded with suspicion and risked being accused of heresy. That view was to change dramatically in the thirteenth century after St Thomas Aquinas (1224–74) had offered another interpretation. He succeeded in persuading the Church that Averroes had been mistaken and that Aristotle had not denied individual immortality. Thereafter the philosophy was whole-heartedly accepted and became part of Christian doctrine. Indeed it became heretical to question or to criticize any part of it.

The practice of natural philosophy

For the Schoolmen the practice of natural philosophy consisted largely in contemplative study of the natural world together with examination of the Scriptures and ancient texts. They believed that such study would reveal God's concern for mankind and would also help to reveal His purposes. In accord with early views (see p. 62) and also in accord with Aristotle's exposition of causation, medieval scholars held that satisfactory explanations of events had to be in terms of purpose, that is they had to be teleological explanations. They did not entertain our present-day view of scientific explanations in terms of prior physical events and causal laws. Medieval natural philosophy differed from modern science in another way: study of events was not separated from other studies – ethics, theology and metaphysics. The Schoolmen thought that natural philosophy was concerned not only with the material world but also with Man's role in that world and with his relation with God.

> The world of the intellect thus had a unity in antiquity that it does not have today. It was not sharply divisible into separate disciplines, such as metaphysics, theology, epistemology, ethics, natural science, and mathematics, but presented itself as a relatively unified and coherent whole.[5]

The holistic view of natural knowledge arose because all creation was believed to be a unity – the work of one God. For medieval thinkers it was axiomatic that human beings were God's favoured creatures and that God had made the earth and all it contained for their benefit. Nevertheless, because the Creation was a unity, man could not be isolated from nature.

Analogy: macrocosm and microcosm

Medieval philosophers argued that an effect must resemble its cause and, since God was the ultimate cause of everything, the entire cosmos must bear traces of the divine hand. Moreover, just because everything must show some sign of being God's work, everything must have some resemblance to everything else. The resemblance was not the overt resemblance of a simple copy, as a portrait might resemble the sitter; it was rather the resemblance displayed by all portraits painted by the same painter.

Hence arose the doctrine that Man, the microcosm, resembled the universe, the macrocosm; both must show that they were fashioned by the divine artificer. In the Middle Ages, and also in later times, the doctrine was used to explain natural events and also to assess philosophical (scientific) theories and discoveries. For example, in the seventeenth century we have the astronomer Francesco Sizi offering the following argument to show why, contrary to Galileo's claim, the planet Jupiter could have no satellites:

> There are seven windows in the head, two nostrils, two ears, two eyes and a mouth; so in the heavens there are two favourable stars, two unpropitious, two luminaries, and Mercury alone undecided and indifferent. From which and many other similar phenomena of nature such as the seven metals etc., which it were tedious to enumerate, we gather that the number of planets is necessarily seven. . . . Moreover, the satellites are invisible to the naked eye and therefore have no influence on the earth and therefore do not exist.[6]

The microcosm/macrocosm analogy was used by scientists we still respect today, for example William Harvey:

> The heart is the beginning of life; the sun of the microcosm, even as the sun in his turn might well be designated the heart of the world; for it is the heart by whose virtue and pulse the blood is moved, perfected, made apt to nourish, and is preserved from corruption and coagulation; it is the household divinity which, discharging its function, nourishes, cherishes, quickens the whole body, and is indeed the foundation of life, the source of all action.[7]

It may be that Harvey hoped that this argument would be especially effective in persuading diehard conservatives to accept his theory that the heart pumped blood round the body but he too must have taken it seriously.

Macrocosm/microcosm arguments lost their force soon after Harvey's day. They failed to persuade when there was no longer a belief in a divine artificer fashioning the cosmos as a potter models clay or a sculptor carves marble. But arguments from analogy have been and continue to be used not only to help in the understanding of scientific theories but also to help in substantiating them. For example the analogy of heat flow with liquid flow was used in the eighteenth century to develop theories of heat transfer; the analogy of light waves with water waves was used in the nineteenth century to explain the transmission of light; the analogy of packets of energy with bullets was used in the twentieth century to develop quantum theory. Indeed the microcosm/macrocosm analogy returned in secular form with the comparison of the Bohr atom with the solar system.

Particular concerns of medieval philosophy

Though natural philosophy was not separated from other fields, and *a fortiori* was not compartmentalized into the branches of science we know today, certain phenomena, the behaviour of light and the nature of motion, were of especial interest. There was also much attention devoted to cosmology, not only because it was concerned with God's Creation but also because it was closely related to Church affairs.

Medieval physics: light

It was held that sunlight illuminated the world just as spiritual light illuminated the mind and soul of Man[8] and since knowledge of truths came directly from illumination by the divine light, i.e. by revelation, it was believed that the study of physical light from the sun might also illuminate the mind. In addition it so happens that reflection and refraction of light can be portrayed in geometrical diagrams that are amenable to mathematical treatment. For these two reasons optics was a favoured field of study.

The Arabs had studied light and their work was known to two British philosophers, Robert Grosseteste (1170–1235) and Roger Bacon (1214–94). Grosseteste was an influential Franciscan who became Chancellor of Oxford University and then bishop of Lincoln; he had access to works – for example the writings of Aristotle – that would have been thought too dangerous for lesser people. He was one of the first Schoolmen to advocate direct observation and experiment and he followed Aristotle in maintaining that inquiry was not just a matter of finding facts; it entailed seeking the reason for the facts.

Bacon also made some direct observations; he described the magnifying effect of a convex lens and is credited with the invention of spectacles. From his reading of the Arabian philosopher Alhazen (died 1093) he probably had the idea that it might be possible to use a lens or lens system to get a better view of the heavenly bodies, the stars and the planets. But this was nothing more than speculation and telescopes were not made until the seventeenth century. Bacon had interests outside the study of light; for example Columbus was influenced by his writings on geography. He was ahead of his time in daring to criticize authority, even the authority of Aristotle. We shall consider some of his views and opinions in the next chapter.

Medieval physics: motion

Aristotle's account of motion was intimately bound up with his cosmology and his views about the nature of material bodies. He held that all such bodies were composed of some or all of the four elements: earth, air, fire and water in varying proportions. These four elements sought their proper positions according to their gravity so that earth and water would naturally tend to sink downwards, whilst air and fire would naturally tend to rise upwards. The direction of motion of any given body would depend on its constitution, that is the elements in it and their proportions, but, without any extraneous force, movement would only be vertically up or down. He said that in their eagerness to reach their rightful places, falling objects would gain speed as they fell and the more dense they were the faster would they fall.

Aristotle said that other sorts of motion, such as the raising of a dense body, restraining the rise of a low-density body, and any form of horizontal movement, were unnatural; therefore they could only occur if there were some propelling agent in contact with the moving body. His view required a special explanation of the movement of projectiles for they seemed to fly through the air without the help of a propelling agent. Aristotle's explanation was that the air in front of a projectile, which was pushed aside by the initial thrust, moved to fill the space that would otherwise form at the rear as the projectile moved forward; therefore extra thrust was added and the motion maintained. He argued that the air had to move in this way in order to prevent a vacuum forming; it was an Aristotelian axiom that nature abhorred a vacuum.

Aristotle's physics is in complete accord with common-sense observation: we see that dense objects fall of their own accord and that low-density objects naturally rise. In our experience very dense objects do fall faster than those that are less dense; the coin does fall faster than the feather.[9] We also know that some propelling agent is needed if bodies are to be moved horizontally and that the push or pull must continue if motion is to be maintained. We can sense the thrust given to an object we throw into the air and we can appreciate that the air ahead must be displaced. We may have observed that if air is removed from a container the sides will collapse inwards so that a vacuum is not obtained. There is little doubt that most of us would accept Aristotle's account of motion if we were unaware of subsequent criticism and of alternative explanations.

Medieval cosmology

From the fourteenth century the accepted cosmology was Aristotle's cosmology. It had needed little modification to be compatible with Christian teaching[10] and had indeed led to an elaboration of the Christian view of a harmonious and hierarchical Creation presided over by God and ministered by His angels.

The cosmos was thought to be closed and finite. It was held to consist of a series of revolving concentric spheres with the immobile earth at the centre. The moon was embedded in the innermost sphere and surrounding it were the spheres of the sun and each of the known planets (Mercury, Venus, Mars, Saturn and Jupiter). Beyond these seven spheres was another carrying all the fixed stars. Aristotle was aware that there was no record of the stars changing their positions *relative to each other*; he envisaged their being permanently attached in the eighth sphere.

As we have seen, Aristotle believed that on earth the natural motion was vertical motion but this was not so in the heavens. He said that above the sphere of the moon all was different; here there was no ordinary matter, composed of the four elements, but all bodies were made of a perfect and unchanging fifth element, the *quintessence*. In addition their natural motion was circular motion. Thus the celestial spheres revolved in circles and the sun, moon and planets moved in complex circles within their spheres. Aristotle's account was developed further by later Ancient Greek astronomers and in AD 150, or thereabouts, Claudius Ptolemy (90–168) constructed an astronomical table, the *Almagest*, which provided a basis for predicting the positions of the planets in the sky. The *Almagest* was used for navigating, for predicting eclipses, for calculating the dates of the equinoxes and the date of Easter.

For medieval interpreters Aristotle's cosmology had a religious significance that went far beyond its use in giving the date of Easter. They regarded the system of spheres as a heavenly hierarchy. Aristotle's ninth sphere, the sphere of the unmoved mover was, for them, the sphere of God in glory. Though they believed that God was ultimately responsible for the heavenly revolutions the spheres were thought to be directly governed by angels. In the *Paradise* of his *Divine Comedy* Dante (1265–1313) describes his ascension to higher and yet more blessed spheres; for though they were all heavenly, the higher spheres were nearer perfection. The ninth sphere, the sphere of God, was absolute perfection. Thus the heavens were a harmonious hierarchy, a magnificent order in which all beings, angels and men, had their right and proper places.

It was believed that though the heavens seemed silent to sinful humanity, in Paradise those who were saved would hear, with God and his angels, the glorious music of the spheres. This vision of the cosmos inspired artists, poets and philosophers throughout the Middle Ages and even into the seventeenth century. In the passage from Dryden (1631–1700) quoted below there is reference to the four qualities: cold, hot, moist and dry, which characterized the four Aristotelian elements. Earth was dry and cold; fire was dry and hot; water was moist and cold; air was moist and hot. In the seventeenth century the allusions in the poem would not have had to be explained.

> From harmony, from heavenly harmony,
>   This universal frame began:
> When nature underneath a heap
>   Of jarring atoms lay,
>   And could not heave her head,
> The tuneful voice was heard from high,
>   'Arise, ye more than dead!'
> Then cold, and hot, and moist, and dry,
>   In order to their stations leap,
>   And Music's power obey.
> From harmony, from heavenly harmony,
>   This universal frame began:
>   From harmony to harmony
> Through all the compass of the notes it ran,
> The diapason closing full on Man.
>
> As from the power of sacred lays
>   The spheres began to move,
> And sang the great Creator's praise
>   To all the Blest above;
> So when the last and dreadful hour
> This crumbling pageant shall devour,
> The trumpet shall be heard on high,
> The dead shall live, the living die,
> And music shall untune the sky![11]

Dryden's readers would not have taken his poem literally, but a hundred years earlier, in the sixteenth century, it was still generally believed that the earth was at the centre of the universe and that the heavenly bodies were carried in their spheres. Thus in *The Merchant of Venice* the young lover, Lorenzo, says to his bride Jessica:

> Look how the floor of heaven
> Is thick inlaid with patines of bright gold:
> There's not the smallest orb which thou behold'st
> But in his motion like an angel sings,
> Still quiring to the young-eyed cherubims;
> Such harmony is in immortal souls;
> But whilst this muddy vesture of decay
> Doth grossly close it in, we cannot hear it.[12]

In Shakespearian times this picture of the cosmos was just beginning to be questioned but in the Middle Ages it was the sober scientific truth; the majestic hierarchy of the heavens and the orderly procession of the heavenly bodies was taken as an established fact. It was supported by Holy Writ and the authorities and by common-sense observation. After all, to us today the earth, solid and firm, does seem motionless and does *appear* to be circled by the stars and the planets. Bearing in mind that there was no other evidence save that which could be seen Aristotle presented an eminently acceptable account of the cosmos. It is true that his cosmology then became intimately bound up with Christian belief but that in itself did not entail that it was wrong. At the time, of course, the apparent interdependence of cosmology and religious belief was held to prove that the Aristotelian system was necessarily correct.

It cannot be too much stressed that in the Middle Ages natural philosophers regarded inquiry as entirely subservient to faith. As indicated above (p. 9) the most reliable knowledge was thought to come through direct revelation and the second most reliable source was the testimony of the Scriptures, followed by the Patristic writings. If there is a sincere and profound belief that the Christian God, as revealed in the Bible, is the source of all truth then it is entirely rational, and certainly not 'unscientific', to accept the support offered by Holy Writ. Such an attitude is not unique to the Middle Ages; until the eighteenth century it was generally thought that the Bible did give an account of nature and that any scientific discovery or theory must necessarily be compatible with it. Today, apart from Fundamentalists,[13] people no longer think that the Scriptures are to be regarded as giving a scientific or factual account of the world. However, as we shall see, our present interpretations of observation, and our assessment of their significance in relation to our scientific theories, are still influenced by metaphysical if not religious beliefs. We are inevitably affected by current social customs and assumptions that correspond to the earlier influence of the Church. Posterity may find these as irrelevant as we find medieval religious beliefs and Church doctrines but Posterity will have its own dogma.

Medieval beliefs

The unquestioned presuppositions of medieval times were as follows:

1 God was the Creator of the cosmos.
2 The cosmos was a closed and finite ordered system maintained by God's care.
3 All created things showed their divine origins.
4 Man the microcosm reflected the universe, the macrocosm.
5 Man was of prime importance, being made in God's own image.
6 Man's first duty was to glorify God and to aspire to a state of grace in order to worship God in heaven in the life to come.
7 Inquiry into the nature of the world and the causes of events was relatively unimportant; but since it might help reveal God's purposes and, through showing His works, enhance Man's reverence, it could have some limited support from the Church.
8 The Church was absolute judge of all truth.
9 Knowledge could be acquired by:
    (a) direct revelation (the divine light);
    (b) by appeal to Authority;
    (c) by syllogistic argument (the light of reason);
    (d) through observation (a poor fourth).
10 Any satisfactory explanation, and all final explanations, had to be teleological explanations.

Dante's *Paradiso* illustrates the medieval world picture supremely well; the lines quoted below show how religious and metaphysical beliefs combine with philosophy in the medieval account of the cosmos. The reference to 'form' and 'matter' which would have been fully understood by Dante's readers, relates to Aristotle's account of the nature of material substances: their passive matter (a mere potentiality) had to be actualized by form. The 'three-stringed bow' is Dante's simile of God's creation of material substances, when both matter and form emerged.[14] Medieval scholars held that the angels were purely spiritual, they were without matter; they had achieved their full potential and were fully actualized as pure form, 'purest act'. But the created cosmos consisted of form and matter, 'pure potency and act', which were indissolubly joined, 'by bonds such as are never loosed'. Beatrice speaks:

> I tell, I do not ask,
> What you would know, for I have seen it there
> Wherein is centred every *where* and *when*
> Not for the sake of gaining for Himself,
> Which could not be, but that his creatures might
> Be able to shine back and say, *I am* –
> In His eternity, beyond all time,
> In His unbounded being, as He pleased,
> The Eternal Love on new loves showed Himself.
> Nor did He lie as it were asleep till then;
> For there was not 'before' or 'after' till
> God's spirit moved upon the waters' face.
> Then form and matter, separate and joined,
> Came into being that had no defect,
> Just like three arrows from a three-stringed bow.
> And as a ray of sunlight shines through glass
> Or amber or a piece of crystal, so
> That there is not an interval between
> Its entering and diffusion through the whole,
> So did the the whole threefold created world
> Spring into being from its Lord at once,
> And there was one beginning for it all.
> Order was concreated and inbuilt
> With substances, and highest in the world
> Were angels, since in them is purest act;
> Pure potency was in the lowest place;
> And, in between, pure potency and act
> Were joined by bonds such as are never loosed.[15]

It would need very cogent new evidence for such a system to be abandoned.

The position in 1300

There was absolute confidence that the immobile earth rested at the centre of a serene and hierarchical cosmos ruled by God and ministered by His angels[16], and that there would be no change in the divine order until the day of Judgement.

2 Old beliefs and new ideas

Roger Bacon

Throughout the Middle Ages the Scriptures and the Patristic writings were sacrosanct and could not be questioned, but some Schoolmen were prepared to look critically at classical writings. One of these was Roger Bacon. As we saw in the previous chapter both Bacon and Grosseteste had based their views, at least in part, on direct observation and both had made discoveries that supplemented Aristotelian physics. Bacon argued that classical writings should not be treated as setting absolute boundaries on what could be known. It was not that Bacon had no respect for Aristotle, or for other secular authorities, indeed he appealed to these authorities to support his contention that no one should rely solely on authority. Nevertheless he advocated a critical approach to established opinion and to established writings. He listed four kinds of impediments to the search for knowledge which are remarkably similar to those discussed by his equally famous namesake Francis Bacon, over three hundred years earlier; there is no evidence that the two were related. These impediments were:

1 Reliance on frail authority, though he stressed that he was not referring to Holy Writ.
2 The influence of custom and habit, 'the long duration of notions'.
3 The pressure of the opinions of the unlearned crowd – this seems to have referred to all his colleagues save for Grosseteste.
4 The temptation to conceal ignorance by a parade of complex terms and a display of apparent learning.

The impetus thory

Roger Bacon did not directly criticize Aristotle's physics but later, in the fourteenth century, various objections to Aristotle's theories about motion were raised. There was particular concern about his explanation of the motion of projectiles, namely that the air pushed aside by the head of a projectile in flight rushes to the rear in order to fill a potential vacuum, thereby maintaining the initial thrust (see p. 10). The explanation was suspect on two counts: firstly doubts were raised as to Aristotle's assertion that nature abhorred a vacuum. Secondly, it was argued that even if he were correct as to the impossibility of a vacuum, his account was still unsatisfactory because he had to postulate that air *helped* the motion of projectiles whereas, in other contexts, he asserted that air *impeded* motion. It was suggested that perhaps motion might be maintained, and even produced, without there being a propelling force directly in contact with the object. William of Occam (1300–49) cited movements caused by magnets acting on iron – the iron moves even though the magnet does not touch it – to show that there could be movement without physical contact between the body set in motion and the moving agent. He also pointed out that iron attracted by a magnet moved very slowly and there could be no question of the air in front being pushed vigorously aside and, with such slow motion, there was no possibility of a vacuum forming at the rear. Therefore, even if Aristotle were right, and nature did abhor a vacuum, there would be no need for air to rush to the back of the iron to fill the space; hence there would be no flow of air to supplement the original magnetic thrust.

At this time there could be criticism of Aristotle's physical theories without risk of censure from the Church, for though his physics was part of an established academic orthodoxy it was not directly related to Christian faith. Furthermore the Church was not unsympathetic to criticism of Aristotle's account of the flight of projectiles because his assertion that a vacuum was an impossibility seemed to limit the power of God. Therefore Occam felt free to revive the impetus theory of motion. The theory had first been proposed in the sixth century by an Alexandrian Greek named John Philoponus. He had suggested that God did not move the heavenly bodies directly but that He had set the spheres revolving by giving them an initial thrust, or impetus. This impetus did not decay with time. Philoponus said that human beings could give an impetus to earthly bodies, but, unlike the divine impetus, the motion imparted by humans died away. He compared impetus to heat in that, just as a hot body lost heat and so cooled, a moving body lost motion and so came to rest. Occam agreed with Philoponus that the impetus given by man would be transient whereas that given by God would be everlasting, and he pointed out that if this were assumed then there was no longer any need to postulate hierarchies of angels to direct the heavenly spheres. He laid down, as a metaphysical and methodological rule, the maxim 'it is vain to do with more what can be done with fewer' (Occam's razor): i.e. simple explanations, involving the fewest intermediaries, are best.

Occam had worked at Oxford but after his death the impetus theory lost favour there and by the fifteenth century Oxford scholars were once more Aristotelians. However the theory was developed further at the University of Paris by Occam's contemporary, Jean Buridan (1297–1358). He drew attention to two important facts that undermined Aristotle's account of motion: firstly that a spinning top rotated without changing its position and therefore could not be moving because of propulsion by displaced air; secondly that a javelin with a flat rear end did not move faster than one with a pointed end, though, if Aristotle's explanation were correct, this ought to happen because the air propelling it from behind would act more effectively. Buridan argued that the motion must be maintained by the initial thrust, i.e. the impetus, and he suggested that all motion was the result of the interaction of impetus and natural inclination.[1]

Later, in the fourteenth century, Nicolas Oresme (1320–82) dared to question Aristotle's cosmology. He revived Aristarchus of Samos's suggestion, made in the third century BC, that the earth was not at rest but rotated daily on its axis, thereby causing night and day and making it seem to us that the sun moved across the sky. Unlike Aristarchus, Oresme did not think that the rotating earth also circled the sun each year. The Church did not regard theories proposing the daily (diurnal) rotation of the earth on its own axis as being so gravely heretical as those that entailed that the earth orbited the sun (annual rotation), for it was only the latter that required the earth to be displaced from its position at the centre of the universe. Occam and Buridan had also been sympathetic to the diurnal rotation theory but Oresme was the first of the medieval scholars to state it explicitly. He suggested that God had set the earth spinning at the Creation, when all the heavenly bodies had been formed and had been placed in their predestined orbits.

Impetus theorists also toyed with the notion that the actual universe might be infinite in extent, not closed and finite as Aristotle had maintained. Oresme considered the possibility of a multitude of world systems, perhaps an infinite number, not only side by side in space but also contained within each other. He surmised that an infinite space was equivalent to God's immensity and might *be* God.[2] Funkenstein thinks that Oresme showed an awareness of the relativity of spatial measurements that has something in common with twentieth-century relativity theories.[3]

Failure to make progress

It is clear that in the thirteenth and fourteenth centuries there was much active critical thought and much discussion of new ideas; the impetus theory was seriously considered by many who rejected the strict scholastic tradition, for example the humanist philosopher and writer Erasmus (1466–1536). But Aristotle's theories remained dominant well into the sixteenth century and were still influential in the early seventeenth century. There were several reasons for the persistence of the scholastic tradition and of Aristotelian theories; some of them were social and cultural, some were economic and some were consequences of current metaphysical and religious beliefs.

The fourteenth century saw the beginning of the end of feudal society, and though the rising commercial and trading communities, with their encouragement of overseas exploration, would soon actively promote the search for knowledge of the world, it was a troublesome time of transition. In addition the Black Death (the plague that almost certainly killed Occam) annihilated a high proportion of the clergy who were the only educated people. Then there was dissatisfaction within the Church, a dissatisfaction which was to lead to the Reformation in the early sixteenth century; the complaints of the reformers and *a fortiori* the final disruption, tended to make the Church establishment sensitive to any implied or overt criticisms of those doctrines that it supported. New ideas about the world would not come from the reformers either; the first Protestant priests were, on balance, rather less tolerant of new ideas than were the Roman Catholics and in the sixteenth century Kepler sought refuge with the Jesuits to escape from protestant persecution. Lutheran Protestants, in particular, tended towards an idealist philosophy and were not interested in knowledge of the natural world. They thought that the human body was corrupt and that nature and all material things were essentially evil so that natural philosophy should not be encouraged.

Everyone accepted that revelation, that is spiritual illumination direct from God, would show truth more certainly and more clearly than any inquiry based on human observation and human reason. Many philosophers would have agreed with Duns Scotus (1265–1308), who followed St Augustine in believing that without divine illumination human beings could know nothing. Those in the higher echelons of the Roman Church were suspicious of change, albeit some of the new ideas were expounded by their own clergy. Bacon, who was a Franciscan friar, had been forbidden by St Bonaventure, the general of the Franciscan Order, to publish an account of his work.

The Renaissance

During the fourteenth century artists and philosophers started to become aware of Greek and Roman art and by the fifteenth century classical art and literature dominated the thought of the day. Under the influence of the classical aesthetics painters broke with the tradition of iconic representation, and classical poetry and drama were highly valued. Yet this appreciation was still essentially medieval in that Ancient Greek and Roman writings came to be revered as 'authorities' so that artists and intellectuals tended to model themselves on the classics rather than seeking originality. Thus painters and sculptors were not supposed to observe the natural world but to imitate the Ancients; poets and dramatists aspired to write in classical style; philosophers commented on Ancient Greek and Roman texts rather than producing new ideas. They were as restricted as those who had earlier been subservient to the authority of the Holy texts. Initially Renaissance concern for the classics probably hampered the development of a critical approach to study of the world as effectively as had the philosophy of the Schools.

Learning was still the concern of a small élite but by the fifteenth century it was not entirely restricted to those in Holy Orders. However, though there were some wealthy and influential lay connoisseurs, for example many of the Medici family, the Church remained the dominant patron. The wealth of the city of Rome was largely dependent on papal revenues (coming not only from the pope's own dominions but also from the whole of the Catholic world), and though Renaissance artists, writers and philosophers did not regard themselves as being subject to the rule of the Church, in the manner of the Schoolmen – some of them were almost atheists – they were aware that anyone who questioned her authority risked impoverishment and loss of position, not only in Italy but anywhere in Western Christendom.

It was going to be necessary to break free yet at first the lessening of Church influence was not wholly advantageous. Freedom from the Church authorities led to a proliferation of superstitions and a revival of beliefs in magic and witchcraft. The Aristotelian logic of the Schoolmen had been narrow but it did give a training in accuracy and in the critical assessment of arguments (see p. 6). When it became unfashionable it was not immediately succeeded by a philosophy or methodology that established a consistent or coherent ordering of thought or encouraged a critical evaluation of new ideas. The old standards were discarded but they were not replaced by new ones so that there were no longer criteria for evaluating philosophical speculations or for appraising theories in natural philosophy. When the logical tradition of syllogistic argument was dismissed as pedantry, fantastic theorizing could run riot; there was no way of distinguishing constructive imaginative speculation from superstition and all ancient legends and myths could be held to have equal merit.

Superstition

Throughout the Middle Ages few would have dismissed witchcraft and black magic as complete nonsense. Though it is probable that the bulk of the clergy and other educated people were sceptical of the wilder stories: witches flying on broomsticks and the cruder accounts of magical charms, almost everyone would have had a certain respect for and fear of witchcraft. The words 'magic' and 'magician' are directly related to 'Magi', the 'wise men', and witches and warlocks were not clearly distinguished from those who practised folk medicine and from local sages. This respect is apparent in the references in Shakespeare's plays, for example it is a wise friar who gives Juliet the potion that leads to the appearance of death. Yet despite some clerical dabblings, the Church wished to deter that interest and to limit the practice of magic; it was held that appeals to occult powers were invocations to the Devil and to the Devil's associates.[4] It was acknowledged that magic could be a potent force and that particular magicians had great power but it was thought that the power was all too likely to be misused. In 1484 Pope Innocent VIII issued a papal Bull against witchcraft; it was intended to save souls from devil worship and idolatry and it led to a series of persecutions and massacres which continued for two centuries. Nevertheless the Magi continued their practices and many of them were honoured and respected.

Astrology and alchemy

Astrology was not held to be evil and was not subject to Church censure; for centuries it had been thought of as part of astronomy, which was itself a recognized branch of learning – one of the quadrivium (see p. 4) – and a genuine science. Princes had their personal astrologers who were usually skilled astronomers and mathematicians as well; for example, John Dee (1527–1608) and Leonard Digges (died

1571), who were both astrologers to our Queen Elizabeth I. It was accepted as a matter of plain fact that the heavenly bodies directly affected mankind. Traces of this belief remain in our language today: for example the illness *influenza* derives its name from association with astrology and belief in the *influence* of the stars on health. References to 'the lucky star' or 'ill-starred destinies' may now be metaphorical but this was not so in the sixteenth century and even in the early seventeenth century. Thus in Shakespeare's *Julius Caesar* (1601) we have:

> When beggars die, there are no comets seen;
> The heavens themselves blaze forth the death of princes.[5]

At the time astrological theories had what we would now call 'scientific status'; they were analogous to our current theories about the effect that sunspots and meteors have on the climate. The Church was not so tolerant of alchemy and it was indeed common knowledge that many alchemists were charlatans[6] living on the greed of their dupes, but alchemy was also practised as a science and as late as the seventeenth century it was thought possible to transmute base metals. Isaac Newton (1642–1727) devoted considerable study to both alchemy and astrology and his earlier contemporary, Robert Boyle (1627–91), thought that he had found the fabulous philosophers' stone which could change all metals into gold.

Magic encouraging science

Belief in the supernatural does not presuppose the harmonious sequence of events that is implicit in the belief that nature is ruled by a perfect and omnipotent God; it does not therefore prompt a search for the divine order. But since the desire to influence the world through magic is based on the hope of controlling events, magic will stimulate inquiry. Today we reject astrology and alchemy but we must recognize that their practice was more than a matter of crude superstition. In relation to the accepted beliefs and presuppositions of the time they could be genuine scientific theories and insofar as they have encouraged observation and experimentation they have helped the advance of science.

The revival of astronomy

The interest in astrology was partly responsible for more careful and more detailed observation of the heavens; astrologers needed to make careful records of the positions of the stars and planets. But maps of the sky were also needed by sailors, for navigation was largely by the sun and the stars. The success of the voyages of discovery to Africa, to the Indies and to the New World depended on maps of the sky being reliable. In addition the Church encouraged astronomers because reliable knowledge of the movements of the stars and planets was needed in order to establish the dates of Christian festivals, and particularly that of Easter Sunday. Lastly there was rising awareness of the need to revise the calendar itself. The standard Julian calender, set up by Julius Caesar, had been based on a year of $365\frac{1}{4}$ days (an extra day being added every fourth year to the 365-day standard year); but by the end of the fifteenth century the calendar was markedly out of step with the solar year which is a little shorter. Thus the seasons, and *a fortiori* the equinoxes, were out of step with the calendar dates; the Julian calendar needed to be modified[7] and the surplus of accumulated days had to be removed.

Aristotle's cosmology gave a theoretical basis to astronomy but, as mentioned in Chapter 1, Ptolemy had altered the Aristotelian scheme so as to improve the basis for predicting the paths of the heavenly bodies. In the *Almagest* the Ptolemaic tables showed how the skies would *look*, that is they 'saved the appearances'. The *Almagest* was valued as an immensely useful practical guide but it was not regarded as having any religious or metaphysical implications. Strictly speaking it was incompatible with Aristotle's account of the heavens but then, as now, natural philosophy (science) can accommodate contradictory theories when they are applied in different situations.[8]

The demand for revision of the *Almagest* began in the fifteenth century at the University of Vienna where nautical almanacs were prepared for Portuguese and Spanish navigators. For the first time astronomical readings were corrected for atmospheric refraction, and mechanical clocks were used to measure the times at which the planets and the stars reached certain positions in the night sky. One of the observers was the artist Dürer (1471–1528). As the data became more accurate the Ptolemaic theory was seen to be less and less satisfactory: predictions based on it were markedly inaccurate so that it could no longer be said to 'save the appearances'. However, though it was acknowledged that the system that had been used for nearly 1,500 years would have to be very substantially modified, there was no thought that it would have to be totally abandoned. It was thought to be a matter of adjusting the *Almagest* so as to make it give predictions compatible with the improved observations. As we have seen there were religious as well as commercial and economic reasons for a reassessment and the Church encouraged the movement for reform.

Nicolas Copernicus was one of a number of distinguished astronomers to whom Rome appealed for help.

The Copernican cosmos

Copernicus (1473–1543) was born to a relatively prosperous and privileged position; his father was a man of means and his uncle was to become a bishop. Copernicus was quiet and diligent; he studied mathematics at Cracow University and by 1500, at the age of 27, he was recognized as a gifted mathematician and was lecturing to colleagues in Rome. He was what we should call an academic. He worked in Italy for some years and there started his revisions of Ptolemy's *Almagest* but in 1512 he left Italy and settled at Frauenberg where he remained for the rest of his life. He had a Church appointment as a canon and he participated in ecclesiastical affairs and in local politics but, encouraged by the Church at Rome, he continued developing his revised cosmology. He came to the conclusion that the sun had to be placed at the centre of the universe and that the planets, and the earth with its ambient moon, must all circle the sun. Thus he proposed fundamental changes, for, according to his scheme, the earth did not only lose its central position, it lost its immobility. Indeed it acquired *three* different kinds of motion. These were: an annual circumcursation of the sun, a daily rotation on its axis, and a gyration of that axis in accordance with the precession of the equinoxes.

Today we speak of the Copernican revolution, yet this was emphatically not how it appeared to Copernicus himself. He had been educated in the scholastic tradition and he was extremely anxious to conform to that tradition and to show that his theory had the support of ancient authorities. He alluded to the writings of classical and of medieval scholars: he drew attention to the heliocentric theory of Aristarchus of Samos (310–230 BC) and to the more nearly contemporary speculations of Nicolas of Cusa (1401–64) as to the possibility of a central sun. Copernicus did not want to claim originality or to be original and he would have been horrified at the suggestion that his theory was revolutionary. Rather he thought of it as a step by step revision of the *Almagest* and he presented it as such. It was as though Ptolemy's scheme had been rewritten in terms of Copernican theory with the minimum of alteration and Copernicus's account can be best understood as a modification of the *Almagest*; a few decades later Kepler was to remark that Copernicus had interpreted Ptolemy rather than nature. For example, the Copernican cosmos, like the Aristotelian and Ptolemaic cosmos, is closed and finite and consists of concentric crystalline spheres. Although he was reluctant to make any alteration Copernicus thought himself well justified in displacing the earth from its central position, and giving it motion, because by this means he was able to avoid using the Ptolemaic equant in the calculations. That device involved postulating unequal arcs of orbit being traversed in equal times so that *non-uniform* circular motion had to be ascribed to some of the heavenly bodies; Ptolemy had used it in order to make predictions more in accord with observations, that is to save the appearances. But to introduce the equant was to propose something that was contrary to the Aristotelian dictum that the only motion natural to the heavens was *uniform* circular motion. Copernicus thought the elimination of such a displeasing irregularity a most important feature of his scheme and he was delighted that he had been able to come closer to Aristotelian harmony. In his eyes such a return was to conform to tradition and also to produce a more elegant mathematical account; it was the reverse of revolution.

But *we* are justified in speaking of the Copernican revolution, for the implications of his new system were to lead to a radically new cosmology and to a fundamental reassessment of the place of the earth – not just as to its physical position but also as to its importance in the cosmos. Moreover, though Copernicus did not appreciate the extent to which he was to undermine the old order, he is entitled to full credit for introducing the new order. He did not forsee what changes must follow, changes not only in the picture of the cosmos but also in physical theories, but he did develop the full mathematics of his theory and he showed in detail how the paths and positions of the heavenly bodies could be calculated. This sets him apart from all his predecessors, from the classical astronomers that he had cited and also from those nearer contemporaries who had speculated as to the possibility of a central sun and a moving earth.

The Copernican scheme was quickly adopted and became the basis for new compilations of astronomical tables for navigation and for prediction. It was much preferred to the *Almagest* for it gave a greatly improved mathematical ordering of the data, and predictions based on it were found to be in better accord with the more accurate astronomical observations that were being made in the sixteenth century. In other words it was far better than the Ptolemaic scheme for saving the appearances. But it was generally held to be *nothing more than* a device for saving the appearances and most astronomers did not accept it as a physical description. For example Erasmus Reinhold (1511–53), who rejected the suggestion that the earth did really move as being incompatible with the Scriptures and with Aristotle, wrote on the title page of his copy of Copernicus's book, *On the Revolutions of the Celestial Orbs*, 'The Astronomical Axiom: Celestial motion is both uniform and circular or composed of uniform and circular motions.'[9]

Copernicus himself did think that he had provided a new physical description; and, as we have seen, he believed that his account was closer to that of Aristotle than was Ptolemy's. But many of his colleagues, like Reinhold, thought that excision of the Ptolemaic equants did not justify a system that removed the earth from its central position and put it in motion. This was to come closer to Aristotle in one relatively minor respect whilst going much farther away in a major matter. In addition there was criticism based on contemporary scientific notions rather than on religious dogma. The Dominican astronomer Maria Tolsani (1470/1–1549) wrote a critique of Copernicus's book:

He is expert indeed in the sciences of mathematics and astronomy, but he is very deficient in the science of physics and dialectic. . . . An astronomer cannot be perfect, in fact, unless he has studied the physical sciences, since astrology [i.e. astronomy] presupposes celestial corporeal natures and the motions of these natures. A man cannot be a complete astronomer and philosopher unless through logic he knows how to distinguish between the true and the false in disputes and knows the modes of argumentation, [skills] that are required in . . . the other sciences. Hence, since Copernicus does not understand physics and logic, it is not surprising that he should be mistaken in this opinion and accepts the false as true. . . . Call together men well read in the sciences, and let them read Copernicus's first book on the motion of the earth and the immobility of the sidereal heaven. Certainly they will find that his arguments have no force and can very easily be resolved.[10]

As we shall see, taken as a physical description, Copernicus's account of the cosmos is incompatible with Aristotelian physics. In Tolsani's time that physics was accepted without question and Tolsani was simply pointing out that if Copernicus had properly understood the current physical theory he could not have suggested that his cosmos was a physical possibility.

Westman says that Tolsani ended his critique with a note that the Master of the Sacred Apostolic Palace, Bartolomeo Spina, had planned to condemn the book, but he died before fulfilling his intention. Westman continues:

As trenchant as Tolsani's critique of Copernicus had been, there is simply no evidence that it received any serious consideration either from the new master or from the pope himself. . . . Tolsani's unpublished manuscript . . . was probably shelved in the library of his order. . . The result was that sixteenth century Catholic astronomers and philosophers worked under no formal prohibitions from the Index or the Inquisition.[11]

For the Church, heresies and heretics were matters of deep concern. All Christians believed that life on earth was but a time of preparation for the life to come and that unredeemed sinners were destined to an eternity of torment.The heretic not only put his own future at risk, he would put the eternal life of others in jeopardy by undermining faith; such corruption was held to be far far worse than murder. It was a major moral duty to save souls from hell and it was an especial duty of the Church and her ordained priests. They were *required* to preach to the heathen and to convert the infidel and they were also required to lead individual heretics back to the Christian fold. Threat of torture and torture itself were held to be justifiable methods of persuasion, for what was a transient earthly agony compared to the everlasting pains of hell? It was an even greater duty to do everything possible to stop heretics from disseminating their evil doctrines and from corrupting others; there was a moral obligation to guard against all potential and possible dangers.

As the Reformation gathered momentum, economic and political factors, connected with Church income and Church influence on the great secular princes, were also operating to stimulate the campaign against heresy. There can be little doubt that the zealots of the Inquisition were strongly motivated by the concerns of this world as well as those of the next. Nevertheless new and unorthodox theories had to be regarded as being potentially subversive of Church doctrine, and therefore as direct threats to the salvation of souls, if they were to attract censure as heresies. On first consideration it can seem surprising that the Church did not condemn Copernicanism (were it to be taught as a true physical description) more quickly; but we must bear in mind that it did not know of the changes that were to come. Perhaps, as indicated by the quotation above, the lack of Church censure was a matter of chance. But in 1543 the subversive influence of Copernicanism could not have been apparent and we can be reasonably confident that however useful it proved, had it been regarded as heretical there would have been swift condemnation.

Why was it thought to be harmless? Firstly it was obvious that it would not seduce the masses, for it was far too abstruse. Copernicus wrote for geometers and astronomers, that is for those who were skilled in mathematics, and, though less complicated than Ptolemy's *Almagest, On the Revolutions of the Celestial Orbs* was still far beyond the capacity of even an educated Renaissance humanist, let alone the barely literate man in the street. When Copernicus wrote, his work was as accessible as, say, Bertrand Russell's *Principia Mathematica* is now. Moreover, though he was an eminent scholar, Copernicus, unlike Russell, was not known outside the academic circles of the day. In the seventeenth century, when the storm broke, the bishop of Fiesole, who wished to put Copernicus in prison, had to be told that he had been dead for over seventy years.

Secondly, in the sixteenth century Copernicus's work, even when understood, was not thought to undermine Church doctrine. As we have seen, the theory was not incompatible with the *spirit* of the Aristotelian system even though there were significant alterations, and it was written in a style harmonizing with the medieval scholastic tradition and with the Renaissance respect for the classics. Copernicus had stressed his reliance on the Ancients and he also appealed to principles of simplicity (Occam's razor) and of mathematical elegance (the removal of the equant). Writing of the earth's motion, he said:

> according to Cicero, Hicetas had thought the earth was moved, . . . according to Plutarch . . . certain others had held the same opinion. . . . When from this, therefore I had conceived its possibility, I myself also began to meditate upon the mobility of the earth. . . . I found at length by much and long observation, that if the motions of the other planets were added to the rotation of the earth, and calculated as for the revolution of that planet, not only that the phenomena of the others followed from this, but that it so bound together both the order and magnitudes of all the planets and the spheres and the heaven itself that in no single part could one thing be altered without confusion among the other parts and in all the Universe.[12]

Copernicus's orthodox and cautious approach, very much in the scholastic tradition, would not in itself have saved his book from censure but his style would not *attract* censure and his overt respect for the classics and his adherence to Aristotelian physics made his work acceptable to contemporary academics. Yet the very fact that his adherence meant that his account could not seriously be taken as a true physical description provided a third reason for the Church to believe that the Copernican system was harmless. To anyone versed in the scientific theories of the times it could be nothing more than a device, albeit highly ingenious and very useful, for saving the appearances.

As Tolsani had appreciated (see quotation on p. 26) Copernicus himself did not realize that his new cosmology could describe physical reality only if Aristotelian physics were completely abandoned; instead he tried to modify that physics. He ended up with an *ad hoc* hybrid which even he knew was unsatisfactory. Thus:

1 He had had to reject Aristotle's postulate of the central position of the earth, but he sought to minimize his departure from Aristotle's account by stressing that he had only displaced the earth *a very little* from the centre of the universe – very little, that is, relative to the size of the whole system of concentric spheres.

2 He supported the Aristotelian view that a condition of permanence was more noble than one of change but he had had to abandon the notion of the quintessence, the special unchanging and incorruptible heavenly element that Aristotle had said pervaded all space above the sphere of the moon. In the Copernican cosmos the earth had the same status as the planets, albeit it possessed the unique dignity of a satellite moon.

3 Aristotle had said that heavy bodies fell to earth because they sought their natural place at the centre of the cosmos and this, of course, was not an explanation that Copernicus could accept. He had to offer another explanation and he suggested that gravity was a consequence of an innate tendency of any part of the earth which had become detached to seek to reunite with the whole:

> I think gravity is nothing else than a natural appetency, given to the parts by the Divine Providence of the Maker of the universe, in order that they may establish their unity and wholeness by combining in the form of a sphere. It is probable that this affection also belongs to the sun, moon and the planets, in order that they may, by its efficacy, remain in their roundness.[13]

Copernicus's teleological explanation depended on the assumption that there was a latent animism in the matter of the earth and of the heavenly bodies, giving rise to natural 'appetency' or natural tendency. Hence, as we see, Copernicus could conjecture that the matter of the sun would tend to seek the sun, matter of the moon to seek the moon and so on. Even at the time, when teleological explanations were expected and when there were no objections to a supposition of animism, Copernicus's account seemed strained and laboured as compared with that of Aristotle.

4 Copernicus had to deal with contemporary scientific objections (objections arising from his acceptance of Aristotelian physics) to his postulate of a moving earth. There were objections to the twenty-four-hour rotation (the diurnal motion) and also objections to the annual revolution round the sun.

Objections to the diurnal motion

Copernicus's contemporaries fully understood that something might appear to be moving though it was really at rest. They appreciated that mere observation of the sun travelling from East to West across the sky did not establish anything more than that the sun moved relative to the earth, and that the same visual effect would be produced if the earth were moving from West to East. But they had no concept of inertial motion: it was thought that if an object in a moving vehicle or ship were thrown up into the air then, when it fell, the vehicle or ship would have left it behind. Hence if the apparent movement of the sun were due to the actual movement of the earth they would expect something thrown vertically upward to fall back to a point further West. Likewise they would think that a bird attempting to fly East would make no headway and that a shot fired towards the East would recoil – for the earth must turn faster than any bird or bullet. Thus the undisputed fact that an arrow shot vertically upward descended to the *same* place, that birds could fly as freely East as they flew West and that bullets fired eastwards did not recoil was, for them, clear proof that the earth must be at rest. It followed that they thought that they had not misinterpreted what they saw and that the sun really did travel from East to West.

It may seem strange that no one had noticed that when objects were thrown upwards in a moving cart or from the deck of a ship at sea they fell back to the same place but in the sixteenth century nothing travelled very fast and inertial motion would not have been easy to notice in a bumpy cart or on board a rolling sailing vessel. Because we have direct experience of inertial motion, for example when a car or train stops or starts suddenly, it is difficult for us to realize that the Aristotelian view, that an object leaving a moving container is no longer affected by the motion it had within that container, is eminently reasonable. Indeed, as we shall see in Chapter 9, we now postulate that the speed of a light ray is independent of the speed of the source of the light.

The verses below describe contemporary objections to Copernicanism, and they also typify the contemporary attitude of amused and contemptuous disbelief:

some brain-sicks live there now-a-days,
That lose themselves still in contrary ways;
Preposterous wits that cannot row at ease,
On the Smooth channel of our common Seas.
And such are those (in my conceit at least)
Those clerks that think (think how absurd the jest)
That neither heav'ns nor Stars do turn at all,
Nor dance about this great round Earthy Ball;
But th'Earth itself, this Massy Globe of ours,
Turns round about once every twice-twelve hours;
And we resemble Land-bred Novices
New brought aboard to venture on the Seas;
Who, at first launching from the shore, suppose
The ship stands still, and that the ground it goes.
So, twinkling Tapers, that Heav'ns Arches fill,
Equally distant should continue still.
So, never should an arrow, shot upright,
In the same place upon the shooter light;
But would do (rather) as (at Sea) a stone
Aboard a Ship upward rightly thrown;
Which not within-board falls, but in the Flood
A-stern the Ship, if so the Wind be good.
So should the Fowls that take their nimble flight
From Western Marches towards Morning's light;
And Zephyrus,* that in the summer time
Delights to visit Eurus† in his clime;
And Bullets thundered from the cannon's throat
(Whose roaring drowns the heav'nly thunder's note)
Should seem recoil: sithens the quick career,
That our round Earth should daily gallop here,
Must needs exceed a hundred fold (for swift)
Birds, Bullets, Winds; their wings, their force, their drift.
Arm'd with these reasons, 'twere superfluous
T'assail the reasons of Copernicus;
Who to salve better of the Stars th'appearance
Unto the Earth a three-fold motion warrants:
Making the Sun the Centre of this All,
Moon, Earth, and Water, in one only Ball.
But sithence here, nor time, nor place doth suit,
His paradox at length to prosecute;[14]

---

* The South East Wind   † The West Wind

Objections to Copernicus's assertion that the earth made a yearly orbit round the sun did not depend on the acceptance of Aristotelian physics but on what might be expected from direct observation of the heavens. They made it difficult to accept the Copernican account as a physical description even after Aristotle's theories of motion had been discarded.

Objections to the annual revolution

Firstly, no annual parallax was observed among the fixed stars, that is their relative positions remained the same throughout the year. Yet if the earth orbited the sun there would be an immense distance between its position at mid-summer and mid-winter (the diameter of the orbit) and, if the Copernican theory were true there ought to be a marked change in the relations between the stars as viewed in summer and in winter. Copernicus said that there was no perceptible change because the stars were so far away that the alteration in the earth's position was relatively insignificant, i.e. the diameter of its orbit was tiny compared to the size of the outer crystalline sphere. We now know that in regard to this objection his answer was essentially right, but in the sixteenth century few could believe that the cosmos was so vast.[15]

Secondly, although Copernicus's theory explained the movements of the planets it would seem that, if it were correct, the planets Venus and Mercury should appear to alter in size much more than they were observed to do; also Venus at least should show phases, just as the moon does.

Small wonder then that the theory was accepted solely as a calculating device to save the appearances, and small wonder that Andreas Osiander (1498–1552), the editor of *On the Revolutions of the Celestial Orbs*, should have introduced the work as such. Osiander emphasized that it was not possible for astronomers to know the true nature of the heavens; they could only devise hypotheses that served as bases for calculating the positions of the various heavenly bodies.

> It is quite clear that the causes of the apparent unequal motions are completely unknown. ... And if any causes are derived by the imagination ... they are not put forward to convince anyone that they are true, but *merely to provide* a correct basis for calculation.[16]

Since the Copernican system appeared so patently impossible, Copernicus's own preface, which followed Osiander's introduction and which made plain that the author *was* offering a physical description, was ignored[17] or ridiculed. Thus Martin Luther (1482–1546) opined:

... the new astronomer, who wants to prove that the earth goes round, and not the heavens, the Sun and the Moon; just as if someone were sitting in a moving waggon or ship were to suppose that he was at rest, and that the Earth and trees were moving past him. But this is the way nowadays; whoever wants to be clever must need produce something of his own, which is bound to be the best since *he* has produced it! The fool will turn the whole science of astronomy upside down. But, as Holy Writ declares, it was the Sun and not the Earth which Joshua commanded to stand still.[18]

Here the objection is based on appeal to robust common sense as well as to the Scriptures.

It must again be stressed that most Christians thought of the Bible as an important source of knowledge about the world until well into the nineteenth century; it was an inspired text, the Word of God, and therefore could not be doubted. Today it is hard for us to understand the very great authority of Holy Writ; it had emotional as well as intellectual power. Thus though there was much contemporary scientific and observational evidence against the Copernican account of the cosmos, evidence that was totally independent of the Scriptures, sixteenth-century philosophers[19] regarded criticisms showing that Copernicanism contradicted the biblical account as no wit less important. Indeed, at the last, Holy Writ had to be rated more highly than any human hypothesis based on human observations and inferences. Hence, when in the seventeenth century the empirical evidence against Copernicanism began to crumble, religious opposition remained.

But this opposition was still to come; when it was first published *On the Revolutions of the Celestial Orbs* was welcomed as a practical manual. It was well received by the Roman Church and was enthusiastically adopted by their Jesuit astronomers.

Post-medieval beliefs

Metaphysical presuppositions and religious faith Belief in the central position of the earth was strong partly because it had the full backing of the Church and the Establishment but also because it was based on very deep-rooted beliefs about mankind's status in the universe. At the end of Chapter 1 we saw that medieval Christians believed that the cosmos was created by God and that Man was a favoured being who had been made in God's image. But believing in the importance of the human race is not dependent on belief in the Christian religion; it is probably a fundamental human trait. Belief in the importance of mankind *gives rise to* religions based on the notion of a benevolent and caring God and is not the *result of* belief in such a God. The Freudian explanation of religious faith as arising from a human need for an all-powerful father figure presupposes a deity who *cares about* mankind. Likewise the belief that Man and the earth are at the centre of the universe antedates any formal religion. Not only Aristotle's but many other ancient cosmologies assume a privileged position for the earth.

Mathematics and the 'simple' explanation   In accordance with the principle of Occam's razor it was believed that simple ('elegant') accounts were best. (That remains a favoured principle even today.) Ptolemy's system became subject to criticism not just because it was becoming inadequate but also because the many *ad hoc* adjustments that helped to lessen some of the inaccuracies made it complex and cumbersome. Maria de Novara, professor of mathematics at Bologna and one of Copernicus's teachers in Italy, criticized the Ptolemaic scheme because it lacked elegance; Copernicus was delighted at being able to dispense with the inelegant equant.

The primacy of teleological explanations and the influence of the Church   In the sixteenth century teleological explanations were still regarded as being the only completely satisfactory explanations. The search was for ultimate explanations in terms of God's purposes though explanations based on appeal to subsidiary purposes also proliferated; we have Copernicus's explanation of gravity in terms of the 'tendencies' of parts of the created universe to join with like parts.

The Renaissance revival of witchcraft and of alchemy led to teleological explanations that did not invoke God directly or indirectly; necromancy undermines the view of God as omnipotent, for the Devil and subsidiary spirits have powers and oppose God's will. Inevitably the Church discouraged the Black Arts and thereby, and perhaps inadvertently, discouraged superstition.

The position in 1550

Sixteenth-century philosophers were well aware that there was no empirical test that could establish *conclusively* that the earth moved or that the sun moved but in the light of current theory and observations then available it was almost certain that the earth must be at rest. Therefore the Copernican theory, though welcomed as a calculating scheme, was ignored as a physical description. It was clear that fundamental changes had to be made to the calculating schema but the scholastic, the Aristotelian, paradigm remained undisturbed.

3   Chaos

Hermes Trismegistus

As we have seen (p. 20) Renaissance humanists came especially to
revere the Ancient Greek and Roman classics as aesthetic and intellectual 'authorities', but they had great respect for all antiquity *per
se*. This was in part because it was believed that the immediate de-
scendants of Adam and Eve had been in direct communication with
God and must inevitably have been profoundly influenced by His grace
as well as His power. It was taken for granted that they must have been
morally better than those who came later so that in those early years
just following the Fall men lived in harmonious peace. Undoubtedly
romantic views of an idyllic past were also influenced by classical
legends as well as by the Scriptures; there was the Greek myth of an
original Golden Age, succeeded by the less perfect Silver Age which
degenerated into the Bronze Age and finally into the even more
corrupt Iron Age. Thus classical legend supported Christian teaching
and, in the fifteenth and sixteenth centuries, it was generally supposed
that there had been a steady moral decline. Hence it came to be
accepted that ideas from the relatively recent past, in particular the
logic and rationalism of the Schools, were less valuable than what was
taken to be the holy mysticism of earlier times.

From the fourth century AD the Hermetic writings, the *Corpus
Hermeticum*, had been revered as a source of the wisdom of the
Ancients and indeed as perhaps the original source of all human
wisdom. The Church Fathers, for example Lactantius (*c*. 240–320),
took them to be the work of one man, Hermes Trismegistus (Hermes
thrice great), who was thought to have lived before the time of Pythagoras, and probably not much later than the Old Testament prophets.[1]
Renaissance scholars inherited and accepted this judgement and surmised that Hermes Trismegistus might have been an Egyptian priest,

for the work reflected Egyptian religion and rites as well as classical philosophy and Christian writings. The allusions to the classics and to biblical themes were regarded as proof that the author had inspired the Ancient Greeks and had foreseen the coming of Christ on earth. Fifteenth-century Christian approval shows in the introduction of representations of Hermes Trismegistus into groups of sages depicted in churches and holy buildings: for example the mosaic pavement at the entrance of the cathedral at Siena (*c.* 1480) shows him flanked by two Sibyls, and there are also paintings of him with various Egyptian gods and Old Testament figures in the Vatican.

Much had been destroyed in the Dark Ages and copies of the Hermetic writings were rare and greatly prized. Cosimo de Medici (1389–1464) was delighted when one of his agents brought a manuscript containing most of the *Corpus Hermeticum* to Florence. He employed the scholar Marsilio Ficino (1433–99) to translate Greek texts into Latin and he thought the new manuscript so important that he directed Ficino to attend to it before embarking on a translation of Plato.[2] Ficino was not reluctant, for he too regarded the *Corpus Hermeticum* as a source of great wisdom. He was particularly struck by its affinities with the book of Genesis and, since there were so many references to Egyptian gods and religious ceremonies, he wondered whether Hermes Trismegistus might have been the prophet Moses.[3]

Ficino's short-lived younger colleague, Pico della Mirandola (1463–94) was also deeply interested in the *Corpus Hermeticum* and especially those sections devoted to astrology, alchemy and occult rites. These were in the *Cabala*, that part of the Hermetic writings concerned with magic arts. Those who studied the texts hoped to acquire secret powers and so to become wise men, or Magi. The Renaissance philosophers had a different attitude to knowledge from that of the Schoolmen: both thought that knowledge was reserved for an élite but the Schoolmen actively encouraged argument in order to clarify and to analyse the premises laid down by the authorities. For the Magi, on the other hand, knowledge was arcane, not to be subjected to critical discussion or logical debate but rather to be revered as a kind of religious magic. The *Cabala* involved the study of spells, of seals and talismans, of the zodiac signs and of their presiding deities.

Renaissance humanists took magic to be a part of wisdom and many of them were very interested in occult practices. Indeed it had attracted some of the medieval scholars: Roger Bacon had concerned himself with magic, but he had been rebuked by the general of his Order[4] and had been sent to prison for some years. In the fifteenth century Pico della Mirandola (see above) was in trouble for dabbling in the occult though he had some protection from the Borgia pope Alexander VI (1431–1503) who was himself interested in astrology. By itself Alexander's papal protection is of no great significance in an assessment of the attitude of the Church for he is described as corrupt and worldly, neglecting the Christian spiritual inheritance.[5] Hence his personal preoccupation with magic rites need not indicate general moral approval of the Hermetic writings and of the *Cabala* among the Church establishment.

It has already been pointed out (p. 21) that there was a certain ambivalence in the attitude of that establishment: the magical practices recounted in the *Cabala* might be suspect but Trismegistus himself was ranked as a pre-Christian prophet and some pious Roman Catholics thought that study of the Hermetic writings might help the counter-Reformation in its fight against protestant heretics. Today we too may be ambivalent in our assessment of magic and its role in the development of natural science. As was mentioned in Chapter 2, the wish to acquire control over events through alchemy and astrology can stimulate observation and even prompt experimental investigation, but revival of such practices and *a fortiori* attempts to control by appeal to charms and incantations can also lead to the undermining of systematic thought and of logical reasoning. Belief in occult powers, in ancient legends and myths may rouse imaginative speculation but it may also lead from fact to fantasy and from unprejudiced inquiry to blind ritual. Both influences show in the effect the *Corpus Hermeticum* had on the development of the new cosmology.

The place of the sun

One feature of the Hermetic writings was the importance accorded to the sun. A section of the text which Lactantius had called *Sermo Perfectus* (the Perfect Word) treats the sun as an intermediary between the divine light and the World, indeed as a second God:

> . . . the Sun, or Light, for it is through the intermediary of the solar circle that light is spread to all. The Sun illuminates the other stars not so much by the power of his light as by his divinity and sanctity. He must be held as the second god. The world is living and all things in it are alive and it is the sun which governs all living things.[6]

We have already noted (p. 9) that early Christian and medieval philosophers regarded physical light as being analogous to the divine spiritual light and that they accorded special importance to the study of light; hence it is not surprising that pre-Christian texts (or rather texts thought to be pre-Christian) deifying the sun would not necessarily meet with disapproval.

The Hermetic writings and Copernicus

Copernicus knew of the *Corpus Hermeticum* and it is possible that his reading of the work prompted him to consider modifying the Aristotelian/Ptolemaic system by placing the sun rather than the earth at the centre. Whether that be the case or no, once he had arrived at this conception, and had developed it mathematically, the central religious and mystical role of the sun in Hermetic writings helped to convince him that his own system was a physical description and was not merely a mathematical construction to save the appearances. Thus in *On the Revolutions of the Celestial Orbs* he wrote:

> In the middle of all sits the Sun enthroned. How could we place this luminary in any better position in this most beautiful temple from which to illuminate the whole at once? He is rightly called the Lamp, the Mind, the Ruler of the universe. . . . So the Sun sits as upon a royal throne ruling his children the planets which circle round him.[7]

Though this was not seen as being heretical, it was after all an echo of the *Sermo Perfecto* which had been commended by Lactantius, it was much more than a metaphor. Copernicus, a devout and sincere Christian, had warmed to the Hermetic teaching and probably regarded it as supporting his orthodox Christian faith. But others interpreted the Hermetic writings differently, seeing them as a purer source of the Christian message which ought to replace rather than support the Gospels. They wished the Church to change its teaching and its doctrines. One of the most ardent advocates of Christian hermeticism was Giordano Bruno.

Giordano Bruno (1548–1600)

Giordano Bruno had been a Dominican friar, but his involvement with Hermetic teachings led to accusations of heresy and he left the order at the age of 28 (in 1576) and no longer wore his Dominican habit. He went from Italy and travelled through the Continent, eventually arriving in protestant England. There he lectured on the Copernican system and on what he said was a purer Christian faith. Bruno thought of himself as a reformer and certainly not as a heretic; he had contemplated dedicating his book *The Seven Liberal Arts* to Pope Clement VIII (1536–1605). Very unwisely, but it seems he did not appreciate the risks he ran, he returned home in 1591 and by May 1592 he was in the hands of the Inquisition in Venice. He was questioned by the Inquisitors for seven years and finally recanted, first in Venice and then at a trial in Rome. It was in Rome that he faced the Jesuit priest (later Cardinal) Robert Bellarmine (1542–1621), who was to correspond with and then interrogate Galileo.

But Bruno soon withdrew his recantation, insisting that there was nothing to recant since he was not a heretic; he said that his writings had been wrongly interpreted. This did not satisfy the authorities and he was handed over to the secular arm of the law and was burned at the stake in 1600. To us, and it would seem to many of his contemporaries, Bruno's hermeticism is a weird *mélange* of mysticism and superstition; clearly he was obsessed by the *Cabala* and by the possibility of appealing to occult powers with seals, talismans and incantations. But he was also deeply concerned to establish what he saw as a better Christianity and to reform the Church; herein lay his heresy.

It was Bruno's religious and metaphysical beliefs, not empirical evidence or mathematical reasoning, that led him to advocate the Copernican theory. He thought that insofar as a dry mathematician was capable of understanding deep religious and metaphysical truths, Copernicus's account of the cosmos was correct but it was, of course, limited. Of Copernicus Bruno wrote:

> To him we owe our liberation from several false prejudices of the commonly received philosophy.... Yet he himself did not much transcend it; for being more a student of mathematics than of nature he was not able to penetrate deeply enough to remove the roots of false and misleading principles and, by disentangling all the difficulties in the way, to free both himself and others from the pursuit of empty enquiries and turn their attention to things constant and certain.[8]

As we have seen, much sixteenth-century opposition to the Copernican theory was based on the accepted science of the day, and Bruno's championship on metaphysical and dubious religious grounds was unlikely to convert practising mathematicians and astronomers still under the influence of Aristotle and of Ptolemy. Bruno made no secret of his opinion that academics were stolid pedants, and were like Copernicus in being unable to understand the implications of the *Corpus Hermeticum* and the higher activities of the Magi. But these same academics regarded *him* as a figure of fun. In 1583 Bruno visited Oxford, where George Abbot, who later became Archbishop of Canterbury, described him thus:

When that Italian Didapper, who intitules himself *Philtheus Iorda-*
nus Brunus Nolanus, magis elaborata Theologica Doctor, &c
(margin: Praefat, in explicatio triginta sigillorum) with a name
longer than his body ... his hart was on fire, to make himselfe by
some worthy exploite, to become famous in that celebrious place.
Not long after returning again, when he had more boldly than
wisely, got vp into the highest place of our best & most renowned
schoole, stripping vp his sleeues like some Iugler, and telling vs
much of *chentrum & circumferenchia* ... he vndertooke among very
many other matters to set on foot the opinion of Copernicus, that
the earth did goe round, and the heavens stand still; whereas in
truth it was his owne head which rather did run round, & his braines
did not stand still.[9]

Abbot went on to say that one member of the audience thought that, in
any case, Bruno's exposition was not entirely original, and later discovered that it had been taken almost *verbatim* from the works of
Marsilio Ficino.

However, even though they scoffed at Bruno, the learned doctors at
Oxford, and in other universities on the Continent, did listen to him
and, of course, they did know of the Hermetic writings. Francis Yates
has pointed out that there is clear evidence of the influence of the
Corpus Hermeticum in the sixteenth and seventeenth centuries in art
as well as in philosophy. It is possible that the character of Berowne in
Shakespeare's *Love's Labour's Lost* is based on Bruno,[10] and perhaps
also the two pedants, Don Armado and Holofernes, who are the foils
of the lovers. Some of the rituals connected with freemasonry may be
derived from the Hermetic writings, and Mozart's *Magic Flute*, which
is concerned with freemasonry, has a temple of Osiris and Egyptian
priests.[11] In Francis Bacon's *New Atlantis* we have a vision of a scientific society ruled by sages of Salomon's House (Magi) and the Father
of Salomon's House rides in a chariot surmounted by a golden sun.[12]
Francis Yates suggests that Louis XIV's title 'Le Roi Soleil' may have
arisen from the influence of the Hermetic writings.[13] It was not until the
early seventeenth century that the relatively recent date of the work
was revealed and though diehards such as Robert Fludd (1574–1637),
who adhered to the animistic tradition, continued to disregard the
evidence, the *Corpus Hermeticum* started to lose influence from then
on.

Today we dismiss animism from science, and tend to think that a
metaphysics involving animistic beliefs cannot contribute to, let alone
provide a foundation for, empirical knowledge. But we have already

seen that it may well have stimulated Copernicus and we shall come to appreciate that it also influenced Kepler and Galileo. Moreover, as Yates has said, the classical physical concept of *mechanical*, as opposed to animal, force perhaps had to develop from animistic notions. She writes:

> Drained of its animism, with the laws of inertia and gravity substituted for the psychic life of nature as the principle of movement, understood objectively instead of subjectively, Bruno's universe would turn into something like the mechanical universe of Isaac Newton, marvellously moving forever under its own laws placed in it by a God who is not a magician but a mechanic and a mathematician.[14]

Our concept of mechanical force has content only because we have experience of forces exerted by ourselves and, by analogy we envisage other people and animals exerting force; at the core it is an animistic concept. In addition, and like our concept of cause, we do not divorce it entirely from a notion of occult necessary connection, even though we may acknowledge that we *ought* to do so. From the seventeenth century onwards empirical explanations have been based on the effects of forces, very often mathematically described, but these forces still have to be postulated as part of a basic metaphysics. We shall be considering this further in relation to Galileo, Descartes and Newton.

The new cosmology in England

Though Bruno's cosmology and metaphysics were ridiculed, not everyone in England was prepared to dismiss the notion that the sun was the central body. Despite the many difficulties inherent in Copernicus's account, most leading astronomers and mathematicians thought that it merited careful study. For example, John Dee, who never committed himself to its physical truth, held that the Copernican scheme required serious consideration and sober discussion and was certainly not to be dismissed out of hand. Dee was acknowledged as a Magus; as we saw (p. 22) he was astrologer to Queen Elizabeth I and he had some sympathy with much in the Hermetic writings. More importantly he was a considerable mathematician and astronomer and could fully appreciate the practical value of Copernicanism for astronomical calculations. Dee's slightly older contemporary, Robert Recorde (1510–58) also had high regard for the Copernican scheme and referred to it in his *Castle of Knowledge*, but Recorde thought that discussion of Copernicanism as a physical possibility must of necessity be very complex and he advised that students should begin by studying the Aristotelian/Ptolemaic scheme. A little later another English astronomer, Thomas Digges[15] (died 1595) came to the conclusion that our cosmos was indeed heliocentric; he went beyond Copernicus in rejecting the crystalline spheres and in proposing an infinitely extended universe. He suggested that the fixed stars were at varying distances (and therefore they could not be embedded in a single outermost sphere) and that they were infinite in number. But, reading his exposition, we are still aware of the influence of the older cosmology and of the animistic tradition:

> This orb of fixed stars extendeth itself infinitely up in altitude spherically, and therefore immovable: the palace of felicity garnished with perpetual shining glorious lights innumerable far excelling our sun both in quantity and quality; the very court of celestial angels devoid of grief and replenished with perfect endless joy the habitacle for the elect.[16]

His accompanying diagram showed the stars scattered at random right up to the edge of the picture, and not fixed to an 'orb'. Boas suggests that it may have been Digges's writings that led to the general belief that despite Copernicus's own view, his cosmology demanded an indefinitely large if not an infinite universe.[17] But as described by Digges this infinite universe was animate; it moved as a living entity, not as a vast machine. From his account we can see that he took it to be a celestial palace which was the abode of angels; moreover the heavenly bodies might themselves be animate.

Undoubtedly the older animistic conception of the cosmos came to be questioned at the same time as the introduction of Copernicanism and the development of heliocentric schemes, but the issue between animism and mechanism did not depend on and was not decided by theories of geo- or heliocentricity, or by notions of an infinite or closed universe. Any combination of theory was compatible with animistic or with mechanistic presuppositions.

The latter part of the sixteenth century saw cosmological theories in a state of flux; Tycho Brahe was an important contributor to the cosmological debate.

Tycho Brahe (1546–1601)

Tycho Brahe was a major figure not only because his astronomical observations were the most accurate obtainable before the invention of the telescope but also because he devised a cosmology which was immune to the philosophical (scientific) criticisms levied against the Copernican scheme but which yet was just as good as that scheme for predicting the paths and positions of the heavenly bodies.[18] Indeed Brahe's cosmos was *mathematically* equivalent to that of Copernicus, though it was physically different. He retained the central and motionless earth round which travelled the sun; but, unlike the Aristotelian/Ptolemaic scheme, the two inner planets, Mercury and Venus, were satellites of the sun (like moons) and the sun, accompanied by these two 'moons', circled both the earth and the earth's own ambient moon (i.e. the 'real' moon). The other planets, Mars, Jupiter and Saturn circled this inner system of the earth, moon and sun (plus its 'moons'), and beyond these were the fixed stars. It must be stressed that Brahe's cosmos was in better accord with the known facts and in better accord with current physical theory than was the Copernican cosmos. For example, if Brahe's was a true physical account, stellar parallax would not be expected since the earth did not change its position in relation to the stars; in addition it did not give rise to physical problems involving the motion of the earth since he postulated that the earth was stationary.

Brahe had no telescope but he made his observations with very large and very carefully designed instruments; they were much better than any others made at that date. He set himself the task of mapping afresh the positions of the brightest stars, making a new starry catalogue which provided him with a basic plan of the heavens. These bright fixed stars could be used as reference points and he was then able to plot the changing positions of the sun, the moon and the planets against the background of stars. In this way he could trace their paths across the sky and so could establish their orbits. Brahe was concerned with astronomical theory as well as with making accurate observations; although he postulated a central and motionless earth, he did not, as we have seen, support the Aristotelian/Ptolemaic scheme. His own theory was more than a mere modification of that cosmology for, as well as having two planets as satellites of the sun, he appealed to recent astronomical observations which undermined the Aristotelian concept of the perfect and unchanging heavens consisting of concentric crystalline spheres. Like all contemporary astronomers Tycho Brahe had observed the 'new star' that had appeared in 1572 and had disappeared in 1574 (it was probably a supernova); he asserted that this phenomenon alone showed that the heavens were not changeless. In addition he pointed out that the path of the comet, that had been observed by astronomers in 1577 could not be accounted for in Aristotle's scheme. For the comet had come into view, passed across the skies, and had then receded and vanished from sight. It was clear, therefore, that it could not have remained under the sphere of the moon where it would always be visible, and yet it could not have been so far away as to remain between the sphere of Saturn and the fixed stars. So, if the Aristotelian theory were correct, the comet would have had to pass through and shatter a series of spheres as it approached and then receded from the earth. This was impossible and hence there could be no crystalline spheres.

Brahe died relatively young in 1601 leaving a vast amount of astronomical data to be assessed. This was the task of his assistant, Johannes Kepler.

Johannes Kepler (1571–1630)

Kepler worked with Brahe at Prague during the last year of Brahe's life and although he was to make a much more revolutionary and more permanent contribution to cosmological theory, he was more deeply influenced by Renaissance mysticism than was his mentor. He was, for example, fascinated by Pythagorean number theory[19] and the related mathematical approach found in Hermetic writings. Yates considers that he probably never learned of the relatively recent date of the *Corpus Hermeticum*.[20] Kepler's passionate conviction that the universe embodied a divine harmony (he believed that there was a music of the spheres) inspired and guided him; but this mystical passion and his belief in a cosmos structured with mathematical symmetry did not lead him to disregard observational evidence. Unlike fantasists such as Bruno, Kepler made a very clear distinction between uncontrolled hermetic mathematical speculations (a playing with diagrams, symbols and numbers) and mathematics as a means of describing what was observed.

Kepler assessed and interpreted Brahe's data and, after Brahe's death, prepared tables of the planets' motions (the Rudolphine Tables, published in 1627). These were much more accurate than earlier tables because Brahe's observations had been so careful and his measurements so meticulous. It was because Brahe had compiled such reliable records that Kepler was able to test mathematical theories of the planetary paths and was at last able to show that the planets revolved round the sun in elliptical orbits. The Rudolphine Tables postulated these orbits.

Yet Kepler had started with the deep metaphysical belief that the planets must follow a circular path and it is a sign of his truly scientific and undogmatic approach that he came to acknowledge that this could not be the case. Before he arrived at the notion of elliptical orbits he had sought others that would be in accord with his conviction that the heavenly bodies must show a harmonious pattern. He subjected himself to the discipline of observed facts but he also had the imaginative insight to create a new theory of planetary orbits. His metaphysical belief in harmony inspired him and made the enormous amount of mathematical work needed to show how the facts confirmed the theory a labour of love rather than mere drudgery. He wanted to show that the universe could be interpreted mathematically and as a harmonious whole. Still influenced by medieval tradition, he also thought that the heavens should be studied to help mankind to be ever more aware of the glory of God the Father, God the Son and God the Holy Ghost. His earliest work, *The Mystery of the Universe*, was published in 1596, before he worked with Tycho Brahe, and shows the influence of his religious and other metaphysical beliefs in the mathematical ordering of nature. In his Dedication to the Archduke of Austria and others, he writes:

I now present to your gracious company . . . a work that though it be small in compass . . . yet treats of a wondrous subject. If you desire maturity – Pythagoras has already treated of it some 2000 years ago. If you desire novelty – it is the first time that this subject is being presented to all mankind by myself. If you desire scope – nothing is greater or wider than the universe. If you desire venerability – nothing is more precious, nothing more beautiful than our magnificent temple of God. . . . St. Paul admonished the Heathens to reflect on God within themselves as they would on the Sun in the water or in a mirror. Why then should we Christians delight less in this reflection, seeing that it is our proper task to honour, to revere and to admire God in the true way? Our piety in this is the deeper the greater is our awareness of creation and its granduer.[21]

and in the text itself Kepler wrote:

Why is it that in adorning the world, God reflected on the differences between the curved and the straight, and preferred the nobility of the curved? Why, indeed? Only because the most perfect builder must needs produce a work of greatest beauty, for it is not now, nor ever was, possible (as Cicero, following Plato's *Timaeus* shows in his book on the Cosmos) that the best should ever be anything but the most beautiful.[22]

and later:

> Thus we come to curved orbits through motion, and to bodies through number and magnitude. We can but exclaim with Plato, that *God is a great geometrician*, and in constructing the planets He inscribed bodies into circles and circles into bodies until there remained not a single body that was not endowed with movable circles internally as well as externally.[23]

This work was written before Kepler had realized that the orbits of the planets were ellipses. He had hoped, even expected, that the orbits would be circles, but Brahe's data could not be disputed and were not compatible with a circular path. Having abandoned that theory Kepler tested serveral other *loci* before finding that Brahe's data were compatible with elliptical orbits. Kepler also formulated mathematical relationships connecting the orbital velocity with the distance from the sun and the distance of each planet from the sun with its period of revolution (the time taken for the planet to complete an orbit). The three relationships, known as *Kepler's Laws*, are quite simple, though very complicated mathematics was required to establish them on the basis of the data. They represent a major advance in cosmology and they have additional importance in that Newton was able to derive his inverse square law of gravitational attraction from them. The laws are:

1 The orbits of the planets are ellipses, with the sun in one focus.
2 The area swept out by the line joining a planet to the sun is proportional to the time taken by the planet travelling the arc of orbit.
3 The squares of their periodic times are proportional to the cubes of the mean distance of each planet from the sun.

Kepler had originally thought that the orbital velocities must be constant, that is that equal lengths of path must be traversed in equal times. Again, Brahe's data showed that this could not be so. However Kepler was gratified to be able to show that his laws did embody some mathematical harmony. Thus his second law showed that even though the planets did not traverse equal distances in equal times, at least equal areas were swept out in equal times. Another consequence of his work, which also pleased him, was that if a cube were inscribed in the orbit of Saturn the orbit of Jupiter would just fit inside it; if a tetrahedron were inscribed in Jupiter's orbit the orbit of Mars would fit; an octahedron inside Mars's orbit would accommodate the earth's orbit; a dodecahedron in the earth's orbit would accommodate the orbit of Venus and an icosahedron inside Venus's orbit would accommodate the orbit of Mercury. This relationship between the orbits of all the then known planets and the five perfect solid shapes is only approximate and of course the subsequent discovery of more planets has destroyed claims for a fundamental symmetry of the solar system based on the perfect solids, but detection of more planets was yet to come and this relationship gave Kepler more joy than the three mathematical laws by which he is now chiefly remembered.

For to him, the connection between the perfect solid shapes and the planetary orbits revealed, indeed gave proof of, the harmony of the created world and of the celestial music of the spheres. So convinced was he of there being a divine mathematical plan that he argued that the Creator had intended the earth to move round the sun in 360 days, not 365¼, a 'disjointed and ignoble fraction', and it was the presence of the sun that had upset the purity of the relation.[24] Kepler likened the universe to the Trinity and for him the sphere was the embodiment of the Trinity; it followed that he held the cosmos to be spherical, closed and finite. Westfall says that:

> The sphere was thus to Kepler more than the shape of the universe. As the image of the divine, it was the form of every being that aspires to perfection assumes, as far as it is able to do so.... The soul, and to Kepler everything was ensouled, pours itself forth from its punctiform abode, both in perceiving external things that surround it in spherical fashion, and in governing its body.... Inevitably he applied the same analogy to light as one of the foremost powers inherent in bodies.

> Kepler insisted that light is not the rays that spread out from luminous and illuminated points. The rays are only the lines of motion. Light itself is the spherical surface that their equal motions constitute, the surface that represents the Son in the trinitarian scheme. Hence in optics as in most of his science, Kepler's contemplation of nature brought him back, not just to theism, but to the very heart of the Gospels. Jesus said, 'I am the light of the world.'[25]

The overtones of animism and the importance of the sun in Kepler's metaphysics indicates the pervasive influence of hermeticism; for example:

> Hence the sun is a certain body in which resides the faculty, which we call light, of communicating itself to all things. For this reason alone its rightful place is the middle point and centre of the whole world, so that it may diffuse itself perpetually and uniformly

throughout the universe. All other beings that share in light imitate the sun.[26]

But Kepler did not endorse Bruno's cosmology, 'that dreadful philosophy', which he thought implied blind impersonal causes rather than a divine ordering.[27] However we can see that his reasons for putting the sun in the centre of the cosmos arose at least in part from his own metaphysical beliefs. It was because he thought the sun must be central that he could not accept Tycho Brahe's cosmology which retained an immobile earth in the centre, even though, as pointed out above, the Brahe scheme was in better accord with current observations and with contemporary scientific theory.

Kepler's universe was essentially Copernican, though with elliptical orbits; for working astronomers and navigators it was an improvement on the Copernican scheme since it was a source of more accurate prediction, but *as a physical description* it was subject to the same criticisms. In order to overcome the scientific objections it would be necessary to reassess concepts of matter and motion and thereby to change physical theories. This was to start with the work of Galileo.

Galileo (1564–1642)

Galileo Galilei, like Copernicus, was a mathematician and, again like Copernicus, he had an established academic reputation when still young. At the age of 25 he became a professor of mathematics at Pisa and three years later, in 1592, he took the Chair of mathematics at Padua, in the republic of Venice. It was here that he worked on the problems of falling bodies and arrived at new laws of motion which were to undermine Aristotelian physics.

His work involved a great deal of ingenious and painstaking experimentation, and it also involved a new conceptual approach to the nature of motion and the relation between force and motion. In accordance with common-sense observation, Aristotle had held that it was necessary to exert some force, a push or a pull, not only to start movement but also to maintain it. Aristotle had said that there were but two kinds of 'natural' motion that did not require motive force: one in the heavens, and one on earth and therefore below the sphere of the moon. Above the sphere of the moon the fifth element, the quintessence, had a natural propensity to rotate eternally along with the spheres themselves; below the sphere of the moon the natural motion of any body (which would be composed of some or all of the four elements) was to move in a straight line towards its proper place (in effect to move vertically up or down according to density).

Galileo made a major break with Aristotelian physics for he claimed that the same laws would apply on earth as in the heavens. He suggested that not only the heavenly bodies[28] but the earth and all bodies on it had a natural circular motion which had been bestowed by God (see third quotation on p. 50) and that they would continue to move round indefinitely, at constant speed, without the need for any further force. However he appealed to the Aristotelian notion of earthly bodies seeking their rightful place to account for their acceleration as they fell to earth. Thus, though he criticized much of Aristotle's physics, Galileo was still influenced by Aristotelian metaphysics and in particular by the latent animism in Aristotle's account of motion. Writing of the general influence of Aristotelian theory, William Shea says that though Aristotle was attacked in the seventeenth century his detractors 'usually retained more of his philosophy than they would have been fond of admitting'.[29]

Galileo supported his ideas by appeal to metaphysical notions of perfection as well as to the authority of Plato and Aristotle. In his *Dialogue Concerning the Two Chief World Systems*, Galileo used Salviati as his spokesman; Salviati concedes that Aristotle was correct in his view that circular motion was more perfect than linear motion and that the world is most perfect:

> I return then to Aristotle.... he ... assumes it as a known and manifest thing that the motions directly upward and downward correspond to fire and earth. Therefore it is necessary that beyond these bodies, which are close to us, there must be some other body in nature to which circular motion must be suitable. This must, in turn, be as much more excellent as circular motion is more perfect than straight. Just how much more perfect the former is than the latter, he determines from the perfection of the circular line over the straight line. He calls the former perfect and the latter imperfect; imperfect because if it is infinite, it lacks an end and termination, while if finite, there is something outside of it in which it might be prolonged.

> I say that in his conclusions up to this point I agree with him, and I admit that the world is a body endowed with all the dimensions, and therefore most perfect.[30]

But he goes on to argue, *contra* Aristotle, that since our world is perfect then everything must be in its proper place and in perfect order and the only possible natural motion, on earth as in the heavens, is circular motion:

if all integral bodies in the world are by nature movable, it is impossible that their motions should be straight, or anything else but circular; and the reason is very plain and obvious. For whatever moves straight changes place and, continuing to move, goes even farther from its starting point and from every place through which it successively passes. If that were the motion which naturally suited it, then at the beginning it was not in its proper place. So then the parts of the world were not disposed in perfect order. But we are assuming them to be perfectly in order; and in that case, it is impossible that it should be their nature to change place, and consequently to move in a straight line.[31]

Salviati suggests that bodies might have moved naturally in a straight line during the construction of the world, i.e. whilst order was being established, and, in medieval and Renaissance fashion, he appeals to the Creator and to Plato:

We may therefore say that straight motion serves to transport materials for the construction of a work; but this once constructed, is to rest immovable – or, if movable, is to move only circularly. Unless we wish to say with Plato that these world bodies, after their creation and the establishment of the whole, were for a certain time set in straight motion by their Maker. Then, later, reaching certain definite places, they were set in rotation one by one, passing from straight to circular motion, and have ever since been preserved and maintained in this.[32]

and a little later:

This assumed, let us suppose God to have created the planet Jupiter, for example, upon which He had determined to confer such-and-such a velocity, to be kept perpetually uniform forever after. We may say with Plato that at the beginning He gave it a straight and accelerated motion; and later, when it had arrived at that degree of velocity, converted its straight motion into circular motion whose speed thereafter was naturally uniform.[33]

We can now appreciate that Galileo's new postulate of natural (what we should now call 'internal') circular motion on earth was at least partly based on and justified by his metaphysical beliefs. He asserted it as a metaphysical *truth*, not merely as a methodological rule, and he used it as a foundation for his physics. It was this physics that overcame many of the contemporary 'scientific' objections to the Copernican theory; for, if circular motion be natural on earth, then a stone thrown vertically upwards will rotate as the earth rotates and so will return to the same place when it descends. Likewise bullets shot eastwards from guns will not recoil and birds will be able to fly East as easily as they fly in any other direction – a major criticism of Copernican theory is no longer valid.

Galileo favoured the Copernican cosmology before he had established his new physics and before he had made discoveries about the heavens with the telescope (see below). It may be that his belief in the central sun and a moving earth prompted him to seek to change physical theory for, like Copernicus, he had feared ridicule if he openly announced that he thought that the Copernican cosmos was a physical reality. However, to the *cognoscenti* he revealed his true opinion. Thus in a letter to Kepler, thanking him for a copy of *The Mystery of the Universe*, Galileo wrote:

> I promise to read your book in tranquillity . . . and this I shall do the more gladly as I adopted the teachings of Copernicus many years ago. . . . I have written many arguments in support of him and in refutation of the opposite view – which however, so far I have not dared to bring into public light, frightened by the fate of Copernicus . . . who though he acquired immortal fame with some, is yet to an infinite multitude of others (such is the number of fools) an object of ridicule and derision.[34]

As well as his new physics, Galileo found support for Copernicanism from his observations with the recently invented telescope. He published these in *The Starry Messenger* of 1610. He claimed that the heavenly bodies could be seen to have flaws and so they were not perfect and unblemished as Aristotle had asserted; for example, craters and mountains would be observed on the moon and there were dark patches on the sun. Moreover the Milky Way was not a light in the sky but a multitude of distant stars so that the universe was very much larger than had been imagined; therefore Copernicus's claim that stellar parallax could not be detected because the stars were so far away (see p. 32) became more credible. The telescope also showed that the planet Jupiter had satellite moons and so provided more evidence to support Brahe's criticism of Aristotle's theory of crystalline spheres (see p. 44). Lastly the telescope revealed the phases of Venus that were to be expected if Copernicus's theory were correct (see p. 32).

Galileo does not appear to have been directly influenced by Hermetic doctrines and though we have seen that he appealed to Platonic ideas of perfection, he did not show the mystical attitude to numbers and to geometrical figures that was characteristic of Kepler. Galileo related his mathematics even more firmly to observation; he thought that mathematics could give an objective description of the world and he went beyond Kepler in developing the view that the only objectively real properties were those that could be directly measured and that could therefore be treated mathematically. These and only these could provide a sound basis for philosophical (what we should now call 'scientific') inquiry. This led him to distinguish them as *primary* qualities, a distinction which would be elaborated by Descartes (see p. 67). Like Descartes, Galileo thought that those qualities that could not be measured, designated as *secondary* qualities, were the results of our sensory responses. Primary qualities were the only intrinsic properties of external bodies:

> To excite in us tastes, odors, and sounds I believe that nothing is required in external bodies except shapes, numbers, and slow or rapid movements. I think that if ears, tongues, and noses were removed shapes and numbers and motions would remain, but not odors or tastes or sounds. The latter I believe are nothing more than names when separated from living bodies, just as tickling and titillations are nothing but names in the absence of such things as noses and armpits.[35]

This is a new approach to qualities, but we can see the influence of Renaissance and medieval thought as he continues:

> And as these four senses are related to the four elements, so I believe that vision, the sense eminent above all others in the proportion of the finite to the infinite, the temporal to the instantaneous, the quantitative to the indivisible, the illuminated to the obscure – that vision, I say, is related to light itself.[36]

But empirical enquiry not only arises from but must return to sense perception and therefore some credence must be given to any sense experience. Moreover, some of the secondary qualities (colours, for example) are dependent on the sense of sight and are notoriously difficult to match and to compare. So there seems no good reason for Galileo to single out vision as being more reliable than the other senses. Indeed elsewhere[37] he argues that we can be misled by what we see. Perhaps he was thinking of vision as the necessary sense for the measurement of distance and of shapes but I would suggest a less 'rational' explanation. In the passage quoted the special place accorded to vision and to the light by which we see shows that Galileo was influenced by the long-established tradition of veneration of light as an analogue of spiritual light and of divine revelation. Medieval and Renaissance influence also shows in his non-rejection of animism; for example in his letter to the Grand Duchess Christina he says that the question as to whether the heavenly bodies are alive or not must be left open:

> among physical propositions there are some with regard to which all human science and reason cannot supply more than a plausible opinion and probable conjecture in place of a sure and demonstrated knowledge; for example, whether the stars are animate.[38]

Though he was inevitably caught up with the metaphysical and, as we shall see, the religious beliefs of his time, Galileo was breaking new ground in his approach to empirical equiry – one based on measurement and mathematics. Explanations were to be in terms of mathematical laws derived from the measurement of 'real' properties. He showed how the descent of falling bodies and the paths of projectiles could be expressed in mathematical terms; the mathematical formulae described what could be observed. His physical theories depended on mathematical reasoning but he tested them by appeal to sense experience. Thus he prepared the ground for a new mechanics, one based on observation, measurement and mathematics. He laid the foundations of classical physics albeit he did not resolve problems concerning basic mechanical concepts: mass and its relation to momentum and force. Burtt says, partly quoting Galileo himself:

> Galileo does not always include weight among the primary qualities ... 'I desire, before passing to any other subject, to call your attention to the fact that these forces, resistances, moments, figures etc., may be considered either in the abstract, dissociated from matter, or in the concrete, associated with matter. Hence the properties that belong to figures that are merely geometrical and nonmaterial must be modified when we fill these figures with matter and give them weight.' He goes on to observe that when a geometrical figure is filled with matter it becomes *ipso facto* a 'force' or a 'moment', unphilosophical terms which he was striving to endow for the first time with exact mathematical meaning.[39]

Behind the new approach: the emphasis on primary qualities, and on measurement and mathematics, there was a new metaphysical assumption, namely that knowledge of the world should be expressed in mathematical terms so that the ultimate and best description of empirical events was in terms of mathematical equations.

It might seem that Galileo's findings and his inferences must convince honest sceptics of the truth of Copernicanism so that only blind academic orthodoxy and religious bigotry delayed the triumph of Copernican cosmology. But this was not the case; Galileo begged the question. His inertial theory was based on metaphysical assumptions that could no more be justified than those of his critics *unless the Copernican theory were assumed to be correct*. Indeed, as we shall see, Galileo's version of Copernicanism was not correct. But even if it had been, his new physics and his telescopic evidence were equally compatible with Tycho Brahe's cosmology. For, though the telescope had shown the universe to be very large, so that stellar parallax might be so small that it would be difficult to detect even if it occurred, it remained the case that parallax had *not* been detected and therefore the earth might really be at rest.[40] In addition, Galileo ignored Kepler's evidence for elliptical orbits. Galileo was perfectly capable of understanding Kepler's abstruse mathematical calculations and it is highly unlikely that he was unaware of Kepler's laws, but it was inconvenient for him to have to acknowledge them, since they were incompatible with his own theory of circular inertial motion. Likewise he disingenuously ignored Brahe's cosmological scheme when considering the Aristotelian/Ptolemaic theory as an alternative to Copernicanism in his *Dialogue Concerning the Two Chief World Systems*. Here he aimed to show the weaknesses of the Ptolemaic cosmos and the strengths of Copernicanism but he was attacking a straw man in arguing against a system that, by 1620, nearly all astronomers had rejected. Galileo did not attempt to tackle the Brahe scheme, the real rival.

In the light of this, the response of the Roman Catholic Church seems less obtuse and dogmatic than many writers have suggested. Jesuit astronomers in Rome were very interested in the new discoveries and the new theories described in Galileo's *The Starry Messenger* and they told Cardinal Bellarmine that they had confirmed Galileo's findings. In 1611 Galileo was welcomed in Rome by the Pope, Paul V. However, even at that time Cardinal Bellarmine made some enquiries as to Galileo's orthodoxy. The cardinal had been involved in Bruno's trial and execution (see p. 39) and he was determined to avoid another confrontation and another burning; contrary to popular belief the Church did not seek to make martyrs – the aim was to persuade heretics to see the error of their ways and to recant.

We are concerned with the conflict between Galileo's basic assumptions, as compared with the assumptions of his critics, not with the details of his quarrels with the Church and with orthodox academics. We shall see that the differences were intensified because all parties had some beliefs in common. Galileo was firmly convinced that the world had been designed and created by the Christian God whose concern for humanity was revealed in the Scriptures. He was just as firmly convinced that the Bible gave true knowledge as were the cardinals and the Pope. It was his faith in God as the perfect and immutable Creator that led him to believe, as Descartes believed, that it was possible to have knowledge of the world that was certain and indubitable; events in the world that God had created and governed must be ordered according to a perfect and therefore immutable divine plan.

Galileo also believed that the Scriptures were a reliable source of empirical knowledge; it was because he was not prepared to accept the *Church's interpretation* of the Scriptures that his attitude was deplored by the clergy. He regarded Protestants as heretics, but it is not difficult to understand why the Roman Catholic hierarchy thought that his own views verged on heresy and, at best, were dangerously arrogant. Galileo himself did not think that he was undermining the Church's authority; perhaps rather naïvely he thought that he could show the Church dignitaries how to deal with the new philosophy. He argued that nature was also the book of God; it ranked with the Scriptures as a source of knowledge and might be less difficult to interpret. By implication, then, natural philosophers who studied nature were in a better position than the clergy to understand the true meaning of God's words in the Bible. Galileo said:

> I think that in discussion of physical problems we ought to begin not from the authority of scriptural passages, but from sense experiences and necessary demonstration; for the Holy Bible and the phenomena of nature proceed alike from the divine Word. . . . It is necessary for the Bible to be accommodated to the understanding of every man, to speak many things which appear to differ from the absolute truth so far as the bare meaning of the words is concerned. But Nature, on the other hand is inexorable and immutable, she never transgresses the laws imposed on her. . . . For that reason it appears that nothing physical which sense-experience sets before our eyes, or which necessary demonstrations prove to us, ought to be called in question (much less condemned) upon the testimony of biblical passages which may have some different meanings beneath their words.

> having arrived at any certainties in physics, we ought to utilize these as the most appropriate aids in the true exposition of the Bible.[41]

Galileo also appealed to what he took to be the views of the early Church Fathers; considering his own lack of theological education the cardinals in Rome must have thought him to be both arrogant and ridiculous. He quoted St Augustine, saying:

'If anyone shall set the authority of Holy Writ against clear and manifest reason, he who does this knows not what he has undertaken; for he opposed to the truth not the meaning of the Bible, which is beyond his comprehension, but rather his own interpretation; not what is in the Bible, but what he has found in himself and imagines to be there.'[42]

It was hardly a tactful way of responding to criticism from the Church establishment and from the very learned clergy, one of whom was Bellarmine. Moreover, as has been shown, Galileo had *not* established the Copernican cosmology. Leaving aside religious and scriptural reservations, the empirical evidence available gave no clear indication as to the truth or falsity of the theory of a sun-centred cosmos. Though the Aristotelian/Ptolemaic theory was discredited the Brahe scheme was as likely to be right as the Copernican. The situation was chaotic and there was a corresponding confusion in the assessment of the Scriptures: what did they tell us about the world? Who should interpret them? Did God provide the book of nature to help mankind to understand his Holy Word, the Bible, or should the Bible help mankind to interpret nature?

The Church was not primarily concerned with the certainty of empirical knowledge or with philosophical (scientific) schemes but with the stability of the Christian religion. It wanted to maintain confidence in the truth of the Scriptures as a firm and sure support for faith and as an essential guide to salvation. In 1640 it still remained the case that for most Roman Catholics the Bible, as interpreted by their Church, gave a true account of the world. Cardinal Bellarmine supported the decision of the Council of Trent (1545–63) which had forbidden any biblical exegesis contrary to what had been agreed by the early Fathers of the Church, and he held that any new cosmological theory should be regarded purely as a calculating device to save the appearances:

The Fathers *do* agree, according to Bellarmine, on a literal reading of the standard passages concerning cosmology. It is therefore a matter of faith because of the unanimity of those who have spoken. Mathematicians should therefore restrict themselves to speaking 'hypothetically and not absolutely', for to speak absolutely would injure the faith and irritate all the theologians and

Scholastic philosophers. Only if there were a strict demonstration would one be permitted to accommodate Scripture absolutely to popular discourse – and Bellarmine was convinced that no such demonstration existed.[43]

Bellarmine died in 1621 but two decades later it was still not possible to show that the sun was at the centre of the system and that the earth moved; the Roman Church could feel justified in its position. Nor did Protestants take a different view; their approach was, perhaps, more holistic but they also believed that the literal meaning of the Bible was fundamental. Westman says:

> additional help was sometimes sought from spiritual or allegorical readings, but the literal, realistic meaning always remained central. Now the literalism of the Reformers was twofold; they believed that the Bible was literal both at the level of direct linguistic reference (nouns referred to actual people and events) and in the sense that the *whole story* was realistic. The bible's individual stories needed to be woven together into one cumulative 'narrative web'. This required the earlier stories of the Old Testament to be joined interpretatively to those in the New Testament by showing the former to be 'types' or 'figures' of the latter. Luther and Calvin were agreed that there was a single theme, a primary subject matter, which united all the biblical stories: the life and ministry of Christ.[44]

This deep and strong belief in the Scriptures is difficult for us to appreciate today and therefore it is difficult for us to understand that appeals to the Bible as evidence for the truth or falsity of an empirical theory were held to be as rational and as objective (perhaps even more objective) as appeals to observation. As Rorty says:

> We are the heirs of three hundred years of rhetoric about the importance of distinguishing sharply between science and religion, science and politics, science and art. . . . This rhetoric has formed the culture of Europe. . . . But to proclaim our loyalty to these distinctions is not to say that there are 'objective' and 'rational' standards for adopting them.[45]

Religious beliefs, like other metaphysical beliefs, provide a framework for interpreting sense experience and members of a community with shared beliefs will interpret observation in the same, or very similar, ways. In the mid-seventeenth century earlier philosophical theories of nature were being severely criticized and this led to a reassessment of many metaphysical beliefs. The basic Christian belief (the Fall and Redemption) were still unquestioned but developments in natural philosophy were starting to undermine those aspects of Christianity that had become dependent on classical Greek and medieval natural philosophy.

Early seventeenth-century beliefs

Some medieval certainties remained but others had been modified and other certainties were developing. The changes were more marked in assumptions related to natural philosophy than in those related to religious belief.

1 There was still strong religious faith, whether Roman Catholic or Protestant: a belief in a caring and omnipotent God who had sacrificed His only son for the redemption of mankind after the Fall. The Bible was still regarded as a holy book and as a source of knowledge, but the role of the Church and her priests as interpreters was no longer unquestioned. Protestants, and also some Roman Catholics, were suggesting that the individual's interpretation of observation was not only relevant but important.

2 The influence of Pythagoras and Plato was as great as, if not greater, than in earlier times; there was admiration of geometrical symmetry and of the circle and the sphere as exemplars of symmetry. There was also admiration of mathematical elegance and of 'simple' equations, and a desire to keep the number of explanatory entities to a minimum in accordance with the principle of Occam's razor. The mystical treatment of numbers inspired Kepler and metaphysical notions of symmetry influenced Copernicus and Galileo.

3 New assumptions about the nature of space arose: it came to be thought of (as most of us think of it today) as the abstract entity presupposed by Euclidean geometry, homogeneous throughout the entire universe. This geometrization of space[46] was accompanied by increasing awareness of the importance of measurement and the beginning of a distinction between primary qualities, seen as measureable and objective, and secondary qualities, seen as non-measureable and dependent on individual sense responses.

4 A consequence of the acceptance of a homogeneous space was that the notion of the same physical laws on earth and in the heavens became acceptable and was eventually assumed without question. Theories based on different natural motions on earth and in the heavens came to be rejected.

5 Matter was coming to be regarded as inert, without any 'vital' qualities. Traces of animism survived well into the latter half of the

century but they became less and less important in natural philosophy, especially in the fields of physics and astronomy.

The position in 1640

Copernicus's *On the Revolutions of the Celestial Orbs* was published in 1543; Galileo died in 1642. Those hundred years had seen the world turned upside down. The marvellous order of the Aristotelian and Christian cosmos was threatened and the common-sense certainty of Aristotelian physics had vanished. Natural philosophy, the social order and religion were in turmoil because fundamental metaphysical assumptions were no longer beyond question.

> A new philosophy calls all in doubt,
> The Element of fire is quite put out;
> The Sun is lost, and th'earth, and no man's wit
> Can well direct him where to looke for it.
> And freely men confesse that this world's spent,
> When in the Planets, and the Firmament
> They seeke so many new; they see that this
> Is crumbled out againe to his Atomies.
> 'Tis all in peeces, all coherence gone:
> All just supply, and all Relation:
> Prince, Subject, Father, Sonne, are things forgot,
> For every man alone thinkes he hath got
> To be a Phoenix, and that then can bee
> None of that kinde, of which he is, but hee.
> This is the world's condition now . . . .[47]

A new order had yet to be established.

4   The search for a new order

The mid-seventeenth century was an unsettled time in Western Europe; nothing seemed stable: the chaos we have remarked in natural philosophy: the conflicting metaphysical beliefs about the nature of the cosmos, about Man's place and status and about the purpose of the Creation were part of a wider disturbance. On the Continent, France, the Netherlands, Spain and the German Principalities were embroiled in the Thirty Years War – an era of sporadic fighting, devastation and misery which in fact lasted for fifty years (1610–60). In Britain the Civil War led to the execution of Charles I in 1649; there was further upheaval after the death of Oliver Cromwell in 1658, though relative calm followed the restoration in 1660. Over a great part of Europe the Roman Catholic Church's counter-Reformation was supported by an active Inquisition, and the heretic Protestant Churches were themselves divided into acrimonious sects. As Donne said, the old-established certainties had been undermined and yet nothing had replaced them. Each man could claim that he spoke truth; philosophies conflicted and mystical fantasies and magical practices abounded; humanity seemed to be degenerating fast and moving ever farther from the Golden Age.

Yet by 1640 Descartes, the principal architect of a new metaphysics, had published some of his writings and in 1642 Newton, the principal builder of classical physics, was born. These two owed much to their predecessors – they stood on the shoulders of giants – and their influence would have been much less without the interest and support of their supremely gifted contemporaries, but it is not unfair to see them as establishing the new order. That order is one that we still, in the main, accept today; many twentieth-century scientists and philosophers take its basic metaphysics as being sacrosanct, and as embodying truths about the nature of empirical inquiry that cannot seriously be questioned. It is a metaphysics that absolutely rejects animism and teleological explanation in that it is assumed that *ultimate* explanations of all physical events must be in terms of preceding physical events and established causal laws. At the last the fundamental metaphysical belief of modern science[1] is that the universe and all that is in it is a vast machine operating in a way that can be described by physical laws.

It must be stressed that neither Descartes nor Newton would have thought that a mechanistic physics could explain human actions. They both believed that every human being had a non-material soul which was the essential person. Human actions were initiated and directed by the soul and could not be explained as being the result of determinate and determining physical laws. Descartes and Newton, like nearly all philosophers of their day, also believed in the existence of an omnipotent non-material God who was not constrained by the causal nexus of the universe He had created. However we shall see that despite the acknowledgement of God's power, the new natural philosophy, and especially the Cartesian approach, implied a purely secular and materialistic explanation of events.

But first we must see how that new philosophy was itself implied by the mathematical approach to nature which can be traced back to Pythagoras and Plato and which appeared with increasing importance in the work of Copernicus, Kepler and Galileo.

Mathematics and the beginning of mechanism

As we have seen, Copernicus valued mathematical symmetry and Kepler had been strongly influenced by mathematics as symbolizing heavenly harmony. Galileo had not been dominated by a mystical view of numbers but he did believe that the world could be described in mathematical terms and therefore that the only meaningful qualities must be those that could be measured and treated mathematically. He thought that only these qualities were objectively 'real'. He said:

> *The real world is the world of bodies in mathematically reducible motions, and this means that the real world is a world of bodies moving.*[2]

For Galileo space (a Euclidean three-dimensional space) and time were ultimate realities and all physical change had to be describable in terms of changes in space and time. This entailed a revolutionary break in the concept of change and therefore in the explanation of change. We may find it difficult to appreciate how dramatic this revolution was because it does not occur to us to explain the behaviour of material objects by appealing to anything but physico/mechanical factors. But, as we saw in Chapter 1, the Aristotelian and the medieval/scholastic view of change was in terms of a 'becoming', of a potentiality becoming an actuality. Renaissance philosophers also saw change in this light: the baby became an adult, the acorn an oak, a base metal (say lead) would in due course become gold. Animate and inanimate nature strove to realize potentiality in actuality, and objects as well as living creatures were regarded as having a 'nature' so that their current state both implied and contained their future state. Hence they were not passive entities and any natural (i.e. not imposed) change in them was seen as part of their own striving to achieve their potential: 'the present state exists unmoved and continually draws into itself the future.'[3]

To us it seems bizarre to think of objects having a purpose, an internal *telos*, that is to be realized by potentiality becoming full actuality or perfection; but that was the way change was conceived from the days of the Ancient Greeks until the early seventeenth century. To fulfil potentiality was to achieve perfection; then there would be no further change for the object would have accomplished its purpose. Indeed in Galileo's writings there are traces of the notion that perfection implies no change; his argument for circular inertial motion is based on the metaphysical premiss that this occurs when perfection is realized and no further change is required (see p. 50). Both Galileo and Descartes used the same metaphysical assumption when they maintained that God must be immutable and His laws unchanging; it was because He was perfect and was pure actuality.

It also seems bizarre to us to think of the present as something static and as drawing the future towards it. This is because we have inherited Galileo's and Descartes's treatment of time and motion and a conception of the universe as a system of bodies in motion. This also leads to a conception of time as a linear continuum: we all move steadily forward in the stream of time, that is along the 'time line', and the infinitely transient present is like a point dividing the past from the future. It is a mathematical point that can be placed where we wish for physical calculations, though, in our individual experiences, it travels remorselessly onwards. On this view, events can be described in terms of the positions of three-dimensional objects in space and time.

Man and Nature

The new approach to the study of the world clearly implied physical determinism though, as already indicated, because human beings were held to have a non-material soul, human actions were not thought to be determined.[4] However, it then followed that human beings were not part of the new natural philosophy. That philosophy did not ignore the living human body *considered as a physical object* because descriptions and explanations of bodily happenings (such as heart beat) could be given in terms of objects in time and space (including the space within the body) but it did lead to the dismissal of mental (as opposed to brain) events from the field of inquiry. Man as a creature with conscious awareness was not a subject for physical study. Descartes thought that human beings were totally different from the rest of Creation since all other living things could be treated as machines which did not possess any inner experiences. Thus as Burtt says in *The Metaphysical Foundations of Modern Physical Science*, Man was separated from, taken out of, nature:[5]

> Instead of causal explanation in terms not unsuited to a metaphysic which regarded man as a determinative part of nature and a link between matter and God, we now, after his banishment from the real world, explain causality solely in terms of forces revealing themselves in the mathematically expressible motions of matter itself.[6]

In addition God was removed, at least from direct participation;[7] He could still be regarded as First Cause, as the Creator Who had planned the world with mathematical perfection and Who had ordained the physical laws of nature, but the very perfection of His Creation implied that He would not change anything.

Descartes (1596–1650)

Descartes's mother died when he was young and at about the age of 10 he was sent to the Jesuit College of La Flèche where he stayed until he was 18. He remained a Roman Catholic, and was sympathetic to the Jesuits, throughout his life though he claimed that all he had learned at the College was mathematics. However, it is clear that he learned much more; for example when he was 15 he had heard of Galileo's astronomical observations with the telescope, observations that had been verified by Jesuit astronomers. He was also familiar with classical authors and knew of the mathematical metaphysical theories of Pythagoras as well as being versed in the works of Plato, Aristotle and the early Fathers of the Church. He also studied the writings of the medieval Schoolmen. Gilson argues that Descartes's own writings show how strongly he was influenced by early Christian and medieval thought and that though he introduced a new philosophy (he is regarded as the father of modern philosophy) many of his ideas were

derived from the Schools. This can be seen in his exposition of theological and philosophical subjects such as free will, the problem of evil,
knowledge of truth and falsehood and innate ideas[8] and also in his
writings on natural philosophy. Gilson compares Descartes's *Les Mé-
teores (The Heavenly Bodies)* with a scholastic treatise[9] and shows
how, despite some differences, the similarities are striking:

> Il y a donc entre les contenus de ces ouvrages, a côté de différences
> l'on ne doit pas négliger, des ressemblances qui demeurent
> frappantes.[10]

After a detailed examination Gilson concludes that there can be no
doubt of Scholastic influence:

> Ainsi l'influence exercée par les méteores scolastiques sur la pensée
> de Descartes n'est pas douteuse.[11]

Descartes's ideal of a mathematical system of certain and indubitable knowledge known to be true by mental intuition (clear and
distinct ideas) is totally compatible with a Schools' philosophy that
valued logical thought as the paradigm of reason (the divine light). He
differed from the Schoolmen and sceptics such as Montaigne (1533–
92) in his confidence (the Church might say 'arrogance') in the powers
of human reason.[12]

There are also grounds for supposing that Descartes was influenced
by hermeticism. Not that he expounded mystical theories of numbers
or offered arguments with overt appeal to a metaphysical notion of
symmetry, but mathematics rests on imaginative insight and Descartes's belief that the cosmos could be described in the language of
mathematics may perhaps be due to his reading of the *Corpus Hermeticum* as well as to the influence of Galileo. Yates[13] suggests that the
three dreams that he claimed had made him realize that he must devote
his life to philosophy are close in mood to a hermetic trance.

These three dreams occurred on the night of 10 November 1619 and
Descartes believed that they could have come only from heaven. In the
first dream he was visited by ghostly presences who terrified him to
such an extent that he felt compelled to walk, although buffeted by a
great wind. He sought refuge in a College which he passed on his way;
the gate was open and he tried to reach a chapel in order to pray. He
saw two men and one of them told him that a Mr N wished to give him
something; Descartes thought that it was a melon. He noticed that all
the people now gathered round him were standing upright whereas he
was still bent and wavering even though the wind had slackened.
Thereupon he awoke and immediately felt a sharp pain which he

thought was caused by an evil spirit. He lay thinking about the punishment his past sins might merit, and about good and evil. Two hours later he fell asleep and had a second dream in which he heard a loud noise which he took to be thunder; on opening his eyes, he saw sparks of fire scattered throughout his bedroom. Soon he had a third dream: on his table he found two books without knowing how they happened to have been placed there. One was a dictionary, the other an anthology of poems entitled *Corpus poetarum*. He opened it and fell on the verse *Quod vitae sectabor iter?* (What road shall I take in life?). At that moment a stranger appeared who showed him a poem starting with *Est et non* (Yes and No). Descartes recognized it and proceeded to look for it in the book of collected poems on his table. Meantime the dictionary disappeared, then reappeared but in a shortened form and he realized also that the anthology was not the edition he knew; it contained a series of small engraved portraits he had not seen before. The visitor and book disappeared but Descartes went on sleeping and, while sleeping, he started to interpret his dreams.

He concluded that the dictionary was the gathering together of all the sciences. The *Corpus poetarum* indicated more particularly the union of philosophy and wisdom for indeed poets use more serious, sensible and better expressed sentences than do philosophers. (As has been remarked, in Descartes's time philosophy included mathematics as well as natural philosophy (science).) This was because divine enthusiasm and strength of imagination allowed the seeds of wisdom to grow better than the philosophers' Reason. The poem *Quod vitae sectabor iter?* showed the good advice of a wise person or perhaps of Moral Theology.

With this he awoke and pursued his interpretation: the poems of the anthology signified the revelation and inspiration that might be granted to him. The poem *Est et Non* – Pythagoras' 'Yes and No' – represented the truth and falsehood of human knowledge and the secular sciences. Descartes was convinced that through these dreams the Spirit of Truth had intended to reveal the treasures of all the sciences to him. The last dream had been pleasant and sweet and marked the future. But the first two were threatening warnings about the errors of his past life, and that was why they were so frightening. The melon represented the charms of solitude filled only with human preoccupations; the wind was nothing else but the Evil Spirit. God had not allowed him to reach the chapel since it was not God's spirit that was pushing him there. His terror in the second dream was remorse for his past sins; the thunder signalled that the Spirit of Truth was coming to take possession of him.[14]

To us, in the twentieth century, much of Descartes's account seems complete nonsense and the fact that the dreams had such a lasting influence on a man of his intellect shows the power of seventeenth-century metaphysics and religious beliefs. For Descartes his dreams of 10 November marked a turning point in his life and he regarded them as moral revelations as well as intellectual stimuli. Their symbolism, the ghostly presences, the Spirit of Truth, the magic books, the engraved portraits, the melon, the wind, were thought by him to be signs of mystical influences. They also led him to place poetry higher than reason. Later, he wrote:

> It might seem strange that opinions of weight are found in the works of poets rather than philosophers. The reason is that poets wrote through enthusiasm and imagination; there are in us seeds of knowledge, as [of fire] in a flint; philosophers extract them by way of reason, but poets strike them out by imagination, and then they shine more bright.
>
> The sayings of the sages can be reduced to a very few general rules.
>
> There is in things one active power, love, charity, harmony.
>
> The Lord has made three marvels: things out of nothingness; free will; and the Man who is God.[15]

There is here a second acknowledgement of poetry but I suggest we take Descartes's homage in a metaphorical sense. Both his mathematics and his philosophy were grounded in reason and he argued that conclusions should be arrived at by clear deductive steps; in his writings he appealed constantly to the notion of clear and distinct ideas and to logic.

However, we can accept that it was imaginative insight as much as reason which led Descartes to apprehend the cosmos as a vast machine operating according to rules laid down by God. Of course divine revelation would give knowledge of those rules but man could also discover them by using his reason. Descartes stressed that knowledge could not come from occult powers, magical incantation or talismans. Hence, though he was obviously influenced by mystical ideas he did not look to them to provide knowledge.

Yet imaginative speculation does have something in common with the logic of the Schools for both suggest that knowledge of the world does not come solely from sense experience. The imaginative conception of the universe as a mathematical system implies that empirical truths can be arrived at in the same way as conclusions of geometrical theorems. Descartes said:

Those long chains of perfectly simple and easy reasonings by means of which geometers are accustomed to carry out their most difficult demonstrations had led me to fancy that everything that can fall under human knowledge forms a similar sequence; and that so long as we avoid accepting as true what is not so, and always preserve the right order of deduction of one thing from another, there can be nothing too remote to be reached in the end, or too well hidden to be discovered.[16]

Like Galileo, Descartes drew a distinction between primary and secondary qualities but, for him, there was only one primary quality, extension. He thought that all other qualities depended on the interaction with our sense organs and so they did not have an objective or independent reality. More importantly, since such qualities could not be apprehended by the intellect alone, they could not be proper objects of knowledge. Descartes delieved that Man was essentially a *thinking* being and only that which could be mentally apprehended could give ground for certain knowledge:

The nature of matter, or a body considered in general, does not consist in its being a thing that has hardness or weight, or colour, or in any other sensible property, but simply in its being a thing that has extension in length, breadth, and depth. For as regards hardness, our sensation tells us no more than that the parts of a hard body resist the movement of our hands when they encounter it; if, whenever our hands moved in a given direction, all the bodies lying that way were always to retreat with the same speed as our hands approached, we should never have any sensation of hardness. Now it is inconceivable that, if bodies did retreat in this way, they would thereby lose their nature as bodies; so this nature cannot consist in hardness. By the same reasoning it may be shown that weight, colour and all other sensible qualities of corporeal matter can be removed from body while it in itself remains in its entirety; so it follows that its real nature depended upon none of them.[17]

It is worth noting that Descartes regarded *weight* (not of course the same as Newton's *mass*, see Chapter 5) as a secondary quality. Like Galileo he had a confused notion of force, a confusion which was to be analysed by Leibniz (see Chapter 5, p. 87), and he had therefore not appreciated that weight was a form of force and that it could be related to extension. Burtt considers that Descartes had also not appreciated that velocity was a measurable dimension of motion and that if he had treated weight and velocity as mathematical dimensions he might have made physics a part of mathematics and achieved his ideal of a deductive system.[18] However, it is difficult to see how any empirical science could be incorporated into a deductive scheme divorced from experience (see also Funkenstein's remark below, p. 69).

Nevertheless, Descartes himself thought that such a system could be constructed. His discussion of the properties of a piece of wax in Meditation II is designed to show that true perception does not depend on the senses but on the understanding:

> I now know that even bodies are not really perceived by the senses or the imaginative faculty, but only by the intellect; that they are perceived, not by being touched or seen, but by being understood.[19]

Whatever may have been his attitude to velocity (speed in a given direction) Descartes certainly regarded motion as a measureable quality and as one which could be apprehended by the intellect; at times he writes as though it were a basic primary quality like extension. In the extract below we should bear in mind that zero motion (i.e. a body at rest) is a mode of the state of motion:

> there is a formal distinction between the motion and the figure of the same body, . . . but nevertheless I cannot think of the motion in a complete manner apart from the thing in which the motion exists nor of the figure in isolation from the object which has the figure; nor finally can I feign that anything incapable of movement has figure.[20]

He explicitly relates his intellectual conception of material objects and of matter to geometry:

> I must make it clear that I recognise no kind of 'matter' in corporeal objects except that 'matter' susceptible of every sort of division, shape, and motion, which geometers call quantity, and which they presuppose as the subject-matter of their proofs. Further, the only properties I am considering in it are these divisions, shapes and motions; and about them I assume only what can be derived in a self-evident way from indubitably true axioms so that it can be accounted as a mathematical proof. All natural phenomena . . . can be explained in this way; I therefore do not think any other principles need be admitted in physics or are to be desired.[21]

'No other principles need be admitted or are to be desired': this is unequivocal. There can be little doubt that Descartes would have *liked* to transform physical science into a branch of mathematics. Indeed he found fault with Galileo for relying on experimental evidence rather than deducing his laws of falling bodies from first principles.[22]

Today we think that Galileo was right; he had sought to confine natural philosophy to the study of primary (measureable) qualities but he did not exclude sense experience. We do not think that Descartes's ideal of deduction from *a priori* premisses can give us empirical (scientific) knowledge. In practice[23] Descartes did not adhere to his ideal and he did carry out some experiments and appeal to observation. But his place as a founder of modern science is not due to his direct contributions to empirical knowledge; it is due, firstly to his mathematical discoveries (indeed Funkenstein thinks that he was 'too faithful a mathematician to be a good physicist',[24] i.e. he was too eager to form abstract systems) and secondly to his establishment of the new metaphysics whereby animism and occult forces were dismissed and physical causal explanations of *how* things happened replaced teleological explanations of *why* things happened.

Space and time

For Descartes the new mechanism appears to have posed no ultimate problems. He held that the universe extended without limit[25] and, since for him extension was equivalent to matter,[26] matter too was indefinitely extended. Moreover, since space *was* matter Descartes did not ponder the notions of absolute space and absolute position. Nor did he debate the problem of absolute time; he held time to be a mode of thinking about duration:

> time . . . we distinguish from duration taken in its general sense and which we describe as the measure of movement, is only a mode of thinking; for we do not indeed apprehend that the duration of things which are moved is different from that of the things which are not moved, as is evident from the fact that if two bodies are moved for the space of an hour, the one quickly, the other slowly, we do not count the time longer in one case than in the other, although there is much more movement in one of the two bodies than in the other. But in order to comprehend the duration of all things under the same measure, we usually compare their duration with the duration of the greatest and most regular motions, which are those that create years and days, and these we term time.[27]

Descartes did not appear to be concerned with how we can know whether or no a motion is or is not regular.

Cartesian dualism

As has been already indicated, for Descartes the human body was a machine, just like the bodies of animals, and subject to the same mechanical laws of nature. But it could also be affected by the mind (spirit, soul) which was a non-material entity and therefore not governed by causal laws. The mind was the essence of the person:

> At this point I come to the fact that there is this consciousness (*or* experience: *cogitatio*); of this and this only I cannot be deprived. *I am, I* exist; that is certain. . . . 'I am' precisely taken refers only to a conscious being; that is a mind, a soul (*animus*), an intellect, a reason. . . . I am a real being, and really exist; but what sort of being? As I said, a conscious being (*cogitans*).[28]

As Burtt has remarked (see above, p. 63) since all human beings were thought to be essentially non-material and spiritual beings they could not be subjects of inquiry for the natural philosopher. The physical body could be studied but mind (spirit, soul) was excluded and was held to be the concern of the Church. Thus Cartesian dualism, implies a fundamental dichotomy between science and religion. This is not to say that Descartes thought that the results of empirical inquiry were irrelevant to Christian teaching and that the Bible had no bearing on natural philosophy. He did stress that mankind should not seek the impossible, namely to discover God's purposes, but he agreed with Galileo that the book of nature, properly interpreted, would be in accord with the Sciptures, properly interpreted – and he offered his interpretations! Nevertheless it was the beginning of secular science and the latent dangers to established religion were appreciated by the Roman Catholic Church; Descartes died in 1650 and in 1664 most of his work was put on the Index.

Descartes had removed human actions, human intentions and human religious aspirations from the field of inquiry. This dichotomy made a mathematically based science possible and made it intellectually manageable. For acceptance of a mechanistic metaphysics implied that empirical problems could be formulated clearly and distinctly and that solutions could be found which could be demonstrated to be true or false (Yes or No). Descartes believed that in due course the nature of the observable world could be known, and known for certain; that certainty would be based on a supreme confidence in the powers of human reason guaranteed by a beneficent and perfect (and therefore non-deceiving) God:

I showed what the laws of nature were; and resting my arguments on no other principles than God's infinite perfection, I tried to prove all the laws that might have been doubted, and to show that they are of such kind that, even if God created several worlds, there could be none in which they were not observed.[29]

The Cartesian conception of 'laws of nature', and of a mechanistic universe, would have been well-nigh incomprehensible to the Ancients or to medieval philosophers. They had little or no experience of machines working independently of human (or animal) power and any regular sequence of events seemed to them to indicate some conscious purpose and activity on the part of some agent. It was precisely the regularity of celestial events which had led the Ancient Greeks and those who followed them to think that the heavenly bodies were animate; we have seen that even Galileo did not exclude that possibility. Likewise, other movements, such as the fall of heavy bodies, had to be explained teleologically.

Descartes proposed and established a new order: not the Greek and medieval hierarchy of matter and spirit but an order within an entirely material system operating according to immutable laws ordained by God. Those laws could be discovered and apprehended by human reason and though in practice inquiry into nature might appeal to observation and experiment it was in principle a purely rational activity, like mathematics. As Jaki says, Descartes's scientific account of the world was an intellectual ideal:

> The world of Descartes was his science and his science was his world. .... His science is the world as it supposedly should be, and such a world stands in one-to-one correspondence to his science. Unfortunately, the real value of the particular world of that specific correspondence was well-nigh zero.[30]

A near contemporary had a different, and in this respect a more modern, view. He did not offer an alternative *metaphysics* but his awareness of the importance of observation and experiment was to leaven Cartesian rationalism and so contribute to the new basis for science.

Francis Bacon (1561–1626)

In the seventeenth century Bacon came to be revered as the founder of the new natural philosophy; his portrait appears on the frontispiece of Sprat's *History of the Royal Society*, published in 1667, and the first Fellows regarded him as their chief inspiration. Yet he cannot be accorded any status as a natural philosopher: he did not even understand the science of antiquity and he certainly did not appreciate the significance of the new ideas of his own time. He was, to say the least, old-fashioned: he did not accept the Copernican theory[31] or the work of Galileo; he did not appreciate the importance of measurement or mathematics; he believed that inanimate bodies possessed spirits;[32] and he believed in the possibility of transmuting metals to gold. However, we must bear in mind that animistic beliefs lingered on and some of Bacon's beliefs were held by several distinguished contemporaries. Indeed later philosophers, such as Boyle and Newton, had some animistic beliefs and, for example, thought that base metals might become gold.

Bacon was revered for several reasons: firstly he argued for freedom from intellectual constraints imposed by 'authority'; in this he resembled his earlier namesake. But he was more consistent than Roger Bacon for he did not appeal to authority to support his view. Secondly he stressed the importance not only of direct observation but of critical and planned experiments; thirdly, and here he was in accord with Descartes, he advocated explanations in terms of what he called (following Aristotle) 'efficient causes', that is physical explanations rather than teleological explanations. The latter are explanations in terms of purpose, what Bacon called (again following Aristotle) 'final causes'.

The challenge to authority

Challenge to authority was challenge to the old order, it contributed to the disruption that we noted in the previous chapter, and it was a necessary precursor of the new order. Bacon's challenge was explicit and elegant. He had sharp words for the Schoolmen:

> This kind of degenerate learning did chiefly reign amongst the schoolmen: who having sharp and strong wits, and abundance of leisure, and small variety of reading, but their wits being shut up in the cells of a few authors (chiefly Aristotle their dictator) as their persons were shut up in the cells of monasteries and colleges, and knowing little history, either of nature or time, did out of no great quantity of matter and infinite agitation of wit spin unto us those laborious webs of learning which are extant in their books. For the wit and mind of man, if it work upon matter, which is the contemplation of the creatures of God, worketh according to the stuff and is limited thereby; but if it work upon itself, as the spider worketh his web, then it is endless, and brings forth indeed cobwebs of

learning, admirable for the fineness of thread and work, but of no substance or profit.[33]

He appreciated the importance of Aristotle's work but argued that he should not be taken as final authority:

> For as water will not ascend higher than the level of the first springhead from whence it descendeth, so knowledge derived from Aristotle and exempted from liberty of examination, will not rise again higher than the knowledge of Aristotle. ... for disciples do owe unto their masters only a temporaray belief and a suspension of their judgement till they be fully instructed, and not an absolute resignation or perpetual captivity.[34]

Critical observation

Bacon advocated *critical* observation of the world; he had little time for credulous acceptance of magic and, in his healthy scepticism he was ahead of his time albeit his criticism of alchemy and astrology (see below) was a criticism of quacks and charlatans, analogous to Ben Jonson's (1577–1637) criticisms in *The Alchemist*. As we have already noted, Bacon did not think that the subjects themselves were nonsensical:

> For as for natural magic whereof now there is mention in books, containing certain credulous superstitious conceits and observations of sympathies and antipathies, and hidden proprieties, and some frivolous experiments, strange rather by disguisement than in themselves, it is as far differeing in truth of nature from such knowledge as we require, as the story of King Arthur in Britain ... differs from Caesar's Commentaries in truth of story. ... So whatsoever shall entertain high and vaporous imaginations, instead of laborious and sober inquiry of truth, shall beget hopes and beliefs of strange impossible shapes. And therefore we may note in these sciences which hold so much of imagination and belief, as this degenerate natural magic, alchemy, astrology, and the like, that in their propositions the description of the means is ever more monstrous than the pretence or end.[35]

There is no truck with arcane mysteries here; Bacon's criticism of magicians could have been written in the eighteenth, nineteenth or twentieth centuries.

Bacon's positive support for critical observation consisted in advocating two points: firstly that observations should be noted and

indexed and secondly that inquiry should be directed to help understanding rather than to immediate usefulness, 'those which give most
light to the inventions of causes'.[36] His emphasis on the importance of
critical observation can be seen as the empirical counterpart of Descartes's stress on the necessity for clear and distinct ideas in reasoning.
Bacon was well aware that it was possible not only for the senses to
mislead initially but also for prejudices to bring about false interpretations. He listed various 'idols' (false notions that were venerated or
accepted without question) which could distort judgement: firstly the
idols of the tribe[37] which influenced all men: false analogy, a love of
system, a desire to see parallels and similarities where there were none
– the human intellect was like an uneven mirror that gave a distorted
image. Then there were the *idols of the cave*,[38] those which were
peculiar to the individual – some men stress resemblances and others
stress difference, some concentrate on detail, others on too broad a
description. The *idols of the market place* were errors of reasoning
arising from the misuse of words to denote something which did not
exist (e.g. *primum mobile*) or to convey an inadequate idea (e.g.
generation and *corruption*).[39] The fourth group, the *idols of the theatre*,
were not so intrinsically bound up with the way men thought; they
came from accepting the authority of others, from reading and from
study, and they were distinctively the idols of the learned. They might
be expressed in high-flown language and what was asserted might well
be supported by academic tradition even though it was false.[40]

Bacon called the first book of his *Novum Organum* 'Pars Destruens'
because its purpose was to destroy false notions and methods of
reasoning. Book II outlined the procedure he recommended: facts
must be collected and arranged. He was aware of the dangers of
induction by simple enumeration (i.e. simply collecting positive instances), what he called 'common induction' (*inductione vulgari*)[41] and
he advocated the comparison of positive and negative instances. Thus
in investigating the nature of heat he compared hot bodies (the positive
instances) with those that were not hot (the negative instances); it was
then possible to see what was contingent and what was necessary for
the phenomenon of heat. By comparison, and by observing if heat
increased or diminished with the accompanying phenomenon, Bacon
believed that the causes and the essential nature could be found; he
concluded that heat was a form of motion. He said that the method was
generally applicable to other investigations and this he called 'true
induction'.[42]

He realized that in the course of inquiry very many instances were
likely to be listed and he suggested that the labour of analysis could be

lightened by considering those cases that illustrated similarity or difference especially well; these were *prerogative instances*. He gave twenty-
seven different kinds of such instances, some are epithets that we still
use: there were *glaring instances*,[43] which had to be treated with
caution (cf. idols of the tribe); there were *travelling instances*,[44] which
varied in degree; there were *clandestine instances*,[45] where the nature
was found in its weakest state and which helped to show the limits of a
phenomenon; there were *crucial instances*,[46] where the observation or
experiment acted as a signpost or *crux*; there were *analogical instances*.[47] Bacon thought that it was more important to seek similarities
than differences for though curiosities might be amusing they were not
of any serious use in promoting knowledge.[48] In this context he was
thinking of the tendency of many of his contemporaries to comment on
the bizarre; naturalists were more interested in animals with two heads
than with one, and Bacon disapproved of this.

Much of Bacon's writings are contributions to scientific method,
contributions which were highly valued, perhaps overvalued, by his
later contemporaries and by scientists of the eighteenth and nineteenth
centuries. But his approach did have implications for the basic metaphysics in that it reaffirmed the role of sense experience in guiding us to
knowledge of the world. There is further contribution to metaphysics
in his discussion of explanation and his treatment of teleological explanation and final causes.

Explanation

Bacon looked for reasons for facts; like Aristotle he contrasted scientific knowledge, knowledge of cause with the simple empirical knowledge of the artisan. He did not doubt that there were ultimate divine
purposes (final causes) but he thought that any search for final cause
and teleological explanation would be fruitless. He said that natural
science could be regarded as a three-part pyramid: the base was
natural history (the collected facts), the middle section was physic
(intermediate explanations and efficient causes) and the apex was
metaphysic.[49] The last was in two parts: firstly formal causes and
secondly final causes. The latter were not fit subjects for inquiry:

> The second part of metaphysic is the inquiry of final causes, which I
> am moved to report not as omitted but as misplaced ... this mis-
> placing hath caused a deficience, or at least great improficience in
> the sciences themselves. For the handling of final causes, mixed
> with the rest in physical inquiries, hath intercepted the severe and

diligent inquiry of all real physical causes, and given men the occasion to stay upon these satisfactory and specious causes, to the great arrest and prejudice of further discovery.[50]

It had been thought that man was not competent to find formal causes either, but Bacon disagreed. He said it was no more impossible than the search for land when far out at sea. He thought that Plato had been mistaken in taking form (that is formal cause seen as the essential nature or Form) to be something absolutely abstracted from matter. Rather it was determined by matter, and:

> if any man shall keep a watchful and severe eye upon action, operation, and the use of knowledge, he may advise and take notice what are the forms, the disclosures whereof are fruitful and important to the state of man.[51]

He thought that the essential natures or forms of animals, plants and even inanimate materials were too complex to be inquired into, but the forms of qualities and of processes might be discovered:

> to inquire the form of a lion, of an oak, of gold; nay, of water, of air, is a vain pursuit: but to inquire the forms of sense, of voluntary motion, of vegetation, of colours, of gravity and levity, of density, of tenuity, of heat, of cold ... is that part of metaphysic which we now define of. Not but that physic doth make inquiry and take consideration of the same natures: but how? Only as to the material and efficient causes of them, and not as to the forms. For example, if the cause of whiteness in snow or froth be inquired, and it be rendered thus, that the subtile intermixture of air and water is the cause, it is well rendered; but nevertheless is this the form of whiteness? This part of metaphysic I do not find laboured and performed: whereat I marvel not: because I hold it not possible to be invented by that course of invention which hath been used; in regard that men (which is the root of all error) have made too untimely a departure and too remote a recess from particulars.[52]

Thus, for Bacon knowledge of forms would come from patient study of particulars but, and this is why he placed it higher than physic, it went beyond particulars.

He ranked mathematics (which he called 'mathematic') with metaphysics (which he called 'metaphysic'), for it dealt with abstractions rather than with particulars. But although he gave it a high place it is clear that Bacon did not appreciate its value; he thought that it could sharpen wits and likened it to tennis which made eye and body quicker but was no great use in itself.[53]

In this important respect Bacon differed from Descartes and from the great natural philosophers, Copernicus, Kepler and Galileo; he trailed behind the new approach. He also differed from them (though here he was in the vanguard) in making no direct appeal to the role of God in the natural world. Descartes had gone further than Copernicus and Kepler when he argued that we could not know God's purposes, and his philosophy implies that the cosmic machine operates without God's interference. But Bacon explicitly stated that 'God worketh nothing in nature but by second causes'.[54] He gave an extensive account of God and the Scriptures in the beginning of his *The Advancement of Learning* and, like all contemporaries interested in natural philosophy, he argued that knowledge properly assimilated would enhance religious faith.[55] But we do not find him asserting that the laws of nature remain constant because God is perfect and therefore immutable. It would seem that, for him, it was self-evidently true and needed no justification.

For Bacon natural philosophy developed as a result of patient, unprejudiced and critical observation; he argued that this would lead to the steady accumulation of facts which would become the bases for subsequent induction of causes. He did not offer any logical or mathematical schema, let alone a grand metaphysical plan. Jaki thinks that Bacon's exposition of natural philosophy was severely flawed by his restriction of the role of metaphysics and in his separation of metaphysics itself from natural theology and any appeal to divine purpose.[56]

> What Bacon called metaphysics was in complete subservience to science. What such metaphysics could do would hardly be of any profit to investigate. What it could not do is very clear from Bacon's efforts in his last ten years. They were largely spent implementing his dream of a definitive encyclopedia of useful knowledge, that is, of science. The effort was a monumental waste of energy.[57]

However Bacon's methodology did and does merit respect and though today induction is not thought to play the major part in discovery that was supposed for nearly three hundred years after his death, his account certainly cannot be dismissed as involving a 'monumental waste of energy'. Bacon showed not only that observation played a necessary part in empirical inquiry but also that clear thinking was needed for the assessment of empirical evidence as much as for logical deduction. Also, as far as it was possible in his day he rejected superstition and metaphysics based on superstition.

Mid-seventeenth-century beliefs

The certainties of medieval times had all but disappeared and the new ideas which would replace them were beginning to emerge, were beginning to be clarified and consolidated and were beginning to form the basis of a new order. That order would eventually be a secular order though, for the time, Christianity and religious faith remained firm. The divine Creator still ruled His cosmos but the new philosophy was starting to undermine belief in His concern for mankind.

1 The notion of a secular science was still latent but the new mechanical philosophy already implied that God did not interfere in His Creation.
2 The material world, as a subject of scientific inquiry, was beginning to be seen as consisting of bodies possessing primary qualities (the only objectively real qualities) and the concept of explanation was changing from being an account of purpose to an account of physical cause.
3 Human actions, controlled by the non-material soul (or mind) were excluded from inquiry; in this sense man was taken out of nature. Teleological explanations, whether appealing to divine purpose or resting on animistic beliefs, were ceasing to be acceptable.
4 Mathematics was being divorced from mysticism and was becoming related to measurement.
5 The notion that natural philosophy might be a logical discipline similar to mathematics was balanced by realization of the importance of observation and experiment.
6 There was increasing confidence in the purely human ability to know and understand the world, and much less emphasis on knowledge through divine revelation.

The position by 1660

Order was starting to emerge out of chaos. The search for knowledge of the world began to be seen as something more than a means of appreciating the marvels wrought by the Creator. There was growing appreciation of what it could signify for mankind's life on earth. As Bacon said:

> the end ought to be, ... to separate and reject vain speculations and whatsoever is empty and void, and to preserve and augment

whatsoever is solid and fruitful: that knowledge may not be as a courtesan, for pleasure and vanity only, or as a bondwoman, to acquire and gain in her master's use; but as a spouse, for generation, fruit, and comfort.[58]

5   The grand design

Knowledge and certainty

We have seen that Galileo and Descartes thought that mathematical laws of nature gave the truest and most objective account of the world; their view was that mathematical description was the ideal of philosophic inquiry. Descartes went further than Galileo because he believed that, in principle, empirical knowledge could be obtained by reasoning alone, and he attempted to present his own empirical knowledge as a deductive system in the confident expectation that ultimately all the laws of nature, and all particular events, would be logically deducible (and predictable) from self-evident premisses. Because that knowledge would be based solely on reason, and would therefore be independent of fallible sense experience, it would necessarily be true. Descartes's criterion of *knowledge* shows that he had inherited the Platonic and Aristotelian standard, namely that a claim to knowledge must be a claim to know for certain, beyond any possible doubt. Aristotle had asserted that only that which *could not be otherwise* should be rated as knowledge, or rather as what was called 'scientific knowledge'.[1] Unlike Plato, Aristotle had thought that observation, sense experience, could be a basis for this scientific knowledge but Descartes disagreed.[2] He argued that the only knowledge that *could not be otherwise* must be based on logical reasoning from self-evident premisses.

Rationalism

Descartes, Leibniz and Spinoza epitomize the rationalist tradition, the tradition that genuine knowledge must be arrived at through the exercise of reason and that information from the senses, if rated as 'knowledge' at all, is an inferior kind of knowledge. This view of knowledge dominated French and much Continental philosophy throughout the seventeenth and eighteenth centuries. Indeed the rationalist criterion of 'scientific' knowledge was accepted by British empiricists, though they disagreed with rationalists as to the primacy of reason.

There were contemporary critics of other aspects of the Cartesian exposition, not only in Britain but also in his own country. For example Descartes's assertion that clear and distinct ideas *guaranteed* truth was questioned; some objected to his identification of space with extension and to his contention that a vacuum was a logical impossibility. It was pointed out that any corpuscular theory, and Descartes himself put forward a corpuscular theory, entails empty space, since there must be space between the corpuscles if they are to *be* corpuscles. Others objected to Cartesian dualism, among them the materialist philosopher Thomas Hobbes (1588–1679) and the idealist, Leibniz (1646–1716). Hobbes thought that soul, mind and spirit could be accounted for in purely physical terms. Leibniz thought that matter could be accounted for in purely mental terms.

Empiricism

The main British empirical tradition was not materialist; most British philosophers were Cartesian dualists. However, they differed from Descartes and were more in sympathy with Galileo, in their opinion that knowledge of the world must depend on observation and experiment and could not be obtained merely from the logical analysis of clear and distinct ideas. We have seen that Francis Bacon had shown how sense experience was to be used and that his writings had such influence that he had been honoured by the founder members of the Royal Society. In fact Bacon's insistence on observation and experiment along with his failure to appreciate the importance of mathematics and imaginative speculation could not in themselves have led to the burgeoning of natural philosophy in the seventeenth century. But Bacon was not the only influence; those who praised him took his recommendations to heart but they also took note of the Galilean approach based on mathematics and measurement and, despite their overt rejection of conjecture,[3] they indulged in imaginative speculation as to causes.

British empiricists had no doubt that sense experience was essential for knowledge of nature even though they accepted the rationalist ideal of knowledge. Hence, since they knew that sense experience was limited and also fallible, they had to concede that knowledge of the world could not be knowledge of the highest kind; it could never be *knowledge that could not be otherwise*. For example, John Locke (1632–1704) held that abstract reasoning was of little use in inquiry into the nature of substances:

> *Experience here must teach me* what reason cannot; and it is by trying alone that I can certainly know what other qualities coexist.[4]

and

> I must apply myself to *experience*: as far as that reaches I may have certain knowledge but no further.[5]

He thought that the only *certainty* to be derived from perception must come from '*the present testimony of our senses*, employed about particular objects'[6] because any further inference (for example a generalization that would refer to objects and events *not* directly observed) could not be guaranteed to be correct. Hence it was not possible to demand logical demonstration in the ordinary affairs of life[7] and he had to admit that natural philosophy could not be a science:

> I deny not that a man accustomed to rational and regular experiments, shall be able to see further into the nature of bodies and guess righter at their unknown properties than one that is a stranger to them; but yet . . . this is but judgement and opinion, not knowledge and certainty. This *way of* getting and *improving our knowledge in substances only by experience* and history, which is all that the weakness of our faculties in this state of *mediocrity* which we are in in this world can attain to, makes me suspect that natural philosophy is not capable of being made a science.[8]

Locke believed (mistakenly) that had we been able to observe the corpuscular constituents of bodies and materials[9] it would have been possible to deduce their properties from 'the present testimony of our senses' and this would enable us to have scientific knowledge. However, as we shall see (Chapter 6) sense experience can never provide logical indubitability and observation of micro-structure can provide no more certainty than direct observation of macro-objects.

Although Locke was a sincere Christian he made no attempt to appeal to God's perfection as a support for his theory of knowledge. For Descartes the truths arrived at by reason and the objective reality of the material universe were guaranteed by God who, being perfect, would not deceive mankind. As we know, Descartes admitted that sense perception was liable to error through human misinterpretation and he appreciated that human reason might also be fallible. But it could be subjected to critical analysis and Descartes was convinced that if reasoning stood up to the test of such analysis then the ideas were clear and distinct and their validity was then guaranteed by God. Locke made no overt reference to a divine guarantor.

The secularization of natural philosophy

The new approach to inquiry was tending to remove God from nature not only in the sense that it became inappropriate to seek God's ultimate purposes,[10] and not only in the sense that God, having created the world and ordained the laws of nature did not then intervene.[11] In addition there was no longer any pretence of basing knowledge on divine revelation;[12] it came to be accepted that human reason and/or human sense perception were the sources of human knowledge.

In earlier times it would have seemed irreverent to rely on a uniformity in the sequence of events and on the constancy of the laws of nature without reference to God's perfection and immutability – Bacon was one of the first to do so. God's grand design was indeed still acknowledged: the movements of the heavenly bodies showed His power and were tributes to His majesty, but there was an implicit assumption of secular causal relations. By the middle of the seventeenth century most philosophers followed Bacon in taking the uniformity of nature to be a self-evident truth. It was not until the mid-eighteenth century that David Hume showed that this 'truth' was by no means self-evident and could not be deductively established (see p. 119).

But this was still to be. In the seventeenth century there were no such doubts. There were problems but there was confidence that they would be solved. Both the rationalists and the empiricists believed that in due course human beings would arrive at a full explanation of natural events through complete knowledge of the laws of nature. As we have seen, Locke, the empiricist, accepted that this knowledge could not embody necessary truth but he did not doubt that the findings of natural philosophers would be utterly reliable, and would have practical if not logical certainty.

The new problems

By mid-seventeenth century the problems involved with the concepts of force and weight were coming to the fore. The Aristotelian concept of force as push or pull is strongly anthropomorphic, though clearly animal force is also part of the concept. But after the introduction of the notion of inertial motion by Galileo, force came to be related to changes in motion rather than to muscular effort. It was appreciated that inanimate bodies could exert force and that the concepts of force and weight were related. Most material bodies were seen to possess weight[13] (gravity); force was necessary to raise them or to move them horizontally and they could exert force as they fell or as they were brought to rest. Nevertheless weight was not at first regarded as an intrinsic property of matter; neither Galileo nor Descartes thought of weight as a primary and objectively real quality. Descartes had explicitly rejected it (see quotation on p. 67) because he thought it was a quality dependent on sense perception.

The principle of inertial motion: Descartes

In Chapter 3 we saw that Galileo had formulated a principle of circular inertial motion which he had justified by appeal to metaphysical assumptions; later Descartes formulated the principle of inertial motion in a straight line. He justified the principle partly by appeal to our direct experience of motion but, like Galileo, he also sought support by appeal to metaphysical and religious beliefs. Descartes was not affected by Bacon's secular approach to natural philosophy and the extracts below clearly show how much Descartes relied on appeals to God's immutability and perfection which he saw as providing support for human inquiry. He pointed out that *without* reflection 'we think more activity is needed for motion than for rest'[14] but, he said, further thought would overcome this prejudice for 'effort is needed not only to move external bodies but also, quite often, to arrest their movement, if it is not arrested by gravity or some other cause.'[15] He concluded that 'motion and rest are simply two different states (*modi*) of a body'.[16] He affirmed that God must be the ultimate cause of all motion and that the amount of motion in the universe must remain constant (an implicit reference to God's perfection and consequent immutability).

> As regards the general cause [of motion], it seems clear to me that it can be none other than God himself. He created matter along with motion and rest in the beginning; and now, merely by his ordinary co-operation, he preserves just the quantity of motion and rest in the material world that he put there in the beginning. Motion, indeed, is only a state (*modus*) of the moving body; but it has a certain definite quantity, and it is readily conceived that this quantity may be constant in the universe as a whole, while varying in any given part.[17]

Referring to the motion of particular bodies he said:

from God's immutability we can also know certain rules or natural laws which are the secondary, particular causes of the various motions we see in different bodies. The *first* law is: *Every reality, in so far as it is simple and undivided, always remains in the same condition so far as it can, and never changes except through external causes.* Thus if a piece of matter is square, one readily convinces oneself that it will remain square for ever, unless something comes to change its shape. If it is at rest, one thinks it will never begin to move, unless impelled by some cause. Now there is equally no reason to believe that if a body is moving its motion will ever stop, spontaneously that is, apart from any obstacle. So our conclusion must be: *A moving body, so far as it can, goes on moving.*[18]

and he developed this into a second law, again justified by appeal to God's immutability:

Any given piece of matter considered by itself tends to go on moving, not in any oblique path, but only in straight lines. . . . The reason for this rule, like that for the last one, is the immutability and simplicity of the operation by which God preserves motion in matter.[19]

Descartes also considered the transference of motion from one body to another, the total quantity of motion remaining constant of course. But he related 'quantity of motion' to the *size*, not the weight, of bodies, though he had a notion of inertial resistance to motion (see quotation, p. 86 below). In the terminology of classical physics Descartes was proposing a conservation of momentum (the product of what we would call *mass* and *velocity*) and he had not arrived at the more fundamental notion of energy and the principle of conservation of energy. Thus his third law (law of nature) was:

When a moving body collides with another, then if its own power of going on in a straight line is less than the resistance of the other body, it is reflected in another direction; but if its power of going on is greater than the resistance, it carries the other body along with it, and loses a quantity of motion equal to what it imparts to the other body. . . . This third law covers all the particular causes of corporeal change . . . I am not now considering whether, or how, human or angelic minds have the power to move bodies.[20]

It is to be noted that Descartes excluded human and angelic forces from his mechanics. Shortly afterwards he referred to inertial motion:

It must be carefully observed what it is that constitutes the power of a body to act on another body or resist its action; it is simply the tendency of everything to persist in its present state so far as it can (according to the first law). . . . what is at rest has some power of remaining at rest; what is moving has some power of persisting in its motion – in a motion constant as regards velocity and direction. This last power must be estimated according to the size of the body, and of its surface, which separates it from others, and the velocity of the motion, and the kind and degrees of opposition of state (*modi*) involved in the collision of bodies.[21]

Decartes related inertia, 'the tendency of everything to persist in its present state as far as it can', to *size*, just as he had related quantity of motion to size. It is of course true that, for a body of a given material, the greater the size, the greater its inertia. But Descartes did not seem to appreciate that a small dense body might have greater inertia than a large one that was less dense; probably this was because he did not regard weight as an objective primary quality whereas he held that extension was. We shall see that for Leibniz the term 'size' represented weight and his appreciation of the importance of the concept of weight was a significant advance towards the concept of mass.

Quite apart from Descartes's vagueness about *weight* his account of the transfer of motion is incorrect because he had no clear concept of what we now call 'energy'. The notion of energy in classical physics is intimately bound up with the notion of force and weight, the latter being the result of gravitational force. Since Descartes had a confused and unanalysed conception of force and weight it was not possible for him to arrive at a clear concept of energy.

The concept of energy: Leibniz

The relationship of velocity to energy and the distinction between momentum and energy was clearer to Leibniz, and his criticism of Descartes shows the part reason can play in making experience meaningful. Leibniz agreed with Descartes that, in collision, and the transfer of motion, motive force would be conserved but said that Descartes had erred in his assessment of what motive force was. Descartes had taken it as being equivalent to *quantity of motion* but, said Leibniz, this was not so.

In the passage below, the terms 'force' and 'motive force' appear. Leibniz's 'force' is equivalent to the terms 'work' or 'energy' of classical physics and the term 'motive force' (which he sometimes calls *vis viva*) is the 'kinetic energy' of classical physics. It is important to bear this in mind because, as we shall see, Newton used the term 'force' in the sense in which it is now used in classical physics. Hence every time 'force' appears in Leibniz's writings I have followed it by 'energy' in brackets. Other words also have their classical equivalents following them. As already indicated, what Descartes (and Leibniz) call 'quantity of motion' is equivalent to the term 'momentum' in classical physics. Leibniz says:

> Descartes, and many other able mathematicians, have believed that the quantity of motion [momentum] – that is the speed multiplied by the size [weight] of that which moves agrees – agrees perfectly with the motive force [energy]. . . . Now it is reasonable that the same force [energy] should always be conserved in the universe. . . . One notes . . . that the force [energy] of a body is diminished only to the extent that it gives some of it to some contiguous bodies, or to its own parts in so far as they have a separate motion. Thus it has been believed that what can be said of force [energy] could also be said of quantity of motion [momentum].[22]

Leibniz goes on to show that this is not so by comparing the force [energy] and quantity of motion [momentum] of two weights of 4 lb and 1 lb. He argues that they will acquire the same force [energy] if the 1 lb weight is dropped from four times the height of the 4 lb weight. But Galileo's laws show that they will not have the same quantity of motion [momentum] for the velocity of 1 lb weight will be only twice the velocity of the 4 lb weight and hence it will have only half the quantity of motion [momentum].[23] He concludes:

> There is, therefore, a great difference between quantity of motion [momentum] and force [energy]; which is what was to be shown. By this one sees how force [energy] must be measured by the quantity of the effect which it can produce; for example, by the height to which a heavy body of a certain size [weight] and kind can be raised, which is very different from the speed which can be given to it.[24]

From his knowledge of Galileo's laws and by clear reasoning, Leibniz showed that a body raised to a certain vertical height acquires a certain force [energy – in this case potential energy] which would be equal to the motive force [kinetic energy] it would have when it fell. The motive force [kinetic energy] would be proportional to the *square* of the velocity whereas the momentum (what *Descartes* has called 'motive force') was proportional to the velocity itself.

Like those of Descartes, Leibniz's arguments presupposed a metaphysical principle of conservation, for he postulated that the total amount of force [energy] remained constant.

Leibniz's metaphysics

Leibniz did not make overt reference to God when discussing physical laws – he was influenced by the secularism developing in the second half of the century – but he did appeal to God's perfection and immutability to justify his metaphysics.

Leibniz and Descartes had different views as to the nature of ultimate reality. We have seen that Descartes was a dualist, holding that there were two different kinds of ultimate substance: matter (with the essential property of extension) and spirit (with the essential property of thought). Leibniz was an idealist monist who held that ultimate reality was non-corporeal and consisted of an indefinitely large number of perceiving and apperceiving[25] spiritual substances, which he called *Monads*. He argued that the very notion of extended matter involved a contradiction: for if matter were continuous and infinitely divisible then there could be no real parts, only arbitrary divisions; but if matter were composed of indivisible ultimate parts then the whole could not be a real unity but merely an arbitrary collection. Such metaphysical theorizing may seem to be of barely peripheral interest to science but much of what Leibniz said is relevant to current physical discussion on the nature of the ultimate constitution of matter: are sub-atomic 'particles' tiny bits of *stuff* or are they *waves*? Have they an objective existence independent of perception or are they mental constructs? Here we shall not debate twentieth-century problems for we shall be concerned with comparing Leibniz's view with those of Newton.

Since Leibniz considered that ultimate reality was non-corporeal he thought that matter was phenomenal, that is, that it had no *ultimate* reality. It followed that what appeared to be interaction between bodies was also phenomenal for there were no real bodies:

> It could therefore be said . . . that one particular substance never acts on another particular substance, nor is acted on by another, if one considers the fact that what happens to each is simply a consequence of its complete idea or notion alone. . . . Really nothing can happen to us apart from thought and perceptions, and all our future

thoughts and perceptions are only consequences . . . of our preceding thoughts and perceptions.[26]

For Leibniz the world *was* our experiences and material objects, including our bodies and the bodies of other people, were but phenomena, albeit well-founded phenomena. Leibniz distinguished them from dreams and visions because there was an orderliness in the sequences of well-founded phenomena. This orderliness was a consequence of the pre-established harmony ordained by God. As we shall see, Leibniz believed that our ideas of time and space only reflected phenomenal relations and that our notion of cause and effect was merely *our* way of relating phenomena. He thought that, in an ultimate sense, everything that had happened, was happening and would happen was nothing more than a mass of perceptions and apperceptions, harmonized by God and part of a timeless, predetermined and divine reality. Leibniz said:

> Now it is God alone (from whom all individuals emanate continually and who sees the universe, not only as they see it, but also in quite a different way from all of them) who is the cause of this correspondence between phenomena, and who brings it about that what is particular to one should be public to all; otherwise there would be no interconnexion.[27]

and a little before this he wrote:

> all our phenomena, that is to say all the things that can ever happen to us, are only consequences of our being. These phenomena preserve a certain order, which . . . means that we are able to make observations which are useful for regulating our conduct, which are justified by the success of future phenomena, and in this we are often able to judge accurately about the future by means of the past. This would be enough for us to say that these phenomena are true, without troubling ourselves as to whether they exist outside us, or whether others apperceive them.[28]

Thus Leibniz regarded natural philosophy as a wholly legitimate study of phenomena and, at the phenomenal level, he thought that it was quite in order to speak of bodies acting on each other and of causal relations. As we have seen, his exposition of motion treated the world *as though* bodies were real entities. As an explanation of phenomena his physics required only the metaphysical presuppositions that there was an orderly succession of events and that there was no further creation and no annihilation.

Leibniz's view of space and time

Leibniz held that space and time had no objective reality but were notions that arose from our ways of relating phenomena. He regarded the common belief in the existence of absolute space as a Baconian idol of the tribe.[29] He argued that since empty space was postulated as being absolutely uniform, parts of space could only be differentiated by the bodies in them, and hence space itself could have no reality, for:

> if space is nothing other than this order or relation, and is nothing whatever without bodies but the possibility of placing them in it, these two conditions, the one as things are, the other supposed the other way round, would not differ from one another: their difference existing only in our chimerical supposition of the reality of space itself. But in truth the one would be just the same as the other, as they are absolutely indiscernible; and consequently there is no occasion to search after a reason for the preference of the one to the other.[30]

Leibniz was appealing to his metaphysical Principle of Sufficient Reason:

> *that nothing happens without a sufficient reason why it should be thus rather than otherwise.*[31]

The Principle applied at the ultimate level in relation to the ordered sequence of perceptions and apperceptions. But it also applied at the phenomenal level and here the concept of space was useful for though there was no *absolute* space, the concept helped us to relate phenomenal bodies.

Leibniz argued that the Principle could also be used to show that there was no absolute time:

> The same is true of *time*. Suppose someone asks why God did not create everything a year sooner; and that same person wants to infer from that that God did something for which there cannot possibly be a reason why he did it thus rather than otherwise, we should reply that this inference would be sound if time were something apart from temporal things, for it would be impossible that there should be reasons why things should have been applied to certain instants rather than to others, when their succession remained the same. But this in itself proves that instants apart from things are nothing, and that they only consist in the successive order of things.[32]

Leibniz and religious belief

For Leibniz God was the Creator of the world and He had established the consistency shown in the sequences of apperceptions. That there was this consistency was, he thought, a *proof* that there must be a divine power,[33] though he stressed that he did not introduce God as general cause to account for all events in a general way.[34] Since Leibniz was a Roman Catholic his God was the Christian God but it is clear that his philosophy had no place for a Redeemer and did not require a God with any particular concern for human affairs. In relation to the phenomenal world Leibniz's view of knowledge was independent of any divine power; he was confident that human reason was capable of understanding the working of the cosmos. The medieval Schoolmen had believed that, with God's help, Man might come to understand Nature but they did not claim that there could be complete understanding; Leibniz did. Thus, as we have seen, he argued that if *we* could not suggest a reason for the Creator creating the universe at a particular time then it *must* follow that time was unreal. Likewise if *we* could find no sufficient reason for placing bodies one way in space rather than another then space *must* be unreal.

Like Descartes, Leibniz postulated a God who did not alter the cosmic machine; he argued that a Creator who needed to intervene in His creation could not be perfect. Writing to Samuel Clarke, he took issue with Newton on this:

> Mr. Newton and his followers have also an extremely odd opinion of the work of God. According to them God has to wind up his watch from time to time. Otherwise it would cease to go. He lacked sufficient foresight to make it a perpetual motion. This machine of God's is even, on their view, so imperfect that he is obliged to clean it from time to time by an extraordinary concourse, and even to mend it as a clockmaker might his handiwork; who will be the less skilful a workman, the more often is he obliged to mend and set right his work. According to my view, the same force and vigour goes on existing in the world always, and simply passes from one matter to another according to the laws of nature and to the beautifully pre-established order.[35]

Leibniz's deity is all-powerful, but He is not so much a Christian God as a guarantor of human reason. As Funkenstein says:

> Only God guarantees the validity of Leibniz's Principle of Sufficient Reason. Leibniz's God is a methodological guarantee for the utter rationality of the world.[36]

The link between physics and metaphysics

Leibniz had appreciated that his notion of energy had metaphysical implications[37] and that it connected the non-corporeal objectively real world of the Monads, and their inner energy,[38] with the phenomenal energy of phenomenal bodies. This latter he might call '*vis viva*', 'derivative force' or 'impetus'. The nature of the connection between non-corporeal energy and phenomenal energy is puzzling, but it did not appear to present problems to Leibniz (see again note 28, p. 89).

The concept of energy was treated very differently by Newton and, not surprisingly, his metaphysics and physics were different. Because Newton was a dualist he thought that the material world was as objectively real as the spiritual world. Like most later-seventeenth-century philosophers he followed Galileo and Descartes in believing that the universe was to be explained in mechanistic and mathematical terms and, despite metaphysical appeals to God's attributes and to God's providence, his approach to physical explanations was secular.

Isaac Newton (1642–1727)

Newton was born at Woolthorpe Manor, near Grantham, and was an undergraduate at Cambridge University. In 1665, the year of the Great Plague, he returned home; some thirty years later he said that it was while he was at home that he developed his physical laws concerning the effects of centripetal force (from hereon we use 'force' in the classical sense and as Newton himself used it) and gravitational attraction. He showed that his laws were compatible with and could be drived from Kepler's laws of planetary motion (see p. 46). He calculated the force of gravity at the surface of the earth from Galileo's laws of falling bodies and the measured distances of the earth from the moon. He could then estimate the speed of the moon in its orbit and show that his calculations were in accord with what was observed, thereby confirming his theory. He did not publish his work until 1687 and it may be that he was not satisfied with his first calculations – there seemed to be an unsatisfactorily large discrepancy between what was observed and what was predicted from the theory.[39] But by 1686 there were more accurate measurements of the distances of the sun, moon and earth and Newton was then able to show that his calculations agreed 'pretty nearly' with observation.

Newton carried out many other investigations: he showed that white light was composed of the rainbow colours, that light rays could produce dark as well as bright fringes and that the rate of heat loss from a hot object was related to the temperature difference with the surroundings; his three laws of motion laid the basis for classical mechanics and dynamics. He was also a mathematical genius; he and Leibniz separately developed the differential calculus. His gravitational theory, which embodied the inverse square law of gravitational attraction,[40] was a grand synthesis. It drew together the apparently independent laws of Kepler and Galileo for Newton had shown that the orbits of the planets in the heavens and the fall of bodies on earth were both the result of the same force of gravitational attraction.

Newton's great genius shows also in his appreciation of the physical and metaphysical problems that his theory produced. At the physical level he was concerned with the concepts of mass, extension, density, force and weight and with ways of relating them by mathematically formulated laws. He developed his own system from consideration of inertial motion and because he used a Galilean methodology based on measurements and mathematics he carried physics[41] much further than had the rationalists. However, neither Newton nor his contemporaries (rationalist and empiricist alike) appreciated the essential role of imaginative speculation and they seemed unaware of their own conjecturing. Newton's famous *hypotheses non fingo* was in reference to surmise as to the nature of gravity (see below, p. 96) and the cause of the gravitational force but it reflects what can be seen as undue reliance on Baconian empiricism. The later-seventeenth-century natural philosophers regarded Bacon as *the* exponent of scientific method and, by the end of the eighteenth century, with rationalism discredited, all philosophers thought of themselves as Baconians. Bacon influenced the nineteenth-century positivists (see Chapter 7) and his insistence on the primacy of observation and the collection and comparison of facts was regarded as the essence of empirical inquiry until well into the twentieth century. Fortunately his precepts, though revered, were never strictly observed; there has always been speculation and Newton's work in particular abounds in imaginative hypothesizing.

We shall see this particularly clearly when we consider Newton's metaphysical theories but his physical theories also involved hypotheses and we need to study these first in order to appreciate the fundamental role of his metaphysical principles.

Newtonian physics and physical concepts

At the physical level Newton was concerned with the concepts of mass, extension, density, weight and force and with ways of relating them in mathematically formulated laws. He took the material world to be objectively real and, like Galileo and Descartes, he distinguished primary and secondary qualities. He did not think that extension was the only primary quality of matter but that solidity (equivalent to hardness and impenetrability) was also primary. Locke's exposition is based on Newton's account of primary qualities, and it is interesting that he presents primary qualities as those that are 'utterly inseparable' rather than as *measureable* qualities. On either view, they were qualities that existed independently of sense experience and had objective reality. Primary qualities were:

> such as are utterly inseparable from the body, in what state soever it be; such as in all the alterations and changes it suffers, all the force can be used upon it, it constantly keeps; and such as sense constantly finds in every particle of matter which has bulk enough to be perceived ... viz. solidity, extension, figure, motion or rest, and number.[42]

By contrast, secondary qualities were:

> such *qualities* which in truth are nothing in the objects themselves but powers to produce various sensations in us by their *primary qualities*, i.e. by the bulk, figure, texture, and motion of their insensible parts, as colours, sounds, tastes, etc.[43]

By 'their insensible parts' Locke meant the minute, and therefore invisible, small bodies (corpuscles)[44] that British empiricists, including Newton, thought were the ultimate constituents of matter. The corpuscles were thought to possess primary qualities, and these were held to be responsible for both the primary and secondary qualities of perceptible materials and bodies. Thus the solidity (i.e. the hardness and impenetrability) and extension of each corpuscle constituted its *mass*, and mass was therefore a primary quality. The mass of a macro-object was the sum of the masses of its constituent corpuscles and hence all material entities had mass, and mass was a primary quality of macro-objects as well as of the minute corpuscles. Newton's use of the notion of inertial mass and his concepts of force (and in particular of weight) presuppose the fundamental and objectively real quality of mass that the corpuscular theory of matter (itself a metaphysical theory) postulates.

Mass and inertia

Descartes had related the inertia of bodies to their size and Leibniz to their weight but Newton related it to mass. And what was mass? Newton said that it was 'the quantity of matter in a body', i.e. the quantity of corpuscles. It would seem he assumed that the corpuscles were of equal density[45] but that in a dense material they would be more tightly packed; hence a small piece of matter could be composed of more corpuscles, and therefore have a greater mass, than a larger piece of a different material. The smaller piece would, of course, have a greater density. Now the density of any given material can vary: if it expands or contracts (as on heating and cooling or with a change of state) the 'packing' of the corpuscles will change. But the *number* of corpuscles will remain the same and so its mass will remain constant. Hence the quantity of matter seems to be a basic property of each particular body. Like all his contemporaries, and like all physicists until the twentieth century, Newton assumed that the mass of a body was in no way affected by its velocity.

Newton accepted the Cartesian principle of inertial motion and then went on to define force as *that which was necessary to overcome inertia*, that is to *change* velocity. Force is necessary to stop a moving body, to start a body moving from rest, to increase or decrease its speed and to change its direction from a straight-line path. It followed that force is needed to keep a body moving in a closed orbit since the straight-line direction of motion is ever changing.

Thus far Newton was following in the footsteps of Descartes, but he went further. He postulated that, for any given body, the change in velocity (the acceleration)[46] would be directly proportional to the force applied and that the constant of proportionality could be taken as the *mass* of the body. Hence if *F* is the applied force, *m* the mass and *a* the acceleration, then:

$$F = ma$$

The new concept of force

That formula represents a methodological rule, perhaps even a meta-physical principle. For we cannot ever *observe* motion free from all interference (true inertial motion) and so we have no direct experience of it; nor can we give a logical demonstration whereby the principle of inertia is established on rational grounds. As we have seen, Galileo and Descartes made it a metaphysical principle, justified by appeal to God's perfection, and this was also Leibniz's view. But Newton treated it as a methodological rule; he used it to measure and compare forces by measuring and comparing the acceleration they produced in known masses. Those masses could themselves be measured by using one constant force, the force of gravity.

Force and weight

Galileo had shown that the acceleration of a falling body was constant; this had been an experimental finding, it had not been deduced from any 'self-evident' premisses or from a metaphysical postulate justified by appeal to God's perfection and immutability. Newton postulated that there was an attractive force between any two material bodies which was directly proportional to the product of their masses and inversely proportional to the square of the distance between their centres of gravity (the inverse square law). As we know, he refused to commit himself to any hypothesis suggesting the cause of this attractive force. This force accounts for the weight of bodies and, applying the inverse square law, it can be shown that the acceleration produced by the force, as a body falls, remains almost constant.[47] Thus Galileo's law of constant acceleration confirms and is confirmed by Newton's law of gravity.

It is possible to measure the acceleration g of falling bodies, and we can then calculate the force with which a body of mass m is pulled towards the earth; it is given by the formula

$$F = mg$$

and this force will be the *gravity* or *weight* of the body. Thus for all bodies *on earth* the weight will be directly proportional to their mass[48] and this means that mass can be inferred from measured weight. It must be stressed that mass is not the same as weight; mass is a primary property of matter that, in classical physics, remains constant for any given body; weight is the result of the gravity pull of the earth. The moon has a much smaller mass than the earth, and therefore less gravity pull, so that a body on the moon *weighs* far less, though its mass is the same. People on the moon can move about more easily than on earth and can carry what, on earth, would be oppressively heavy equipment. Likewise in space, where there is negligible gravity, a body of any mass will have negligible weight; this is the phenomenon of weightlessness experienced by spacemen.

So Newton had tackled the problem of force and with it the problem of weight and he had done so by making the two methodological assumptions referred to above: he assumed the principle of inertia and he assumed that the force necessary to overcome inertia was proportional to the *mass* of the body concerned; in effect mass was equivalent to the inertial resistance of matter. Force could now be divorced from its anthropomorphic overtones; it could be objectively measured from the acceleration produced in a given mass and it could be *defined* as the product of mass and the acceleration produced in that mass.

But are we not in a circle here? For how do we measure mass? We derive it from weight. And how do we assess weight? As a force. Thus:

$$F = ma \text{ (definition)}$$

Therefore

$$m = F/a$$

But also

$$m = \text{Weight}/g$$

So we can take any body and find its weight in terms of some arbitrary standard – the pound or the gramme – and then from our measurement of g we can calculate the mass of that body.[49] We can then calculate what force would be needed to produce a given acceleration, a, in that mass – perhaps horizontally on earth, or as a projectile or a space rocket. We expect these calculations to be in accord with what we observe but if the acceleration we calculate does not occur we do not regard this as invalidating the law $F = ma$, we assume that there must be some other force (positive or negative) that we have not allowed for. This is because we have *defined* force in terms of acceleration so that the relationship $F = ma$ is not a genuine empirical law.

Newton, of course, was aware of this and was worried by it since he appreciated the metaphysical problems arising from his approach to the concepts of acceleration and force. He was particularly concerned about the attractive force between bodies at a distance for it seemed as though that force must operate across empty space. Critics, especially the followers of Descartes, accused Newton of reintroducing the occult powers which had so recently been discredited. His supporters, such as Samuel Clarke, suggested that the attractive force was an innate property of matter but though Newton himself entertained this idea he was not willing definitely to commit himself to that explanation – he framed no hypotheses.

Physical and metaphysical problems

As we have seen, force has to be calculated from acceleration, and forces can only be compared by comparing the accelerations they produce on a body of given mass. Now how do we measure acceleration? It is change of velocity in unit time and to measure *changes* in velocity we have to be able to find velocity and we must do this by measuring distances covered in a given time. Thus these measurements are the basis for the calculations necessary for finding acceleration and force. Newton appreciated that this posed problems at the metaphysical level.

Absolute space

If we assume a homogeneous space extending indefinitely in all directions then the position of a lone object cannot be specified, for position has to be related to something, for example another object. Likewise the concept of *change of position* can have no significance for a lone object. If we assume just two objects, then if their relative positions change are we to say that only one moves? If so which one? Or do both of them move? The answer depends entirely on what we decide to adopt as our point of reference. If we choose one of the objects then the other one moves relative to it; if we choose some other point of reference (say the mid-point of the straight line joining the two objects) both objects might change their position relative to that point and then both could be said to have moved. Questions about such movements present methodological problems for physics but to answer them we have to make metaphysical assumptions about points of reference.

In our experience there are an indefinitely large number of objects in space; so that in every day life we take reference points that are convenient; for example, a room, in reference to the objects in it, the earth in reference to cities and rivers, and the fixed stars in reference to movements of the heavenly bodies. But is there an *absolute* reference point? Can space itself provide a reference so that *in principle* even the position of a lone object could be established? If this were so, then, even though human beings might not know any absolute position, their physics could be based on the assumption that there were absolute as opposed to relative changes of position and therefore absolute as opposed to relative motions. We may recall that Leibniz had rejected the concept of space (as an ultimate reality) because he held that it would be impossible to identify parts of space without reference to bodies. As we shall see, Newton took another view.

Absolute time

There is an analogous problem in relation to the measurement of time. From the days of Aristotle it had been appreciated that the concept of time was significant because the things in the world change; they change in appearance and/or position and we are able to appreciate the passing of time because things change. If nothing whatever were observed to change we would have no way of measuring time; in effect we would be in a Sleeping Beauty situation where, within the enchanted palace, time 'stood still'.

Time is measured by relating it to sequences of similar events. Galileo was said, wrongly as it happened,[50] to have used his pulse to time the swings of the pendulum in the cathedral at Pisa. This would not have been very accurate because pulses are not completely regular. But how do we know this? By comparing pulse rate with a *more regular* sequence; Galileo did not have a watch and in his day the accepted sequences such as the annual orbit of the sun and the nightly rise of the Dog Star (Sirius) marked time periods that were inconveniently long for measuring a pendulum swing. Yet, though more regular than a pulse, these sequences are not absolutely regular. How do we know? It can only be by comparison with something else. The most regular sequence we can take (today we rely on atomic vibrations) is shown to *be* the most regular because it most consistently correlates all other time intervals; this is our only way of testing regularity. Our mathematical/scientific and now our common-sense concept of time as a steady stream in which 'the present' moves forward along the time line at a constant rate depends on there being events. Without events and therefore without any change, it has no empirical significance. Is it then illegitimate to appeal to the notion of an absolute and perfectly regular flow of time as an ideal, albeit an unattainable ideal?

Newton's metaphysics

Newton believed that there were indeed absolute positions in space and that there was a perfect, regular flow of time.

He conceived of space as establishing absolute positions, so that any portion of *space* (as opposed to any body in space) was fixed:

> As the order of the parts of time is immutable, so also is the order of the parts of space. Suppose those parts to be moved out of their places and they will be moved (if the expression may be allowed) out of themselves. For times and spaces are, as it were, the places as well of themselves as of all other things. All things are placed in time as to order of succession; and in space as to order of situation. . . . And that the primary places of things should be movable is absurd. These are therefore the only absolute places; and translations out of those places are the only absolute motions.[51]

He conceded that we human beings have to be content with measuring relative position and relative motion:

But because the parts of space cannot be seen or distinguished from one another by our senses, therefore in their stead we use sensible measures of them. For from the positions and distances from any body considered as immovable, we define all places; and then with respect to such places, we estimate all motions. . . . And so, instead of absolute places and motions, we use relative ones.[52]

Newton did not argue the case for absolute time, he took it for a fundamental metaphysical postulate, but he appreciated that it had to be distinguished from the time that we were able to measure; he called the latter 'relative time', 'apparent time' or 'common time'. Thus:

Absolute time and mathematical time, of itself, and from its own nature, flows equably without relation to anything external, and by another name is called *duration*; relative, apparent and common time is some sensible and external (whether accurate or inequable) measure of duration by means of motion which is commonly used instead of true time.[53]

He realized that there was no way for us to know that our 'sensible measures' were measuring the absolute flow of time:

it may be that there is no such thing as an equable motion, whereby time may be accurately measured. All motions may be accelerated and retarded, but the flowing of absolute time is not liable to any change. The duration or perseverance of the existence of things remains the same, whether the motions are swift or slow, or none at all; and therefore this [absolute] duration ought to be distinguished from what are only sensible measures thereof.[54]

It is interesting to compare this with Descartes's account of time (quotation on p. 69) and Leibniz's (quotation on p. 90). Descartes was well aware of the practical point, that time had to be measured by motion and that the 'most regular' was the best to choose, but he did not address either the question as to how we could assess the regularity or the question of an absolute standard. Leibniz dismissed the notion of absolute time because it gave rise to problems in relation to his Principle of Sufficient Reason. Newton, though more secular in his exposition of physical events, based his metaphysical assumptions on appeal to God, a God more mysterious that the guarantor of perfect uniformity required by Descartes and of intellectual rationality postulated by Leibniz.

Newton's metaphysics and religion

Newton believed that absolute space and absolute time were aspects of God, and that God was directly concerned with forces (*a fortiori* the force of gravity) and with the causal laws of nature. This God did not detach Himself from His creation. Newton surmised that space might be a manifestation of God; he called space 'God's sensorium' and although he did not mean 'God's brain' since, for him, God was non-corporeal, he did think that that God was essentially immanent in space and was involved in His creation. Funkenstein says:

> But what is the subject in which time and space as absolute predicates inhere? What reality would they have (as they must) if all bodies were annihilated (as God can do)? From early on Newton maintained that space and time are explicatory predicates to God's omnipresence and eternity, since these attributes should be understood literally and unequivocally. The presence of God in space allowed him not only to act in space . . . but to be the actual carrier, or subject, of force between bodies. And finally, space is indeed a *sensorium Dei*, a 'sense organ' of God. . . . We ought not to say that all things *are* in God or participate in him, since God has no body. . . . the relationship between God and entities in space (creatures) is analogous to that between sensing subject and his sensations . . .

> [BUT]

> whereas our sensations . . . enter the sensory . . . from outside it; this is not the case at all with God's sensory. In respect to God, 'outside' and 'inside' the *sensorium* cannot be viewed as *two* places: they are the very same space. Space is the place of objects and at the same time the place of God's intuition of these objects. . . . Newton used the different properties of space to show how God is in things 'by essence, power and knowledge'.[55]

As we see, Funkenstein considers that for Newton God was in some sense the means of transmitting force across space. Newton had originally surmised that the transmission might be through some etherial medium but he decided that there were cogent physical objections:

> Against filling the heavens with fluid medium, unless they be exceeding rare, a great objection arises from the regular and very lasting motion of the planets and comets in all manner of courses through the heavens. For thence it is manifest that the heavens are void of all sensible resistance, and by consequence, of all sensible matter . . .[56]

> [A fluid would] serve only to disturb and retard the motions of those great bodies and make the frame of nature languish. . . . And as it is of no use . . . so there is no evidence for its existence and therefore it ought to be rejected.[57]

The last sentence shows a firm empiricism and a rejection of unnecessary entities in the Occam tradition. It is also interesting to note that Einstein's reasons for dismissing the notion of an ether (see pp. 171–2) are very similar to those of Newton.

Newton did think that there would be occasions when God would have to intervene in the ordering of the world and, as we saw in the quotation on p. 91, Leibniz had derided this. Newton's belief in God's present concern for His creation and present activity also permitted a role for God's providence and, as Newton thought, gave some escape from determinism.

By now it may seem absurd to contend that Newton, the natural philosopher who thought his exposition of the Creator's grand design gave proof of His existence, was a secular scientist. Not only did his reliance on the constancy of his laws of nature depend on God's will, but his metaphysics directly involved God in nature. One of Newton's arguments for relating God so closely to space and for denying the Cartesian assertion that matter (body) was equivalent to extension (so that it was logically impossible for there to be a vacuum) was to counter the atheistic notion that God was not the First Substance. He said:

> We are not able to posit bodies without at the same time positing that God exists and that he has created bodies in empty space out of nothing. . . . But if with Descartes we say that extension is body, are we not opening the way to atheism? . . . Extension is not created but was from eternity, and since we have an absolute conception of it without having to relate it to God, we are able to conceive that it exists though imagining at the same time that God is not. (This is all the more so) if the division of substance into extended and thinking is legitimate and perfect, then God would not contain in himself extension even in a pre-eminent manner and would therefore be unable to create it. God and extension would be complete and absolute entities and the term substance would be applicable to each of them in the same sense.[58]

We know that Newton finally concluded that space itself was part of the divine; his physics required a metaphysics of absolute space and time in that it implied a fixed and absolute reference for position and an ideally regular flow of time. We have seen that he took these absolutes to be aspects of God. He also allowed for God's providence: God *could* intervene and suspend the laws governing His mathematically inspired cosmos, though this was a rare event:

> although God was sovereign over a world that he created and, in principle, could suspend or change natural laws to accomplish a special purpose, in practice he did not tamper. . . . He was a God of general providence and only rarely, in the case of miracles, a God of special providence. The needs of the individual are thus subordinated to the general laws by which God maintains the common good.
>
> Mechanists employed the sovereignty of God to impose laws of nature . . . laying the conceptual basis for mathmatical physics. The sovereign redeemer of Luther and Calvin became the sovereign Ruler of the world machine. The Reformers' search for assurance of salvation gave way to the assurance of scientific explanation.[59]

Funkenstein thinks that even metaphorical corporeal references to God's attributes prepared the ground for His annihilation:

> It is clear why a God describable in unequivocal terms, or even given physical features and function eventually became all the easier to discard. As a scientific hypothesis, he was later shown to be superfluous; as a being he was shown to be a mere hypostatization of rational, social, or psychological ideas and images. . . . God lost his body in Christian theology . . . and . . . regained it in the seventeenth century. Once God regained transparency or even a body, he was all the easier to kill.[60]

As with Descartes and Leibniz, we have here to distinguish between Newton's own personal religious belief – he was a sincere though highly unorthodox Christian[61] – and the implications for his natural philosophy. He, above all others, made natural philosophy into a rational practice, where yet there was scope for creative imagination and indeed awe and wonder.[62] God was transcendent but he believed that our human capacity was of the same kind as God's though not so powerful:

> the difference between divine and human knowledge became quantitative rather than qualitative. God may possess infinite knowledge, ours is finite; God knows all at once intuitively, our thinking processes are discursive. Yet what we know, we know exactly as God knows it – it is, in fact, the same act of knowledge by which we and God know something.[63]

Hence Newton, who had formulated the laws describing the motions of the heavenly bodies could write of the Cause of the system (i.e. God):

> To make this System therefore, with all its Motions required a Cause which understood, and compared together, the Quantities of Matter in the several Bodies of the Sun and Planets, and the gravitating Powers resulting from thence; ... and to compare and adjust all these Things together, in so great a Variety of Bodies, argues that cause to be not blind and fortuitous, but very well skilled in Mechanics and geometry.[64]

God has to be a mathematician skilled in mathematics as we understand mathematics, though infinitely more adept than us.[65] Of Newton, Westfall says:

> A tradition of natural philosophy that had stood for two thousand years had been rejected and a new beginning had been made. ... At his hand, Christianity felt the touch of cold philosophy.[66]

and

> it was the rise of modern science that confronted Christianity on the most critical ground, its claim to give an account of reality ... the enchanted world of the medieval church dissolved right away.[67]

The same view that science and in particular Newtonian science had reduced the world to a cold system completely describable in mechanically mathetmatical terms is presented by Burtt:

> The general picture of the universe ... was that which had already been constructed by the great mathematical metaphysicians who had preceded him. ... it was of the greatest consequence for succeeding thought that now the great Newton's authority was squarely behind the view of the cosmos which saw in man a puny irrelevant spectator ... of the vast mathematical system whose regular motions according to mechanical principles constituted the world of nature. The glorious romantic universe of Dante and Milton, that set no bounds to the imagination of man as it played over space and time had been swept away. Space was identified with the realm of geometry, time with the continuity of number, ... The really important world outside was a world hard, cold, colourless, silent and dead; a world of quantity, a world of mathematically computable motions in mechanical regularity.[68]

This is a distorted account of Newton's own philosophy but it is a not unreasonable view of the classical scientific approach, especially in the physical sciences. In Newton's lifetime the full implications of mechanism were not realized. The world was *beginning* to be seen as a world of primary qualities but God was still revered as the Designer-Creator, maintaining His laws of nature for the benefit of mankind.

Beliefs at the close of the seventeenth century

1 There was still the conviction that *knowledge* should be certain and indubitable. Rationalists thought that it was possible to have such knowledge of the world because it could be found through the use of reason. Empiricists insisted on the necessity for sense experience (observation) and, though they thought that indubitable knowledge might be attained in principle, they believed that it was unattainable in practice.

 Nevertheless they thought that empirical knowledge fell not far short of certainty and they had absolute confidence in the Newtonian laws of nature.
2 In general, natural philosophers were dualists and believed that matter was a separate substance from mind; but the only objectively real qualities of matter were the primary qualities.
3 The Christian God was coming to be worshipped as a mathematician and designer rather than as a redeemer. He guaranteed order and consistency. The implication that he had become little more than a metaphysical postulate was not yet appreciated.

The position in 1700

Order had come out of chaos. At last men were discovering God's grand design and as they learned more and more so they must have deeper reverence for their creator. Quite different in tone from Donne's *First Anniversary* lines (above, p. 59), written in the seventeenth century, is Addison's 'Ode' of 1712:

> The spacious firmament on high,
> With all the blue etherial sky,
> And spangled heav'ns, a shining frame,
> Their great original proclaim:
> Th'unwearied sun, from day to day,
> Does his Creator's power display,
> And publishes to every land
> And work of an almighty hand.

Soon as the evening shades prevail,
The moon takes up the wondrous tale,
And nightly to the listening earth
Repeats the story of her birth:
Whilst all the stars that round her burn,
And all the planets in their turn,
Confirm the tidings as they roll,
And spread the truth from pole to pole.

What though, in solemn silence, all
Move round the dark terrestrial ball?
What though nor real voice nor sound
Amid their radiant orbs be found?
In reason's ear they all rejoice,
And utter forth a glorious voice,
For ever singing as they shine,
The hand that made us is divine.[69]

This was another kind of music of the spheres, music for the ear of reason.

6   The age of reason

Newton and Descartes

Newton's laws and theories were the basis of physics in Britain well before the end of the seventeenth century. But on the Continent, and especially in France, the Cartesian system was still preferred. It was not until the middle of the eighteenth century that Voltaire (1694–1778) persuaded the French to accept Newtonian physical theory and Descartes was superseded. By the end of the century Newton dominated the field; he was thought to have discovered the fundamental laws of nature and his influence was such that the few astronomical observations that seemed to be incompatible with the predictions made by Newtonian physics were regarded as anomalies for which an explanation would ultimately be found.

Though Cartesian mechanics, the Cartesian vortex theory and the Cartesian picture of the cosmos as a plenum had all been rejected one important metaphysical postulate remained: it was believed that the laws of nature were immutable. It followed that the causal relations deduced from these laws represented necessary connections between physical events and therefore that effects could be logically deduced from causes.

The influence of religion: British belief

In the eighteenth century, as in the seventeenth century, the great majority of natural philosophers in Britain were sincere Christians, albeit many of them were nonconformists rather than Anglican and some, like Newton, were so highly unorthodox that they would have been regarded as heretics by Roman Catholics and also by conventional Anglicans. Although there was no persecution comparable to the Inquisition, British nonconformists were at a political and social disadvantage: the Test Acts[1] excluded them from universities and therefore they could not enter the professions of law and medicine. But this very disadvantage had a beneficial effect in that it encouraged the development of new fields of learning. Nonconformists set up Dissenting Academies where students devoted themselves to subjects related to natural philosophy.

Furthermore, it has been suggested that there were intrinsic features of protestant nonconformity that would in themselves tend to stimulate and encourage inquiry into nature. Robert Merton has argued that even though the early protestant reformers were hostile or, at best, neutral to natural philosophy their puritan values indirectly encouraged the study of nature.[2] Hooykaas has pointed out that the regard for independent and critical thought, and the anti-authoritarianism which is characteristic of nonconformism, was also likely to promote inquiry and a search for explanation of events.[3] Lastly there is little doubt that many of the nonconformists, who were serious and devout, believed, as had their forebears, that they should devote themselves to natural philosophy because they would thereby help to reveal the splendour of God's works and His care for His Creation.

The Argument from Design: Christian

The belief that God created the cosmos for the benefit of mankind has biblical origins, but the discoveries of the seventeenth century and especially the cosmic organization revealed by Newton were held to show divine order and harmony so clearly that any sceptic who was made aware would be compelled to believe that there was a (Christian) God. From the seventeenth century onwards, from Robert Boyle (1627–91) to William Paley (1743–1805), and indeed well into the nineteenth century, the findings of natural philosophy were held to *prove* the existence of God and God's providence. In the heavens there was the mathematically ordered movement of the planets and the comets; on earth there was the wonderful variety of plants and animals, beautifully made to live in their habitats and also to be of use to mankind. It was in this way that not only God's power and glory but also His care and concern were made manifest by natural philosophy. The Argument from Design was an important, perhaps the most important, part of natural theology; it purported to show that it was rational to be a believer and irrational to be a sceptic.

The Argument from Design: deist

Many who accepted the Argument from Design as demonstrating that there was a God, and a beneficent God, were not prepared to accept that He was the Christian Redeemer; they were deists. One notable deist was Thomas Paine (1737–1809). Paine rejected Christianity on account of the inconsistencies (and weak morality) apparent in the Bible but he argued that the natural world did indeed give proof that a God existed. He said:

> THE WORD OF GOD IS THE CREATION WE BEHOLD; it is in *this word*, which no human invention can counterfeit or alter, that God speaketh universally to man.[4]

and

> Do we want to contemplate his power? We see it in the immensity of the creation. Do we want to contemplate his wisdom? We see it in the unchangeable order by which the incomprehensible Whole is governed. Do we want to contemplate his munificence? We see it in the abundance with which he fills the earth. Do we want to contemplate his mercy? We see it in his not withholding that abundance even from the unthankful. In fine, do we want to know what god is; search not the book called Scripture, which any human hand might make, but the Scripture called Creation.[5]

Paine quoted Addison's 'Ode',[6] pointing out that it was based on Psalm 19. He said:

> What more does man want to know than that the hand or power that made these things is divine, is omnipotent? Let him believe this, with the force it is impossible to repel if he permits his reason to act, and his rule of moral life will follow of course.[7]

It was *rational* to be a deist.

It will be remembered that in the seventeenth century, Locke, though he somewhat grudgingly granted that knowledge of the world might be obtained through revelation (see Chapter 5, note 12) did concede that there were some propositions that were above reason; these were articles of faith and only revelation could give grounds for assent.[8] By the eighteenth century this position was no longer tenable; all propositions had to have the support of reason if they were to be accepted. Thus natural theology which, in the seventeenth century, had been seen as a *prelude* to revelation and as a subsidiary support for revelation, came, in the eighteenth century, to be seen as *replacing* revelation. For those to whom the Bible seemed irredeemably irrational natural theology was acceptable for it had the support of natural philosophy (science). For many, deism superseded Christianity.

Divine design and divine laws

Seventeenth- and eighteenth-century natural philosophers, whether Christian or deist, thought that they were *discovering* the divine laws of nature. Those laws were not taken just as descriptions of what was observed and observable, and *a fortiori* not as accounts of events as we human beings could understand them. Rather they were regarded as the objective rules that controlled the universe. They had a prescriptive force and were analogous to human laws, save that they applied universally and they *could not be broken*. This conviction is expressed in Kempthorn's hymn of 1796:

> Praise the Lord! ye heavens adore Him,
> Praise Him, Angels in the height;
> Sun and moon rejoice before Him,
> Praise Him all ye stars and light.
>
> Praise the Lord! for He hath spoken;
> Worlds His mighty voice obeyed;
> Laws, which never shall be broken,
> For their guidance He hath made.
>
> Praise the God of our salvation;
> Hosts on high His power proclaim,
> Heaven and earth and all creation,
> Laud and magnify His name![9]

The rise of secularism

The design revealed by natural philosophers was thought to show clearly that there was a designer who executed a harmonious plan and that there was a general concern for the divine Creation. But the new philosophy did not have any place for God's *particular* providence (a care for individuals) nor for 'our salvation'. The concept of God was of an entity who was responsible for the creation of the world and for the uniform succession of events. As has already been pointed out natural philosophy also depended on the metaphysical assumption that human beings could understand the workings of the cosmos. Unorthodox Christianity and deism can be regarded as consequences of that new metaphysics rather than as a direct result of the *discoveries* of natural philosophers.

Even though the majority of philosophers were dualists, and believed that body and mind were two separate and distinct substances, natural philosophy inevitably came to be associated with materialism because explanations of events were sought in terms of purely physical laws, i.e. by appeal to reactions between physical bodies and to forces engendered by bodies. The secularism that was latent in the seventeenth century became explicit in the eighteenth century, especially in France. Whilst the British philosophers were Christian or deist, the French were deist or atheist. Atheists admitted that natural philsophy showed design and possibly a First Cause but was it necessary to postulate an *anthropomorphic* god? Voltaire is reputed to have said that if horses had a god he would be like a horse. Moreover was not the conventional (even the deist) concept of God redundant? It was on methodological grounds that Laplace rejected the postulate of God as an unnecessary hypothesis.[10]

The Christian and deistic notions of a personal God had in fact been rejected in the seventeenth century by Spinoza and we shall consider his views because he *retained* those aspects of the deity that were needed to provide a metaphysical as well as a methodological basis for science.

Spinoza (1632–77)

Most of his contemporaries regarded Spinoza as an arch-atheist, one who had overtly rejected any deity. This may seem strange to us since Spinoza, who was committed to the rationalist doctrine that knowledge had to be logically indubitable, considered that he had demonstrated that God *necessarily* existed. But Spinoza's concept of God was far, far, removed from the Christian concept of a Being caring for mankind and almost as far removed from the god of Descartes, Newton, Leibniz and other deists for whom God was a non-corporeal and supremely rational power. Spinoza's God was an infinite being whose existence arose from His[11] essential nature, so that He was *self-caused*. Spinoza said:

> By that which is *self-caused*, I mean that of which the essence involves existence, or that of which the nature is only conceivable as existent.[12]

Spinoza used the word 'substance' for 'that which is self-caused'; substance was something that *was* or *existed* solely on account of itself. In the quotation below I have italicized the 'is' to bring out Spinoza's meaning:

> By *substance*, I mean that which *is* in itself, and is conceived through itself: in other words, that of which a conception can be formed independently of the conception of another thing.[13]

Substances had qualities and Spinoza used the term 'attribute' for quality or property. On the basis of his definitions he demonstrated that God was the only substance and that God possessed all attributes to an infinite extent. Moreover as an infinite being God must have an infinite number of attributes although *we* could know only two of them: the attribute of extension and the attribute of thought. Since God was the only substance the cosmos *was* God, that is everything was part of (an aspect of) God. It followed that all individual and particular entities were simply modes of God, that is they evinced aspects of God's attributes:

Individual things are nothing but modifications of the attributes of God, or modes by which the attributes of God are expressed in a certain fixed and determinate manner.[14]

Each human body, for instance, was a mode of the divine attribute of extension and human thoughts and minds were modes of the divine attribute of thought. Human actions, and for that matter all events, could be described as interactions between material bodies *or* as a succession of ideas (thoughts); the two were *necessarily* in harmony because they were different ways of describing the one substance: from its aspect of extension and from its aspect of thought:

The order and connection of ideas is the same as the order and connection of things . . .

Hence God's power of thinking is equal to his realized power of action – that is, whatsoever follows from the infinite nature of God in the world of extension . . . follows without exception in the same order and connection from the idea of God in the world of thought . . .

substance thinking and substance extended are one and the same substance, comprehended now through one attribute, and now through another. So, also, a mode of extension and the idea of that mode are one and the same thing, though expressed in two different ways.[15]

Spinoza's metaphysics is a double-aspect form of monism in that there is only one ultimate reality and, as far as we are concerned, it has two aspects: extension and thought.

Implications for science

Like all seventeenth-century philosophers Spinoza was confident that human beings could understand the world that was accessible to them, i.e. in its two aspects. Therefore his philosophy supported the view that empirical inquiry would be successful. His exposition gave both matter and mind objective reality so that any study of the material world, or any mode of extension, was paralleled by thoughts or ideas of that mode, 'a mode of extension and the idea of that mode are one and the same thing.' Spinoza's thesis implies that all ideas of material entities have an objective reality and this would include the idea of causal relations between entities: 'the order and connection of ideas is the same as the order and connection of things.'[16] Spinoza agreed with Leibniz that all events, the order of things *and* the order of ideas, were predetermined. It followed that God himself was predetermined; the world could not be other than what it was.

> God cannot . . . be said to act for freedom of the will, any more than the infinite number of results from motion and rest would justify us in saying that motion and rest act by free will.
>
> *Things could not have been brought into being by God in any manner or in any order different from that which has in fact obtained.*
>
> *As I have thus shown more clearly than the sun at noonday, that we have no objective justification for calling things contingent . . .*[17]

For Spinoza it was *logically* impossible that God could be other than He was, and therefore it followed that it was logically impossible that the course of the cosmos, the modes of the attributes of God, could be a matter of chance. He believed that knowledge of the world, and therefore natural science, depended on rational analysis.[18] His philosophy is absolutely in accord with the emerging philosophical view of the universe operating like a perfect machine governed by fixed laws. But since his notion of God was so different from the rational deity of both Christians and deists, it was not surprising that he was regarded as an atheist and that his double-aspect theory was treated as a pernicious form of materialism.

Eighteenth-century materialism and the Enlightenment

The materialist believes that matter is the only fundamental substance and that all events, including thoughts and consciousness itself, can be completely described in terms of interactions between material particles. As expounded in England by Hobbes, materialism postulates that the ultimate explanations of events in the world must be in terms of interactions between particles in accordance with causal laws. Though never so popular as dualism, materialism had considerable support in the eighteenth century, particularly from French philosophers of the Enlightenment such as Voltaire (1694–1778), Diderot (1713–84), D'Alembert (1717–83), Holbach (1723–89) and La Mettrie (1709–51). For the Enlightenment philosophers materialism also carried social implications and Gellner[19] thinks that it is by no means clear that these were compatible with their philosophical outlook; however we shall not be concerned with that issue here.

Voltaire was the foremost as well as the earliest Enlightenment philosopher; he had been influenced by sceptical and iconoclastic writers such as Bayle (1647–1706) and Fontanelle (1657–1757). Voltaire visited England in 1727, the year that Newton died and, as mentioned earlier, he promoted Newtonian physics in France. He also warmed to the empiricist philosophy of Locke and was sympathetic to English deism. Although he was sceptical of the existence of an anthropomorphic God (see above) he did not, like some of his younger contemporaries such as Diderot and D'Alembert, become an atheist.

Holbach also had great influence in his day; in his *Système de la Nature*, published in 1770, he argued that the materialist view of nature was not only correct factually but also *morally right* and that any religion or doctrine suggesting the existence of a non-material soul or spirit was wrong and harmful. Gellner says:

The particular object of attack is not merely the Christian, and in particular the Roman Catholic vision of the world, but also what the author considers its buttressing by 'modern' philosophers (above all, Descartes and his followers): the main dualistic doctrines to the effect that there is an independent thinking substance in addition to extended matter and that there are modes of knowing other than through the senses. In general, one might say that what is under attack is any doctrine that impugns the unity and exhaustiveness of nature – any doctrine that adds an extramundane religious realm to the totality of nature or that introduces some fundamental rift or discontinuity inside it (such as the discontinuity between matter and thought or between determined and free events).[20]

Holbach argued that matter did not have to be given by a spiritual power because it was in itself capable of motion; in effect he made Leibniz's first entelechy, which Leibniz had said was a property of non-corporeal Monads (see p. 88), into a property or attribute of matter. For Holbach the capacity for motion was analogous to mass in that both were intrinsic to the nature of matter.

the essence of matter is to act: if we consider its parts, attentively, we shall discover there is not a particle that enjoys absolute repose.[21]

We say this motion is a manner of existence, that flows, necessarily, out of the nature of matter; that matter moves by its own peculiar energies; that its motion is to be attributed to the force which is inherent in itself.[22]

If nature had been viewed uninfluenced by prejudice, they must have long since been convinced that matter acts by its own peculiar activity; that it needs no exterior communicative force to set it in motion.[23]

Holbach appealed to Newtonian mechanics and to the principle of inertial resistance to change of motion to support his thesis that matter had an inherent capacity for motion:

A body that experiences an impulse, an attraction, or a pressure of any kind, if it resists, clearly demonstrates by such resistance that it reacts; from whence it follows, there is a concealed force, called by these philosophers *vis inertia*, that displays itself against another force; and this clearly demonstrates that this inert force is capable both of acting and reacting. In short, it will be found, on close investigation, that those powers which are called *dead*, and those which are termed *live* or *moving*, are powers of the same kind; which only display themselves after a different manner.[24]

Matter-in-motion had existed from all eternity:

If, therefore, it be asked, whence came matter? It is very reasonable to say it has always existed. If it be inquired, whence proceeds motion that agitates matter? the same reasoning furnishes the answer; namely that as motion is coeval with matter, it must have existed from all eternity, seeing that motion is the necessary consequence of its existence – of its essence – of its primitive properties, such as its extent, its gravity, its impenetrability, its figure &c.[25]

By 'primitive properties' Holbach meant what has elsewhere been called 'primary qualities'. He chided philosophers who thought that there must be some external cause of motion, saying:

They have not forsaken this error, although they must have observed, that whenever a body is left to itself, or disengaged from those obstructions which oppose themselves to its descent, it has a tendency to fall or to approach the centre of the earth, by a motion

uniformly accelerated; they have rather chosen to suppose a vision-
ary exterior cause, of which they themselves had but an imperfect
idea, than to admit that these bodies held their motion from their
own peculiar nature.[26]

The dynamics are weak here; perhaps it is permissible to conflate mass
with force, for inertial resistance to motion is what Newton had
regarded as the essence of *mass*, but Holbach seems to ignore the fact
that gravitational force is the result of an *interaction* between (at least)
two masses. Moreover he came close to endowing matter with purpose; we may be reminded of Copernicus's account of gravity as a
'natural appetency' (see quotation on p. 29). Copernicus believed that
this had been endowed by God; Holbach substituted Nature:

Had man but paid proper attention to what passed under his review,
he would not have sought out of Nature, a power distinguished from
herself, to set her in action, and without which he believes she
cannot move. . . . But if by Nature be understood what it really is, a
whole of which the numerous parts are endowed with various
properties, which oblige them to act according to these properties;
. . . there is no necessity to have recourse to supernatural powers.[27]

and:

the sum total [of diverse matter, its properties and manner of acting,
and the systems constituted by them] we call *nature*. . . . Thus nature
in its widest sense, is the grand total resulting from the assembly of
the different materials, their combinations, and the different movements we see in the universe.[28]

There was also a narrower sense of 'nature', referring to individuals –
what Spinoza had called 'modes':

Nature in its narrow sense, or as applied to each individual being, is
that which follows from its essence, that is to say, the properties,
combinations, movements, and manner of acting which distinguish
it from other beings.[29]

Holbach had a determinist view of events, like that of Spinoza, and
in giving matter activity he came close to a dual-aspect theory of the
world, though he would have resented being accused of metaphysical
speculation. Gellner says that in the preface of his *Système de la Nature*
Holbach wrote dismissively of:

the pursuit of the transcendental, the desire to indulge in metaphysics rather than in physics. Man despises realities in order to

contemplate chimeras. He neglects experience and fails to cultivate his reason, but feeds instead on conjectures and systems.[30]

The possibility that *mind* might be a property of inert matter had been entertained by Locke[31] but this was a speculation as to the possibility that God might endow a particular piece of matter with the capacity to think; Locke did not suggest that this capacity was an inherent property of matter

The incorporation of mind into matter, and the denial of immaterial spirit, was elaborated in the writings of Julien Offray de la Mettrie (1709–51). In his book *Man a Machine* he extended the Cartesian thesis that animals were nothing but complex machines (with no souls) to include human beings. Like Holbach, he thought that matter was innately active so that mental activity did not necessarily denote a different and immaterial substance:

> The human body is a machine which winds its own springs. It is the living image of perpetual movement. Nourishment keeps up the movements which fever excites. Without food, the soul pines away, goes mad, and dies exhausted. The soul is a taper whose light flares up at the moment before it goes out. But nourish the body, pour into its veins life-giving juices and strong liquors, and then the soul grows strong like them.[32]

La Mettrie dismissed attempts to make the soul a special and separate substance; it was, he said, just a feature of our material body. He argued that people were what they were partly as a result of the food they ate.

> Raw meat makes animals fierce, and it would have the same effect on man. This is so true that the English who eat meat red and bloody, and not as well done as ours, seem to share more or less in the savagery due to this kind of food, and to other causes which can be rendered ineffective by education only.[33]

Since the soul was an aspect of the body, La Mettrie suggested that a strong body would indicate a vigorous mind. Hence the well-known differences between the sexes, and the superiority of the male, could easily be explained:

> The soul follows the progress of the body, as it does the progress of education. In the weaker sex, the soul accords also with delicacy of temperament, and from this delicacy follow tenderness, affection, quick feelings due more to passion than to reason, prejudices and

superstitions, whose strong impress can hardly be effaced. Man, on the other hand, whose brain and nerves partake of the firmness of all solids, has not only stronger features but also a more vigorous mind. Education, which women lack, strengthens his mind still more.[34]

Although he was a materialist La Mettrie did believe that there was a supreme being, though not one who required or expected adoration:

I do not mean to call in question the existence of a supreme being; on the contrary it seems to me that the greatest degree of probability is in favor of this belief. But since the existence of this being goes no further than that of any other toward proving the need of worship, it is a theoretic truth with very little practical value.[35]

Exclusion and the conflict thesis

Eighteenth-century natural philosophers regarded inquiry into the nature of the world as a secular *practice* even if they might use the results of their inquiries to illustrate and support the Argument from Design. The exclusion of God from scientific explanation has been almost total; ever since and insofar as there have been explanations based on appeal to a deity or to transcendental powers they have tended to impede progress or even to reverse it. It is for this reason that the notion of a conflict between science and religion commands support. However, though we may grant incompatibility between religious and scientific accounts of the world we need to bear in mind that metaphysical beliefs have always underpinned scientific inquiry. Some of these do not involve appeal to a higher power but, as we have seen, many are supported by religious beliefs (though not necessarily arising directly from them) and they continue to be necessary even though religious doctrines are ignored or rejected.

Materialism and scientific explanation

Many of the philosophers of the Enlightenment were primarily natural philosophers (scientists): Holbach wrote on chemistry and related subjects, La Mettrie studied natural philosophy and then became a physician. They held that the world was to be explained in terms of interactions between material particles according to scientific laws, and this view of scientific explanation still dominates our scientific thought and methodology today. Although in this century some scientists have had doubts about the validity of strict causal laws, largely as a consequence of new conceptions as to the nature of matter and its relation to energy (it is accepted that the cosmic machine is much more complex than the concepts of classical physics allow) the criterion of explanation remains materialistic.

This view was already latent in seventeenth-century natural philosophy and was made overt in the eighteenth century. The other major assumption, one that we have seen was presupposed by Bacon, was that Man was a rational being whose search for the ultimate truth about the world would eventually be successful.

Yet a small cloud in the sunny sky of confidence was about to appear for, in the eighteenth century, the power of human reason itself, and *a fortiori* the role of reason in relation to empirical events, was to be challenged.

David Hume (1711–76)

As we have seen, Descartes considered that the uniform course of nature depended on the immutability and perfection of God and since Descartes did not doubt that God *was* immutable and perfect he did not doubt that the laws of nature were absolute and invariant. There are hints that reasoning from cause to effect was not a matter of logical deduction in the works of later philosophers, for example Locke[36] and Berkeley (1685–1737).[37] But the real challenge came with Hume.

Hume was sceptical as to the existence of a deity and he certainly did not wish to appeal to divine perfection as a guarantee of the constancy of the laws of nature. He pointed out that we had no logical reason to assume that the previously observed course of events would continue or that causal relations of the future would be the same as those in the past. The lack of logical certainty applied as much to common-sense generalization such as 'Fire burns' or 'Bread nourishes' as it did to scientific laws such as the inverse square law of gravitational attraction. Moreover Hume's sceptical arguments showed that it was not possible to claim indubitable knowledge even of particular objects and materials currently being observed. For example, we look at a glass of water and *perceive* its colour and shape and we claim to *know* that the glass is brittle and would break if dropped, that the water would quench our thirst, would boil if it were heated and would turn to ice if cooled. We claim, on the basis of direct perception of *some* qualities that there are others also present; the very words we use such as 'glass' and 'water' have significance because a theory of regular association of properties is presupposed.

In the quotation below Hume conceded that in respect of relations of ideas (for example mathematics) we may be entitled to claim certain knowledge (he came to doubt even this later); but the truth of statements concerning matters of fact could never be established as logically indubitable. This was because the contrary of every statement of fact could not imply a logical contradiction and so remained at least a logical possibility.[38]

All the objects of human reason or enquiry may naturally be divided into two kinds, to wit, *Relations of Ideas*, and *Matters of Fact*. Of the first kind are the sciences of Geometry, Algebra, and Arithmetic; and in short, every affirmation which is either intuitively or demonstratively certain. . . . Propositions of this kind are discoverable by the mere operation of thought, without dependence on what is anywhere existent in the universe. Though there never were a circle or a triangle in nature, the truths demonstrated by Euclid would for ever retain their certainty and evidence.

Matters of fact, which are the second objects of human reason, are not ascertained in the same manner; nor is our evidence of their truth, however great, of a like nature with the foregoing. The contrary of every matter of fact is still possible; because it can never imply a contradiction, and is conceived by the mind with the same facility and distinctness, as if ever so conformable to reality. *That the sun will not rise tomorrow* is no less an intelligible a proposition, and implies no more contradiction than the affirmation, *that it will rise*. We should in vain, therefore, attempt to demonstrate its falsehood.[39]

Hume said that all our reasonings on matters of fact were founded on causal relationships and our knowledge of these was based on appeal to past experience (our own or that of others). Any attempt to provide a logical justification of our reliance on past experience must itself be based on appeal to past experience and therefore must beg the question.

In the main Hume's contemporaries ignored his challenge. This was partly because they failed to appreciate the nature of his criticism: they thought that he was denying the existence of causal relationships whereas, as we have seen, he was pointing out that there was no logical justification for our conviction that they would continue to hold. In addition he was distrusted as a sceptic and atheist for he had also attacked the validity of the Argument from Design as proof of the existence of God. Practically all British philosophers were Christian and many Continentals were at least deists; both groups thought that the Argument from Design was incontrovertible (see quotations from

Paine on p. 109 above). Therefore, Hume was either ignored or was regarded with active hostility.[40]

Today Hume's criticism of the rational basis of empirical knowledge is still largely ignored by scientists but what has come to be known as 'Hume's problem' is much discussed by philosophers. It is relevant to note that Hume questioned even the right to assert that there was a *probability* of an empirical generalization being true in the future. He pointed out that there can be no basis for estimating statistical probability based on a number of positive instances in relation to the whole, for when making scientific investigation the number of *unobserved* instances must be indefinitely large and therefore always so much greater than the number of observed instances as to make the statistical probability of a law being true effectively zero.

On the other hand Hume did *not* think that statements concerning matters of fact had no standing. Although reasoning based on causal relationships could not be logical demonstrations it did not follow that we should not be guided by past experience and by laws of nature based on past experience. The only kind of statements that he considered worthless were those that were supported neither by logic nor by experience, that is metaphysical statements.

> When we run over libraries . . . what havoc must we make? If we take in our hand any volume; of divinity or school metaphysics, for instance; let us ask, *Does it contain any abstract reasoning concerning quantity or number*? No. *Does it contain any experimental reasoning concerning matter of fact and existence*? No. Commit it then to the flames: for it can contain nothing but sophistry and illusion.[41]

It was Kant who took up Hume's challenge. He tried to resolve the problem of justifying our reliance on causal laws and he also tried, with greater success, to rehabilitate metaphysics.

Kant's response to Hume

Immanuel Kant (1724–1804) was one of the few contemporary philosophers who understood Hume's thesis and appreciated its importance as an attack on the reliability of empirical knowledge. He did not publish until he was nearly 60 years old and although he was born only thirteen years later than Hume there was no direct communication between the two men. Kant had been brought up in a strictly religious family and, unlike Hume, he retained a great respect for religious faith, but he was far too intellectually honest to deny the force of

Hume's arguments. He appreciated that the problem of justification could not be resolved by appeal to divine perfection and immutability.

Kant suggested that all our empirical knowledge was knowledge of a phenomenal world that *we* had constructed. We could know nothing of ultimate reality (things-in-themselves), whether that reality was material, spiritual or both or neither of these. This phenomenal world that we were aware of was only perceived as an objective reality because we had organized our perceptions according to certain intuitions and concepts that were common to all human beings. He said:

> Experience rests on a synthesis according to concepts of an object of appearance in general. Apart from such a synthesis it would not be knowledge, but a rhapsody of perceptions.[42]

Kant offered an entirely new assessment of empirical knowledge; he was not merely insisting on the need for interpretation of our sensations, as Descartes had done, nor was he developing the empiricists' view of impressions and ideas as *representations* of the world; he did not think that even the most simple impression was 'given'.[43] He suggested that the process of arriving at knowledge from sense occurred in two stages. First our sensations were organized in accordance with our innate intuitions of space and time; this was necessary before they could be consciously appreciated even as *subjective* experiences. Secondly, and in order to be appreciated as objective experiences (i.e. referring to the world rather than to ourselves) they had to be structured according to certain concepts; one of these was the concept of physical objects, another was the concept of causality. It followed that what we took as the objectively real world *had to be* a world of physical objects interacting according to causal laws. It was, said Kant, a Copernican revolution in philosophy:

> Instead of all our knowledge conforming to objects, let us suppose that all objects conform to our knowledge.[44]

Though the intuitions and concepts enabled us to have objective experiences and to make judgements about the phenomenal world we had constructed with their help, it did not follow that our knowledge was completely independent of sense experience:

> Notwithstanding the independence of our pure concepts of the understanding and principles of experience, notwithstanding indeed the apparently greater extent of their use, nothing can be thought through them outside the field of experience, because they can do nothing but merely determine the logical form of the judgement in respect of given intuitions; and as there is no intuition

whatever outside the field of sensibility, these pure concepts have no meaning whatever, for there is no means of exhibiting them *in concreto* ... our understanding is not a faculty of intuition but merely a faculty of the connection of given intuitions in our experience. Hence experience must contain all the objects of our concepts, but beyond it all concepts will be without meaning as no intuition can be subsumed under them.[45]

For example, the concept of causality would have no meaning unless we had had sensations, which were then built into *subjective* experiences by our intuitions of space and time; these would be subsumed under concepts, among them the concept of causality, to yield *objective* experiences of interacting phenomena:

> Without sensibility no object could be given to us, without understanding no object could be thought. Thoughts without content are empty, intuitions without concepts are blind.[46]

Kant appreciated the force of Hume's criticism of metaphysics; he realized that metaphysical judgements could not be established as true or false by appeal to logical argument or to experience and that metaphysical speculation could be, and often was, nonsensical. Nevertheless, because metaphysical judgements were presupposed by factual judgements a justification had to be found:

> Whether metaphysics is to stand or fall, and thus its existence, now entirely depends on the solving of this problem. A man may propound his assertions in metaphysics as plausibly as he will, heaping conclusions on conclusions to suffocation; if he has not first been able to answer this question satisfactorily, I have the right to say: this is all vain groundless philosophy and false wisdom. You speak through pure reason, and presume as it were to create concepts *a priori*, not merely by analysing given concepts but by giving out that you are making new connections ... and you imagine you have insight into them independently of all experience; how do you arrive at all this and how will you justify such pretensions?[47]

For Kant metaphysical judgements were like empirical judgements in that they told us something new, made 'new connections' (he called such judgements *synthetic judgements*); but metaphysical judgements were also like logical judgements in that they did not rest on appeal to sense experience (he called such judgements *a priori judgements*). So significant metaphysical judgements were *a priori synthetic judgements* and Kant realized that he had to show that such judgements were possible. At the last we have to say that he failed in his purpose. For example he thought that he had shown that certain causal laws of science were *a priori* synthetic judgements and necessarily true but he did not succeed. For, even if we grant that the concept of causality must subsume our experiences if they are to be objective, it does not follow that any *particular* causal law is indubitable. Again, Kant argued that mathematical relations, such as $5 + 7 = 12$, were *a priori* *synthetic* judgements but this is not the case; arithmetical equations can be shown to be true by logical analysis and therefore are not synthetic judgements. Kant believed that our intuition of space *must be* of Euclidean space and therefore that phenomenal space must be Euclidean; likewise he believed that we had to describe phenomena in terms of Newtonian mechanics so that Newton's laws were necessarily true. We now know that these beliefs are false; not only can we conceive of objects in non-Euclidean space but we hold that space *is* non-Euclidean; not only can we conceive of a non-Newtonian mechanics, we now know that Newtonian mechanics is not strictly correct.

Nevertheless Kant's analysis has given us great insight into the nature of sense experience and objective reality and it has given us better understanding of the complex assumptions that underlie observation. Warnock says:

We are no doubt inclined to think of space and time as being simply 'given' features of the world. It is just the case that we find ourselves in a space of three dimensions, and that events occur successively in a single and irreversible time order. But Kant points out that there are further considerations which seem to be inconsistent with the idea that all this is a mere fact about the world. . . . we are evidently prepared to make assertions about space and time for which, if these are mere assertions of fact, we surely have not the necessary evidence. . . . that there is only *one* space; what evidence have we for so vast a claim? We take it to be certain that in any part of the universe the nature of the temporal sequence will be the same as in our vicinity; but by what right . . . ? It appears, then . . . that we do not really treat assertions about space and time as ordinary assertions of fact – as assertions to which alternatives are perfectly conceivable and for which we require the warrant of empirical observation. . . . it appears rather that we approach the universe with the postulate that whatever it may anywhere contain, its contents *shall* be in three-dimensional space, and that whatever events may at any time be found to occur, they *shall* all have their places in a single time series, and it appears also that this postulate is for us the only one that is fully and genuinely intelligible.[48]

Now of course it may be that there will come a day when we *can* conceive of different multi-dimensional spaces in the universe, and, with the development of relativity theory, our notions of time sequences are already modified. But two points made by Kant stand: first we need to have some metaphysical framework and secondly our sensations can give us intelligible experiences only if they conform to our framework. Our world, the world we experience through our senses, the world that is investigated by science, is, to a much greater extent than was appreciated before Kant's time, constructed by us. That is why, in our search for knowledge and understanding of our world, we cannot consign metaphysics to the flames.

Beliefs at the close of the eighteenth century

1 Lip service might be rendered to God but science itself had become a secular activity in that it was believed that explanations must be in terms of interactions between material bodies.
2 On the other hand, and despite Hume, it was generally believed that the order which science revealed was a proof that nature had been fashioned by a divine hand.
3 Again despite Hume, there was belief in the uniformity of nature, that events in the world (though possibly not human actions) were *determined* by the causal nexus.
4 It was conceded that truths about the world might not be logically necessary truths but there was confidence that immutable laws of nature were steadily being discovered. It was believed that Newtonian mechanics gave indubitable knowledge of the behaviour of material bodies.
5 There was complete confidence in human reason and firm belief that all truths could be understood and rationally justified.

The position in 1800

The eighteenth century saw the emergence of natural philosophy as what we, today, call 'science'. The general methodology of inquiry was similar to what it is today: to make conjectures as to explanatory theories, to observe, to measure and to attempt to describe physical events in mathematical terms. This was an ideal, but one which was being realized for physics and astronomy. Conjectures were constantly put forward but, as in the seventeenth century, the role of imagination was underestimated and it was often subsumed by reason:

Imagination, which, in truth,
Is but another name for absolute power
And clearest insight, amplitude of mind,
And Reason in her most exalted mood.[49]

Only a few poets presented a different view, and this was very far from
the mood of science:

To see a World in a Grain of Sand,
And a heaven in a Wild Flower,
Hold infinity in the palm of your hand,
And eternity in an hour.[50]

7 The age of experience

From natural philosophy to science

As we have seen, originally 'science' meant 'certain and indubitable knowledge'; hence Locke's assertion that natural philosophy could never be a science.[1] Science had also been contrasted with art where 'science' was the word for theoretical truth and 'art' stood for practical and traditional skills. The study of nature and the search for explanations of events was called 'natural philosophy' because, at first, the study of what could be observed in the world was seen as part of a more general inquiry into what human beings could know and about how they should live. It was part of a search for general understanding, and therefore it was a part of philosophy – seen as the love of wisdom. Our present view of *science* as a more limited subject with a characteristic methodology based on observation and planned experiment, on critical interpretation and generalization, and on conjectures leading to hypotheses and to explanatory theories, has developed in the last three hundred years. Hence the change from natural philosophy to science represents more than a change of name. It shows a change in attitude to the nature of empirical knowledge and to how it is to be found.

There is reference in 1725 to science as a term 'usually applied to a whole body of regular or methodical observations or propositions . . . concerning any subject of speculation',[2] and by the middle of the nineteenth century its present meaning was established so that the word 'science' gradually came to be used instead of 'natural philosophy'. Thus in 1867 W. G. Ward wrote:

> We shall . . . use the word 'science' in the sense which Englishmen so commonly give to it; as expressing physical and experimental science to the exclusion of theological and metaphysical.[3]

It was in the nineteenth century also that the empiricist thesis that knowledge of the world must be based on observation was firmly established; there was confidence that perception could be truly objective and independent of theory and that, by taking care, other laws of nature, as absolute and as certain as Newton's laws of motion, would be revealed. Nineteenth-century scientists did of course acknowledge the vital role of mathematics and many of them appreciated the role of imaginative insight; but Baconian empiricism, that is observation and inductive inference from observation, remained the rock basis. This is apparent in the writings of John Stuart Mill (1806–73). Mill, like Bacon, had no direct experience of inquiry but just as Bacon had influenced seventeenth-century natural philosophers, so Mill influenced nineteenth-century scientists. He was the principal nineteenth-century exponent of the inductive method and his *Philosophy of Scientific Method* and his *System of Logic* were generally regarded as giving a definitive account of scientific inquiry. However there was not complete unanimity; William Whewell argued that metaphysics underlay all interpretation of sense experience and he also thought that Mill's exposition of scientific method did not adequately account for discovery.

William Whewell (1794–1866)

Whewell did not deny that induction was an integral part of scientific method and that generalizations and laws might be inferred from observations of particular events, but he maintained that observations were meaningful only by virtue of certain Fundamental Ideas that were independent of perception and of past experience:

> The *Senses* place before us the *Characters* of the Book of nature; but these convey no knowledge to us, till we have discovered the Alphabet by which they are to be read.

> The *Alphabet*, by means of which we interpret Phenomena, consists of the *Ideas* existing in our own minds; for these give to the phenomena that coherence and significance which is not an object of sense.[4]

and

> Ideas are not *trans*formed, but *in*formed Senstions; for without ideas, sensations have no form.[5]

Whewell's Fundamental Ideas are analogous to Kant's Concepts[6] and Whewell held them to embody necessary as opposed to contingent truths. Thus, like Kant, he thought that Euclidean geometry was necessarily true; he said it was based on a Fundamental Idea of space; he thought that Newtonian mechanics expressed necessary truths because it was based on Fundamental Ideas of motion, causality and force.

Whewell accepted Hume's arguments showing that experience provided no justification for the belief in a necessary connection between cause and effect but his conclusion differed from that of Hume and was similar to that of Kant: he said that because we are intuitively certain of the validity of causal laws our idea of necessary connection must be a Fundamental Idea, independent of experience and giving significance to experience:

> We see in the world around us a constant succession of causes and effects connected with each other. The laws of this connection we learn in great measure from experience, by observation of the occurrences which present themselves to our notice, succeeding one another. But in doing this, and in attending to this succession of appearances, of which we are aware by means of our senses, we supply from our own minds the Idea of Cause. This Idea . . . is not derived from experience, but has its origin in the mind itself.[7]

and

> That this Idea of cause is not derived from experience, we prove . . . by this consideration: that we can make assertions involving this idea, which are rigorously necessary and universal; whereas knowledge derived from experience can only be true as far as experience goes, and can never contain in itself any evidence whatever for its necessity. We assert that 'Every event must have a cause' and this proposition we know to be true, . . . we cannot suppose it to be false in any single instance. We are as certain of it as of the truths of arithmetic or geometry. We cannot doubt that it must apply to all events past and future, in every part of the universe, just as truly as to those occurrences which we have ourselves observed.[8]

Whewell also argued that the notion of substance, the *substratum* in which qualities inhered, was a Fundamental Idea:

> We unavoidably assume that the qualities and properties which we observe are properties of *things*; – that the adjective implies a substantive; that there is, beside the external characters of things, something *of which* they are the characters. An apple which is red, and round, and hard, is not merely redness, and roundness, and hardness: these circumstances may all alter while the apple remains

the same apple. Behind the appearances which we see, we conceive something of which we think; or to use the metaphor which obtained currency among the ancient philosophers, the attributes and qualities which we observe are supported by and inherent in something: and this something is called a substratum or *substance*, that which stands beneath the apparent qualities and supports them.[9]

By the mid-nineteenth century this had become an old-fashioned view; it had been subject to criticism for over a hundred years and, as we shall see, it was to be criticized further. But in some other respects Whewell was ahead of his contemporaries. He appreciated the vital importance of imaginative conjecture and he stressed that scientific knowledge was not attained merely by observation and inference from observation; the scientist had to contribute something from himself and that progress depended on invention. For Whewell induction as practised by the scientist was not simply a matter of inference, however critical and controlled, from 'some' to 'all'; the most important feature was the formation of a new conception. New conceptions were, he thought, *superinduced* upon the facts[10] and so bound them together; he called the binding 'colligating' and the bundle so formed a 'colligation'.

Whewell did not think that colligations were arrived at by chance; the observer's mind must have been prepared in order to become aware of what was latent in the facts. He pointed out that the act of invention was often overlooked because once a new concept was established it would seem self-evident. He also appreciated that a new colligation (in effect a new hypothesis) had to be supported by evidence provided by observation; he assumed that such evidence could do more than support, it could verify and so act as proof. Thus he took one aspect of induction to be a process of verification and, for him, the logic of induction consisted in showing the conditions of proof. The other aspect of induction was invention, the invention of the hypothesis itself, and so scientific discovery was a matter of invention not of logic.[11]

The creative aspect of scientific inquiry was consistently minimized by Mill and, to be fair to Mill, we must bear in mind that the greatest scientists of the seventeenth, eighteenth and nineteenth centuries had not fully appreciated that their laws and theories had been arrived at largely as a result of imaginative speculation. From the time of Galileo natural philosophers had aspired to be guided by logical and mathematical reasoning and by direct appeal to observation. Speculative conjecture had become suspect, for it was believed to lead to explanation based on occult forces and in terms of occult purposes rather than to factual descriptions implying physical causes.

Although by the nineteenth century the rationalist criterion of knowledge, that of logical certainty, had been rejected, it was still believed that factual certainty was possible. As we have seen Whewell followed Kant in basing empirical certainty on the notion that experience *had to be* in conformity with Ideas and Concepts that were intrinsically bound up with the nature of human thought. They both believed that in this way Hume's objections to claims for knowledge could be overcome. Mill, on the other hand, considered that he had solved Hume's problem in a different way. He said that *insofar as human experience was concerned* certainty could be attained through a precise methodology of observation and critical assessment. Mill's analysis persuaded most of his contemporaries that Hume's objections could be ignored, that science was entirely rational and that carefully tested scientific laws and theories were impregnable.

John Stuart Mill

Mill amplified and extended Bacon's methodology, incorporating eighteenth-century philosophical views on perception and on causation. He stressed that he had learned much from Whewell, though he disagreed with Whewell's account of the colligation of facts; he argued that colligation was not a matter of invention for the so-called 'new concept' was already contained in the facts and the colligation was merely a new description.[12] In addition he absolutely rejected the notion of Fundamental Ideas, maintaining that all knowledge, even mathematical knowledge, came from sense experience. Like Whewell he thought that mathematics and Euclidean geometry embodied absolute truths but he did not accept that the indubitability of what he called 'the laws of number' and 'the laws of space' depended on anything other than experience; in his view it was a mistake to think that their necessity derived from structures imposed by human thought:

> In the laws of number, then, and in those of space, we recognise in the most unqualified manner, the rigorous universality of which we are in quest. Those laws have been in all ages the type of certainty, the standard of comparison for all inferior degrees of evidence. Their invariability is so perfect, that it renders us unable even to conceive any exception to them; and philosophers have been led, though ... erroneously, to consider their evidence as lying not in experience, but in the original constitution of the intellect.[13]

He was aware that it was not possible to use the laws to provide explanations of events, for from the laws of number and space only laws of number and space could be deduced;[14] it was therefore necess-ary to find some other law that would have the same invariability. For Mill this was the law of causation, the very law that Whewell (see above) had treated as a Fundamental Idea.

Mill knew that he could not simply assume that the law had no exceptions, as Bacon had implicitly assumed, and since he would have no truck with Fundamental Ideas he could not use them as guarantors of truth. He appealed to experience; he asserted that established laws of succession of events could be observed to hold universally and invariably and he argued that this was enough proof of their in-dubitability. He stressed that he was not seeking to demonstrate any metaphysical notion of *causality*, 'a mysterious and most powerful tie',[15] his concept of cause rested entirely on the notion of invariability of succession.

> Between the phenomena, then, which exist at any instant, and the phenomena which exist at the succeeding instant, there is an in-variable order of succession; .... To certain facts, certain facts always do, and as we believe, will continue to succeed. The in-variable antecedent is termed the cause; the invariable consequent, the effect. And the universality of the law of causation consists in this that every consequent is connected in this manner with some particular antecedent, or set of antecedents.

> On the universality of this truth depends the possibility of reducing the inductive process to rules. The undoubted assurance we have that there is a law to be found if we only knew how to find it, will presently be seen to be the source from which the canons of the Inductive Logic derive their validity.[16]

By 'Inductive Logic' Mill meant 'scientific reasoning'; inferring gen-eral laws from particular observations.

He qualified his claim in that he did not assert absolute universal certainty, let alone logical certainty. He granted that there might be other parts of the universe where the law of causation did not hold and that there might have been earlier times and there might be future times when it was not or would not be applicable. What he maintained was that *as far as our experience was concerned* it could be trusted. He evaded Hume's criticism by arguing that it was not necessary to have a logical proof because our experience provided ample evidence of the reliability of inductive inference. Even with the restriction of validity to human experience Mill's argument is suspect but we shall not pursue the matter here; it is sufficient for our purposes to note that Mill treated the law of causation as an absolute truth when developing his theory of scientific method.

We may contrast Mill's assessment of the law of causation with his assessment of laws of association of properties for in the latter case he did not claim certainty even within the limits of our experience. Thus he rejected the view that there must be an invariable association of properties and, along with that, the notion of an essential nature and the Baconian account of 'form'.[17]

> The Methods of Induction applicable to the ascertainment of causes and effects, are grounded on the principle that everything which has a beginning must have some cause or other; . . . . But in an inquiry whether some kind (as crow) universally possesses a certain property (as blackness), there is no room for any assumption analogous to this. We have no previous certainty that the property must have something which constantly coexists with it; must have an invariable coexistent in the same manner as an event must have an invariable antecedent.

> To overlook this grand distinction was, as it seems to me, the capital error in Bacon's view of inductive philosophy.[18]

However, Mill did concede that observed associations of properties could be accepted as empirically valid, that is they could be treated as invariable until such time as further observation might show them to be false,[19] for he appreciated the need for classification. A classifying scheme must be based on the assumption that properties are reasonably constant and that they remain associated in constant manner. Thus for Mill the laws of association of properties were to be treated as methodological principles whereas the law of causation was a metaphysical principle. He maintained that particular causal laws, when firmly established, were indubitable laws of nature.

Mill differed from the positivists, for their professed aim was to avoid completely any appeal to abstractions such as causality. Positivists held that explanations based on such appeals were metaphysical explanations and represented a primitive stage of human thought.

Positivism

Auguste Comte (1798–1857) put forward the thesis of positivism as a basis for social reform: he said that human society should be reorganized as a result of a scientific approach to social problems.[20] Comte thought that not only social problems but all problems could be solved by applying the methods of science and so he stated that the primary aim of positivism was 'to generalize our scientific conceptions and to systematize the art of social life'.[21] He followed the tradition of the Enlightenment and indeed he did not suggest that his thesis was original. Positivism, he said, was founded on the scientific approach shown in the work and writings of scientists and philosophers such as Galileo, Descartes, Bacon and Hume. This was appreciated by Mill, who said:

> The philosophy called Positive is not a recent invention of M. Comte, but a simple adherence to the traditions of all the great scientific minds whose discoveries have made the human race what it is.[22]

Comte not only welcomed and endorsed the methodology of science, he also advocated a socialist and far more egalitarian society and so his thesis was associated with radical, even revolutionary, reform. Insofar as science was associated with positivism it too was held to be radical and potentially subversive. There is analogy here with the seventeenth-century Establishment attitude to science (then natural philosophy) as a subversive study potentially threatening both Church and State. However, as we have seen, there was not a simple antagonism between science and religion; many seventeenth-century natural philosophers were profoundly religious and had seen their researches as contributing to natural theology by providing evidence that supported the Argument from Design. Likewise many nineteenth-century scientists were very conventional and used their scientific findings either to support the status quo or to show that a hierarchical society was inevitable and that attempts to reform it were futile and dangerous. Nevertheless I think it must be conceded that both natural philosophy and science were bound to be indirectly subversive and to undermine established attitudes, because they encouraged a spirit of critical inquiry and the questioning of accepted dogmas.

Positivism was directed towards the management of practical affairs and Comte asserted that increased efficiency and successful reform depended on rational (scientific) thought. He said:

> all Positive speculations owe their first origin to the occupations of practical life. . . . The importance that we attach to theories which teach the laws of phenomena, and give us the power of prevision, is chiefly due to the fact that they alone can regulate our otherwise

blind action upon the external world.... From its first origin in mathematics and astronomy, it has always shown its tendency to systematize the whole of our conceptions in every new subject which has been brought within the scope of its fundamental principle.... the Positive spirit can embrace the entire range of thought without lessening or rather with the effect of strengthening its original tendency to regulate practical life.[23]

This is a grandiose claim; Comte held that the Positive spirit, in effect the scientific spirit, represented the ultimate pinnacle of human speculative thought. There had been two earlier stages: theological followed by metaphysical:

> our speculations upon all subjects whatsoever, pass necessarily through three successive stages: a Theological stage, in which free play is given to spontaneous fictions admitting of no proof; the Metaphysical stage, characterized by the prevalence of personified abstractions or entities; lastly, the Positive stage, based upon an exact view of the real facts of the case.[24]

By 'theological' Comte meant speculative accounts and explanations in terms of active spirits, gods or a single god; by 'metaphysical' he meant the stage in thought when explanations were in terms of reified abstraction, not a god but a power or force; for example, vitalism, essence or plastic nature. By 'positive' Comte meant accounts and explanations in terms of the succession of observed events or phenomena. For him appeals to causality and to the notion of causal laws were tainted with metaphysics.

Positivist thinking, the reasoning from objective facts, would, in Comte's view, extend the scientific approach to all fields of human inquiry: inanimate objects, the natural world, social and even moral problems. He said that instead of philosophy including science, science would come to embrace philosophy:

> All knowledge is now brought within the sphere of Natural Philosophy; and the provisional distinction by which, since Aristotle and Plato, it has been so sharply demarcated from Moral Philosophy, ceases to exist. The Positive spirit, so long confined to the simpler inorganic phenomena, has now passed through its difficult course of probation.... All our notions of truth are thus rendered homogeneous, and begin at once to converge towards a central principle. A firm objective basis is consequently laid down for that complete co-ordination of human existence towards which all sound philosophy has ever tended.[25]

Comte's claim that the scientific method can be successfully applied to all problems was new but, since his time, it has had much support. It is associated with the belief that true knowledge, and *a fortiori* scientific knowledge, is independent of metaphysics. This view may be seen as a development of Hume's criticisms, for Hume had asserted that metaphysical writings contained 'nothing but sophistry and illusion'.[26] Probably influenced by Hume, the Enlightenment philosophers in France had also thought that at best metaphysics was unimportant. It was generally accepted that facts were the basis of science and that, as regarded scientific inquiry, metaphysics was unnecessary and probably damaging.

Positivism and causality

We have already noted that positivists did not wish to entertain explanations based on appeal to causes or to causal laws. Comte said:

> The true Positive spirit consists in substituting the study of the invariable laws of phenomena for that of their so-called Causes, whether proximate or primary; in a word, in studying the *How* instead of the *Why*.[27]

He and his disciples thought that only orders of succession should be sought, what they called 'Laws of Phenomena', and they objected even to the word 'cause'.

Mill did not agree; as we have seen he distinguished laws of association of properties, mere empirical laws, from the more fundamental laws of succession (which *he* called 'causal laws') that he took to be the laws of nature. Mill argued that Comte made no distinction between empirical laws, which carried no hint of necessity, and the basic laws of nature which *within the range of our experience* were necessarily true. Of Comte he wrote:

> He sees no difference between such generalizations as Kepler's laws, and such as the theory of gravitation. He fails to perceive the real distinction between the laws of succession and coexistence which thinkers of a different school call Laws of Phaenomena, and those of what they call the action of Causes.... There are ... two kinds of uniformities of succession, the one unconditional, the other conditional on the first: laws of causation, and other succession dependent on those laws.[28]

It is interesting that Mill treated Kepler's laws as mere empirical generalizations and seems to have failed to appreciate that they can be mathematically derived from the gravitational theory which he acknowledged to be a law of nature. However we are not here concerned with criticizing this aspect of Mill's exposition, his point was that at least some physical laws or theories were effectively guiding principles and could be relied on absolutely. He thought that it was because Comte did not acknowledge that there were ultimate laws that he had failed to present a proper inductive logic on which to base positivist methodology.

However Comte did not think that positivism was concerned solely with applications to science; he had a wider view of its scope than had Mill. For Comte positivism involved not only intellectual but spiritual advance, and he argued that it would supersede religion; in the quotation below the Convention is the revolutionary tribunal, still a vivid memory in mid-nineteenth century France:

> I have now explained the principal purpose of positive Philosophy, namely, spiritual reorganization; and I have shown how that purpose is involved in the Positivist motto, Order and Progress. Positivism, then, realizes the highest aspirations of mediaeval Catholicism, and at the same time fulfils the conditions, the absence of which caused the failure of the Convention. It combines the opposite merits of the Catholic and the Revolutionary spirit, and by so doing supersedes them both. Theology and Metaphysics may now disappear without danger, because the service which each of them rendered is now harmonized with that of the other, and will be performed more perfectly.[29]

Comte regarded the moral aspect of positivism as more important than the intellectual aspect;[30] he said it was a religion, with Humanity replacing God.[31] He forecast that in time philosophers would become priests of Humanity[32] and it would be through science that men would come to know the nature of Humanity, this Great Being.[33]

Systematic positivism

Comte had said that the aim of positivism was to systematize the art of social life (see above, p. 134) and positivism as an all-embracing philosophy came to be known as 'systematic positivism'. In England it was developed by Herbert Spencer (1820–1903). Systematic positivists followed Comte in holding that all knowledge was attainable through scientific inquiry and they argued that since the method was the same the results of all inquiries could be brought together and integrated into one grand epistemological system. Such a synthesis would fulfil Comte's aim and must be the ultimate task of positivists.

Positivism and science were mutually supportive, each contributing to the prestige of the other. Both were based on confidence in human capacities, and especially confidence in human reason, and both were intimately involved in the notion of progress. One assumption that underlay nineteenth-century thought was the assumption that not only was knowledge increasing but that the world, and mankind as part of the world, was inevitably improving – in the moral sense as well as in the material sense. The medieval and Renaissance belief that there had been a steady deterioration from the Age of Gold (see the beginning of Chapter 3) was dismissed. Mandelbaum says:

> the thought of both Comte and Spencer was dominated by the view that there had taken place, and was taking place, a progressive development of man and society. This conception of history . . . was deeply rooted in nineteenth-century thought; . . . there is one further point which must be noted in order to account for the appeal of Comtean positivism in particular. In the eighteenth century it had been an important article of faith that intellectual enlightenment provided a basis through which societies might be transformed. This heritage of the Enlightenment was widely shared in England and in France during the nineteenth century, and was not the property of any one school of thought; however no other philosophy of history made claims as bold as Comte's. . . . To those who tended to link intellectual enlightenment and social reform, and who also placed the empirical sciences in the forefront of knowledge, the Comtean system had tremendous appeal.[34]

Critical positivism

Despite the appeal of Comte's system and despite the confidence in progress, the attempt to find a single all-inclusive scheme of knowledge came to be criticized. A less comprehensive positivism, *critical positivism*, was suggested. From the mid-nineteenth century critical positivism was favoured by scientists and philosophers; its aims were twofold:

> to analyse the foundations of scientific knowledge . . . [and] . . . to examine the true sources and meanings of all concepts which tended to be used in an uncritical, metaphysically charged manner.[35]

Like systematic positivists, critical positivists held that the scientific approach was the only route to knowledge and they too dismissed metaphysics as primitive superstition. This rejection of metaphysics influenced those nineteenth-century scientists who were not otherwise sympathetic to positivism. It was considered improper to produce speculative hypotheses, for they might corrupt the process of inquiry, i.e. the diligent search for facts. Metaphysics tended to be associated with conjectures based on outmoded theories such as vitalism, the transmutation of the species, diluvial geological theories and phrenology. It was not appreciated that conjectures as to wave transmission through ether and fields of force, let alone postulates such as the conservation of matter, the conservation of energy and the constancy of mass, were based on metaphysical assumptions.

Positivism and the notion of substance

We have seen that positivists were criticized by Mill for failing to distinguish causal laws from empirically established regularities. Positivists preferred the term 'description' to 'law' though they stressed that a description could also be a basis for prediction. Their view of the concept of substance was analogous to their view of the concept of cause or causal law: they thought that references to substance were confusing and should be avoided.

The word 'substance' has several different meanings but in relation to scientific explanation it is to be taken in Whewell's sense (see quotation on p. 129) and signifies an underlying constituent of matter and of all material bodies. From medieval times and earlier the observed properties of a body were thought of as being bound together or supported by its *substance*, rather like plums in a plum pudding. With the general acceptance of the corpuscular theory of matter in the seventeenth century and the development of the notion of primary and secondary qualities,[36] substance came to be regarded as the substratum of the individual corpuscles, the medium supporting their primary qualities of extension, solidity, etc. Locke, who elaborated this view, also pointed out that since substance itself had no qualities it must be inherently unknowable:

> if anyone will examine himself concerning his *notion of pure substance in general*, he will find he has no other *idea* of it at all, but only a supposition of he knows not what support of such qualities which are capable of producing simple *ideas* in us; . . . If anyone should be asked what is the subject wherein colour or weight inheres, he would have nothing to say, but the solid extended parts; and if he were demanded what is it that the solidity and extension adhere in, he would not be in much better case than the *Indian* . . . saying that the world was supported by a great elephant, . . . asked what the

elephant rested on, ... his answer was a great tortoise; but being again pressed to know what gave support to the broad-backed tortoise, replied, something, he knew not what. ... The *idea* then we have, to which we give the general name substance, being nothing but the supposed, but unknown, support of those qualities we find existing, which we imagine cannot subsist ... without something to support them.[37]

However, although he showed that substance was intrinsically unknowable (we could have no *idea* of it) Locke did not deny that there was a substratum. Even in the nineteenth century what was essentially the medieval view (modified by a corpuscular or atomic theory) was still supported by some.[38]

Mill took a position similar to Locke and he acknowledged Whewell's contention that we had an intuitive belief in an underlying substance; he was content to leave the problem of the ultimate nature of matter to the metaphysicians.[39] He was anxious to stress Locke's point, namely that all we can know about objects is the sensations (the *ideas*) they give to us.[40] He argued that whatever the nature of ultimate reality, as far as we were concerned material bodies could be treated as collections of actual and possible sensations:

Matter, then, may be defined as a 'permanent possibility' of sensation. If I am asked whether I believe in matter, I ask whether the questioner accepts the definition of it. If he does, I believe in matter. ... In any other sense than this I do not. But I affirm with confidence that this conception of matter includes the whole meaning attached to it by the common world. ... The reliance of mankind on the real existence of visible and tangible objects means reliance on the reality and permanence of possibilities of visual and tactile sensations.[41]

Positivists went further than Mill for they repudiated the term 'substance' just as they repudiated the term 'cause'. Thus Ernst Mach (1838–1916), a later nineteenth-century positivist who had great influence on the young Einstein, held that objects should be treated as collections of sense experiences (sense data). The concept of substance was, he thought, a mirage, 'that obscure mysterious lump which we involuntarily add in thought'.[42] Twentieth-century logical positivists such as A. J. Ayer (1910–89) when writing *Language, Truth and Logic*, argue that our involuntary belief in substance arises not so much as a result of intuitive theory but as a consequence of the grammar of our language.[43]

Phenomenalism

In the quotation above, Mill presented the philosophical theory of matter known as *phenomenalism*, the theory or thesis that all references to physical objects are logically equivalent to, and can be translated without loss of meaning into, statements about actual or possible sense experiences. Phenomenalism has much in common with Berkeley's idealist theory of matter, known as *immaterialism*, but it is more radical than Berkeley's doctrine because Berkeley (1685–1753) had maintained that though physical objects had an existence independent of *human* perceptions yet, even when not observed by any person they would continue to exist as God's perceptions. As Ayer has pointed out this gives them a different status from actual or possible human percepts for 'to say of something that it is perceived only by God is to say that it is not, in any ordinary sense, perceived at all.'[44]

Mill did not invoke God and nor did the nineteenth-century positivists and there are fatal objections to their phenomenalism. Ayer has shown that 'Statements about physical objects are not formally translatable into statements about sense data.'[45] He points out that our concept of physical objects (and indeed of physical materials) is based on a theory that we all arrive at spontaneously as a result of our sense experiences; that theory goes beyond what can be established by sense perception and hence transcends any finite collection of statements about sense experiences. However, Ayer's criticism was not raised in the nineteenth century and at that time phenomenalism was acknowledged as a possible philosophical theory of matter (though not one that was accepted by the majority). Hermann Helmholtz (1821–94) elaborated a highly idiosyncratic form of phenomenalism, arguing that since physical objects appeared as they did as a consequence of human senses, what we could know was inevitably limited by our sensory capacities. Hence our sense experiences could be nothing more than symbols for an unknown reality. Writing of Helmholtz, Mandelbaum says:

> according to him, the specific nature of what we experience is not to be identified with anything existing independently of us any more than the written name of a man is to be identified with that man himself. However, the fact that we can note an orderly connection among our sensations gives us the possibility of knowledge, which is the discovery of patterns of relationship among sensory elements.[46]

The banishment of metaphysics

Positivists thought that scientific inquiry should be treated as inquiry into the ordering and predicting of potential and actual sense experiences; this was the way to abolish metaphysical speculations as to the nature of matter. Nevertheless Helmholtz and his supporters thought that though sense experiences themselves were but symbols they did relate directly to the world. It followed that though ultimate reality could not be known, the observed relations of sense experiences reflected real relations in nature. Mach himself came to deny this, and by the 1890s he was suggesting that even the relations might be no more than reflections of our own expectation and therefore we ought not to assume that our laws of nature described an objective reality, even in symbolic form.[47] It was not surprising, he said, that we came to think that notions such as *substance, cause, time* were independent entities, but this was to cherish an illusion. For:

> All physical ideas and principles are succinct directions, frequently involving subordinate directions, for the employment of economically classified experiences, ready for use. Their conciseness, as also the fact that their contents are rarely exhibited in full, often invests them with the semblance of independent existence. Poetical myths regarding such ideas, – for example, that of Time, the producer and devourer of all things, – do not concern us here. We need only remind the reader that even Newton speaks of an *absolute* time independent of all phenomena, and of absolute space – views . . . which are often seriously entertained today. For the . . . inquirer, determinations of time are merely abbreviated statements of the dependence of one event upon another, and nothing more. . . . Instead of referring events to the earth we may refer them to a clock or even to our internal sensation of time.[48]

We shall see how Einstein took Mach's view of time to heart.

Mach argued that our various sense impressions by which we were aware of phenomena were the *elements* from which our world was made. The term 'sensation' could be used when we were concerned with the direct effect on our bodies and he admitted that, in a sense, the world *was* our sensations:

> Let us look at the matter without bias. The world consists of colors, sounds, temperatures, pressures, spaces, times, and so forth, which now we shall not call sensations, nor phenomena, because in either term an arbitrary, one-sided theory is embroiled,

but simply *elements*. The fixing of the flux of these elements, whether mediately or immediately, is the real object of physical research. . . . we call *all* elements, in so far as we regard them as dependent on this special part (our body), *sensations*. That the world is our sensation, in this sense cannot be questioned.[49]

The collapse of positivism

If science is reduced merely to the ordering of sense experiences then there seems no reason to accept the positivist thesis that its methodology is a model for all inquiry or indeed for any. Would not introspection be as appropriate? And how can positivists account for the role of mathematics in science? As we have seen, Mill, though not a positivist, had maintained that mathematical knowledge was derived from experience; Mach also thought that it was empirically based and that, in effect, it was a system devised to make counting more efficient. He said:

> The greatest perfection of mental economy is attained in that science which has reached the highest formal development, and which is widely employed in physical inquiry, namely mathematics. Strange as it may sound, the power of mathematics rests upon its evasion of all unnecessary thought and on its wonderful saving of mental operations.[50]

The strangely autonomous character of mathematics arose, said Mach, from the fact that many great men had contributed to the subject so that any one individual had access to the intelligence of others.

> By communication, the experience of *many* persons, individually acquired at first is collected in *one*. The communication of knowledge and the necessity which everyone feels of managing his experience with the least expenditure of thought, compel us to put our knowledge in economical forms. But here we have a clue which strips science of all its mystery, and shows us what its power really is. With respect to specific results it yields nothing that we could not reach in a sufficiently long time without methods. There is no problem in all mathematics that cannot be solved by direct counting. But with the present implements of mathematics many operations of counting can be performed in a few minutes which without mathematical methods would take a lifetime.[51]

Now theories based on the mathematical treatment of non-Euclidean space, of classes of infinities, of notions of limits and of imaginary numbers are not concerned with counting and yet, even in

Mach's day, these were beginning to influence scientific inquiry. In their desire to banish metaphysics positivists had applied a Procrustian sword reducing mathematics to nothing but counting, and science to little more than classification – a natural history of sense experience.

If thrown out of the house, metaphysics has a tendency to re-enter through the back door. Even if science and mathematics could be adequately assessed in positivistic terms there would still be metaphysical assumptions underlying the scheme of knowledge expressed entirely in terms of sense experiences. Mach's account of *elements* is in effect an account of a form of idealism – all that can be known are ideas, the mental experiences.[52] Moreover that position involves metaphysical assumptions: the assumption that there can be fruitful exchange of information about personal sense experiences and the assumption that there can be agreement as to what experiences have occurred and what will occur.

This criticism of positivism is totally independent of scientific discoveries; any philosophy grounded on personal and individual experiences runs the danger of collapsing into idealism and collapsing further into solipsism. However, as we shall see, the problems of later-nineteenth-century scientists helped to show the inadequacies of positivism more clearly and, by the twentieth century, the necessity for underlying metaphysical assumptions was plain.

Beliefs at the close of the nineteenth century

1 By the end of the century science was characterized as an intrinsically secular subject. It was regarded as independent of religion rather than as being anti-religious. Arguments from Design still had popular appeal but were no longer intellectually respectable.

2 There was still a Baconian belief in the paramount importance of observation and experiments and, despite Whewell, creativity was undervalued. However, the importance of mathematics was fully realized.

3 Mill's philosophy of science was dominant and there was also strong positivist influence. It was generally accepted that science ought to be free of metaphysics and metaphysical speculation.

The position in 1900

Science was thought to have become independent of philosophy, and scientific inquiry was seen as being essentially different from philosophical speculation. The methodology of science: observation, experiment, measuring and mathematics came to be regarded, and not only by positivists, as the exemplar of inquiry.

8   Problems: energy and ether

The nature of heat

As we saw in Chapter 4 (p. 74) Bacon thought he had shown that heat was a form of motion. But despite his prestige another theory came to be favoured[1]. It was held that heat was a material substance, probably some sort of fluid and possibly an element. Some philosphers, for example Robert Boyle, tried to show that heat had weight so that bodies were heavier when they were hot. Others, who did not consider weight to be an essential property of matter, (see quotation on p. 67) suggested that heat was weightless so that bodies remained the same weight however hot or cold they became. There was no general agreement; indeed for a short time there was yet another theory which suggested that there were two different fluids, one producing heat and the other cold, though by the eighteenth century it had become generally accepted that cold was a deficiency of heat. The fluid responsible for heat was called 'caloric' and the caloric theory of heat survived into the nineteenth century.

By then that theory was losing favour for Bacon's theory of heat had been revived and developed by Count Rumford (1753–1814). He offered more cogent experimental evidence than Bacon's to support the thesis that heat was motion. For example he showed that an indefinitely large amount of heat could be obtained from friction on metal, as in the process of boring a cannon. He pointed out that if heat had been a fluid it would eventually have been used up and it would have been impossible to generate what was virtually a never-ending supply.

Some years later Robert Mayer (1814–78) showed that in the tropics venous blood was nearly as red as arterial blood (it is oxygen which makes arterial blood red) so in hot places the body uses less of the oxygen in its blood. It was known that heat was produced by oxygen reacting chemically in the tissues and Mayer concluded that in the tropics less oxygen was used because the body needed less heat. He also noted that more oxygen was used if animals were active (they breathed more deeply and more quickly) and he suggested that there was a connection between heat obtained from oxygen and bodily activity. Hence from another very different source there were indications that heat had a close connection with motion.

Heat and energy: the First Law of Thermodynamics

Some fifty years after Rumford, James Prescott Joule (1818–89) established that there was a quantitative relation between heat and energy which he called the *mechanical equivalent of heat*. Energy can appear in a number of different forms and Joule's work showed that heat was one of the forms of energy. In 1847 he formulated the Law of Conservation of Energy, a law also known as the First Law of Thermodynamics. This states that though energy may change its form the total amount in any closed system must remain constant so that energy cannot be created or destroyed. Since the universe itself is a closed system the First Law asserts that the amount of energy in the entire cosmos cannot change or be changed. Joule himself believed that the law was a divine decree:

> the grand agents of nature are, by the Creator's fiat, indestructible; wherever mechanical force is expended an exact equivalence of heat is always obtained.[2]

and in a lecture of 1847 he said:

> We might reason, *a priori*, that ... absolute destruction of living force cannot possibly take place, because it is manifestly absurd to suppose that the powers with which god has endowed matter can be destroyed any more than they they can be created by man's agency.[3]

Joule's appeal to divine constancy is in the same spirit as that of Descartes and of Leibniz (see, for example, quotation on p. 84 and first quotation on p. 85). For Joule and his contemporaries and successors the First Law of Thermodynamics was not an empirical law that would be subject to correction but a metaphysical postulate. Experimental findings were interpreted so as to conform to it; they could not show it to be false.

The Second Law of Thermodynamics

Well before 1847 Sadi Carnot (1798–1832) had studied how mechanical work was obtained from heat in heat engines, such as steam engines. It was clearly desirable to have greater knowledge of how to make efficient engines because an efficient engine would require less heat and would consume less fuel and be cheaper to run. In order to eliminate consideration of the inevitable heat losses due to friction Carnot decided to calculate the performance of an ideal (frictionless) engine. Initially he thought that such an engine would be reversible, that is it ought to be possible to work the machine backwards with no more expendititure of heat, but from theoretical considerations (an ideal engine could not, of course be constructed) he was able to show that a frictionless engine would not be reversible.

Carnot favoured the caloric theory of heat; he compared the energy available from the heat of a heat engine to the energy available from water cascading down a waterfall: the energy from the heat engine was related to the temperature drop between boiler and condenser just as the energy available from a waterfall was related to the height from which the water descended. Moreover, just as water will not flow naturally up hill so heat will not pass naturally up a temperature gradient, i.e. from the colder to the hotter. This is why even an ideal heat engine is not reversible.

Carnot died young, a victim of one of the nineteenth-century cholera epidemics, but his work was developed by Rudolph Clausius (1822–88). It was Clausius who formulated the Second Law of Thermodynamics: heat will only yield useful energy as it passes from a hot body to a cooler body. It follows that if bodies are all at the same temperature, however high, there is no energy available for use.

The metaphysical implications of the two Laws of Thermodynamics

The two laws are:

First Law: energy cannot be created or destroyed; the amount of energy in the universe is constant.
Second Law: useful energy can be obtained from heat only if there is a temperature gradient.

We have seen that though the First Law was suggested by inquiry into the relation between heat and energy, the notion of constancy embodies a metaphysical principle and the law is used to *interpret* experimental findings rather than being supported by those findings.

The Second Law had emerged as a consequence of speculation as to how an ideal engine might behave, and since an ideal engine cannot be made the law is in some ways analogous to Newton's law relating force to mass and acceleration (see p. 95) which rests on an ideal concept of motion free from all interference. It is also analogous to the law of causation. We have seen (see p. 132) that Mill granted that there might be other parts of the universe and there might be other times when causal laws could not be established but he stressed that *as far as our experience was concerned* the law of causation could be relied on absolutely. In practice Mill ignored his own caveat and, along with everyone else, he treated the law of causation as a metaphysical principle. Indeed although positivists (see p. 136) jibbed at the notion of cause their Laws of Phenomena were little but reformulations of the causal principle. Once accepted and established, the Second Law of Thermodynamics had the same status; it too was a metaphysical principle.

Since temperatures naturally tend to equalize by heat flowing from hot to cold it would seem that the entire universe must, in due course, come to the same temperature. It has been estimated that this will be about $-270\,°C$, only $3\,°C$ above the absolute zero of temperature and very cold indeed. But the final temperature is immaterial; the relevant consideration is that if the temperature everywhere is the same then no useful energy can be obtained. Kelvin (1824–1907), among others, pointed out that if the Second Law were accepted then the universe was doomed to a heat death. But this would be a long time coming and of more immediate interest were the implications of the First Law of Thermodynamics.

The age of the earth

From calculations based on his reading of the Old Testament, Archbishop Usher (1580–1656) had asserted that the earth was a little under six thousand years old, having been created in 4004 BC. This figure was generally accepted throughout the seventeenth century because at that time there was no reason to call it into question. But during the eighteenth century the study of rocks and fossils made it probable that the earth was very much older than the Scriptures appeared to show. The Enlightenment philosopher Georges Buffon (1707–88) openly suggested an age of seventy-five thousand years and privately he surmised that it was likely to be even greater, perhaps some three million years. By the nineteenth century it was generally accepted that the earth was very considerably older than the Archbishop had calculated.

In 1859 Charles Darwin (1808–82) published his *Origin of Species*, a work showing that the enormous number of different plants and animals might have a common ancestry. Others had suggested this and had pointed out that there were similarities between groups of species, but Darwin was the first to put forward a reasoned explanation as to how species might change and how new species might emerge. We shall not be concerned with the biological sciences here except insofar as they relate to physics but it is on this account that Darwin's theory does need to be introduced. Evolution through natural selection requires a very long time, hundreds if not thousands of millions of years. Any evidence showing that the earth is very old, very much older than the three million years conjectured by Buffon, makes Darwinian evolution at least a possibility. Any evidence that the earth cannot be more than a hundred million years old tends to show that the theory cannot be correct. Darwin himself did not look for evidence of an ancient earth; he simply asserted that it had to be very old. This can be compared with Copernicus's assertion that the fixed stars must be very far from the sun, and hence stellar parallax is not detected (see p. 32). Although at the time of publication there was no reason *not* to postulate an ancient earth, quite soon afterwards considerations based on the First Law of Thermodynamics seemed to show that the planet could not be nearly as old as Darwin's theory required.

It is reasonable to assume that the earth originated as a mass of molten rock and on that assumption Kelvin calculated that it would have cooled to its current temperature in no more than one hundred million years. Hence in its solid state the earth could not be more than a hundred million years old[4] and for much of that time it would have been far too hot to support life. Thus the First Law, asserting that extra heat cannot be created, appears to rule out the possibility of evolution through natural selection. In 1894 the President of the British Association for the Advancement of Science opted for Kelvin's estimate and Darwin's theory was threatened.

But not for long. The discovery of radioactivity in 1896 showed that the earth had been and would continue to be warmed by radioactive emissions from its core. It is important to appreciate that had radioactivity remained undetected it would not have been possible to accept the theory of evolution through natural selection. The laws of thermodynamics were treated as fundamental presuppositions and any scientific theory that was incompatible with one or both would necessarily be rejected.

Detection of radioactivity saved Darwin's theory; but where did radioactive energy come from? It was suggested it might be from ether waves.

The ether

The word 'ether' or 'aether' is Greek for the blue of the sky; in medieval times it was held to be equivalent to the quintessence, the element that Aristotle had said made the material of the heavenly bodies (see Chapter 1, p. 11). In the seventeenth century the term had been appropriated by Descartes. As we have seen (see p. 69) Descartes had held that matter was equivalent to extension so that, in his view, a vacuum was a logical impossibility. He asserted that the ether filled the apparently empty spaces of the heavens and that so-called empty space was a plenum. A whirling motion is possible in a plenum and Descartes said that the etherial particles formed swirling vortices which could carry round grosser matter, in particular the heavenly bodies. He said that the ether was also the medium for the transmission of forces of attraction and repulsion, such as magnetism, which operated across space. He dismissed all hypotheses based on appeal to forces acting at a distance, for in his view there had to a material medium to transmit any force.

The ether and the nature of light

Robert Hooke (1635–1703) had suggested that light might consist of vibrations of ether and not long afterwards Christian Huygens (1629–95) proposed that light rays might be treated as ether waves. But the wave theory of light was not generally accepted, largely because it was not favoured by Newton. Newton preferred a corpuscular theory, a theory that light rays consisted of streams of tiny particles which were emitted from the source rather like bullets from a gun. He rejected the wave theory on empirical grounds because he thought that the observed behaviour of light, in particular refraction and dispersion (the rainbow colours obtained by passing white light through a prism) were much better explained by a corpuscular theory. Moreover he refused to accept the logical necessity for an ether permeating space, at least partly because he had metaphysical and religious reasons for opposing Descartes's contention that a vacuum was a logical impossibility. Newton said that if, as Descartes asserted, extension were to be equated with matter, then because extension was prior to God, and could be conceived without thought of God, matter would also be prior to God and independent of God. He was not prepared to accept this:

> We are not able to posit bodies without at the same time positing that God exists and that he has created bodies in empty space out of

nothing. . . . But if with Descartes we say that extension is body, are we not opening the way to atheism? . . . Extension is not created but was from eternity, and since we have an absolute conception of it without having to relate it to God, we are able to conceive that it exists though imagining at the same time that God is not. (This is all the more so) if the division of substance into extended and thinking is legitimate and perfect, then God would not contain in himself extension . . . and would therefore be unable to create it. God and extension would be complete and absolute entities and the term substance would be applicable to each of them in the same sense.[5]

Here we see a metaphysical assumption about extension 'we have an absolute conception of it', embedded in religious belief; both were presupposed by Newton's physics.

Newton did not reject the notion of ether entirely and though he did not think that it carried light waves he conjectured that perhaps, as a matter of fact and not of logical necessity, there could be some tenuous material suffusing what appeared to be empty space. It might fill not only the heavens but might also permeate material bodies, passing between their constituent corpuscles. Then perhaps ether bonding would account for the cohesion of material bodies. He wondered also whether the composition of the ether might vary; just as air could contain varying amounts of water vapour so ether might contain varying amounts of etherial spirits adapted to produce electricity, magnetism and gravitation.

Newton stressed that any medium pervading space must have a very low density, 'be exceeding rare' (see quotation on p. 152); he calculated that, on average, an ether could not have a density greater than 1/700,000 that of air. He estimated that at such a low density there would be no detectable alteration in the orbits of the planets for at least ten thousand years though, inevitably, they would be gradually slowing down. He did not regard the universe as a perfect frictionless machine; he thought that God's supervision was required. Many of his contemporaries, for example Leibniz, (see p. 91) ridiculed such a notion; they said that it was absurd to suggest that God would not make a perfect cosmos. But Newton took a different view, relating divine supervision to divine immanence:

The Deity endures for ever and is everywhere present, and by existing always and everywhere, he constitutes duration and space. . . . [He] governs all things and knows all things that are, and can be done. . . . Who, being in all places, is more able by His will to move the bodies within His boundless uniform sensorium, and thereby to form and reform the parts of the universe, than we are by our will to move the parts of our body.[6]

For Newton, God's control of the world was not to be compared with the craftsman's control of his machine; his God was not merely the Creator of the world, He was within the world.

Though both Newton's and Descartes's physics depended on overt metaphysical assumptions and religious beliefs, Newton's theories of nature were tied to observation whereas Descartes's sought support from logical analysis. This is apparent in their attitudes to the ether. For Descartes the ether was a logical necessity, for Newton it was an empirical hypothesis. Such a hypothesis could be abandoned if it proved not to provide a helpful explanation of what was observed. For all his speculations as to the nature of the ether it is clear that Newton was not fully convinced that it existed. He said:

> Against filling the heavens with fluid mediums, unless they be exceeding rare, a great objection arises from the regular and lasting motion of the planets and comets in all manner of courses through the heavens. For thence it is manifest that the heavens are void of all sensible resistance, and by consequence, of all sensible matter.

A fluid would:

> serve only to disturb and retard the motions of those great bodies and make the frame of Nature languish.

It might not be necessary to postulate an ether:

> And as it is of no use ... so there is no evidence for its existence and therefore it ought to be rejected.[7]

We do not know whether Newton came to a final conclusion as to the existence of the ether. He did speculate about the possibility of ether being an intermediary between light and ordinary matter and he also wondered whether heat might result from disturbances in the ether. But he was convinced that light did not consist of ether waves and his influence on eighteenth-century scientific thought was so powerful that the wave theory of light was ignored and there was little speculation as to the nature of the ether.

Revival: ether and the nature-philosophers

Interest in the ether revived in the early nineteenth century as a result of two different approaches to inquiry, based on very different metaphysical assumptions. One was that of the German nature-philosophers, typified by the poet Johann Wolfgang von Goethe (1749–1832). The nature-philosophers were reacting against the materialistic and, as they saw it, atheistic presuppositions of the Enlightenment and also against the mechanistic views of nature implicit in Newtonian physics. Goethe, for example, repudiated Newton's explanation of colour in terms of the dispersion of white light; in his *Theory of Colours*, published in 1810,[8] he argued for an explanation of colours based on Aristotle's theory that colour was a result of white light mixing with other materials. Goethe's account is of no consequence in current physical theory though its highly subjective and mystical treatment of the subject is of some interest when considering psychological reactions to colours.

The key feature of nature-philosophy was its rejection of the classical scientific view of the world as a machine; nature-philosophers held that this view was not so much wrong as irrelevant. They were influenced by medieval and Renaissance beliefs[9] and much of their doctrine reminds us of Hermetic incantations and seems close to mumbo-jumbo today. Their metaphysics presupposed an ultimate reality based on vitalism rather than on mechanism. In their view true understanding of the world had to be based on the appreciation of the presence of an inner vital activity analogous to the inner mind and spirit of each human being. It was an animistic philosophy and, like Aristotle, they made no sharp distinction between animate and inanimate bodies. Like him they also held that all ultimate explanations had to be teleological explanations,[10] explanations in terms of purpose.

Lorenz Oken (1779–1851) was one of the nature-philosophers; he put forward the suggestion that matter had originated from the ether under the influence of electrical and magnetic forces. He surmised that when it was first formed matter was inanimate and that animate structures emerged later. He wrote:

> As the whole of nature has been a successive fixation of aether, so is the organic world a successive fixation of infusorial mucus-vesicles, the mucus is the aether, the chaos of the organic world. . . . The infusorial mucus mass originated at the moment when the planets succeeded in so bringing together and identifying all the elementary processes that they were all together or at one and the same time in every point.[11]

Nature-philosophers were closely associated with the philosophy of Georg W. F. Hegel (1770–1831) and Friedrich Schelling (1775–1854); this was not so much on account of their mysticism (as we have seen

Newton's writings could be mystical) but because their basic meta-physical presupposition, vitalism, and their view of ultimate explanation being in terms of purpose, were incompatible with the mechanistic basis of nineteenth-century science and totally alien to the spirit of positivism. Nevertheless some of them contributed to ortho-dox science and their speculations as to the nature and function of the ether helped to rekindle interest in the subject.

Ether and the wave theory of light

The second approach leading to a revival of interest in the ether came from within orthodox science, and was a result of the work of Thomas Young (1773–1829). Young modified and developed Huygens's suggestion that light rays were wave disturbances. Any wave consists of vibrations of a medium, so that for there to be waves there must be something to vibrate. Since light rays travel through the apparently empty space of the heavens (and also through any artificially created vacuum) it follows that if a wave theory of light is even to be enter-tained it is necessary, as Huygens had appreciated, to postulate the presence of some pervasive medium. It seemed obvious that the ether must be that medium.

Huygens had thought that light waves were like sound waves, *longitudinal* vibrations, and he therefore pictured the ether oscillating backwards and forwards in the direction of the light ray. At first Young favoured Huygens's view but by 1817 he had come to the conclusion that light waves were more likely to be like water waves so that the ether would vibrate at right-angles to the direction of the light rays; these would be *transverse* vibrations. Although his theory was ridi-culed when he first proposed it and then ignored, in a relatively short time there was a change and by 1825 the corpuscular theory was superseded. It was accepted that light rays were waves in the ether.

Electromagnetism and the electromagnetic theory of light

In the first quarter of the nineteenth century another German nature-philosopher, Hans Christian Oersted (1771–1851) showed that mag-netic fields were associated with electric currents and also that moving magnets could produce effects similar to electric currents. These find-ings harmonized with the underlying ethos of nature-philosophy which presupposed that the various physical forces: electrical, magnetic, gravitational and chemical were different aspects of the World Spirit and therefore were necessarily interrelated.

Though orthodox scientists did not seek explanation in terms of the activity of a World Spirit or of a vital essence the notion of an underlying unity of physical forces appealed to them also. Oersted's work was continued by the French physicist André-Marie Ampère (1775–1831) who showed that a circular coil of wire carrying an electric current could be treated as a magnet, one face of the coil acting as a North Magnetic Pole and the other as a South Magnetic Pole. Soon after, Michael Faraday (1791–1867) was able to show that an electric current could be produced in conductors if there were fluctuating current in other nearby conductors. These *induced currents* also showed that magnetism and electricity were intimately connected.

In 1846 Faraday was able to demonstrate a relationship between magnetism and light and he conjectured that the ether might be a vehicle for magnetic forces and also a vehicle for light. He too was attracted by the notion that the ether might link different kinds of forces; in 1851 he wrote:

> it is not at all unlikely that if there be an ether, it should have other uses than simply the conveyance of radiations.[12]

In suggesting that magnetic forces and light might both be carried in ether Faraday anticipated Clerk Maxwell's electromagnetic theory of light. It was Maxwell (1831–79) who developed the theory of electromagnetic fields; these could be regarded as distortions of the ether which were produced in the space around electrically and magnetically charged bodies. In 1861 he proposed a mechanical model in which the ether was portrayed as being made up of whirling magnetic vortices and electrically charged idle wheels. He surmised that in an electromagnetic field[13] the vortices would become twisted and displaced but that they would recoil back to their original positions when the field was not there. In a paper of 1865 he wrote:

> The electromagnetic field is that part of space which contains and surrounds bodies in electric or magnetic conditions. It may be filled with any kind of matter, or we may endeavour to render it empty of all gross matter . . .
>
> There is always, however, enough of matter left to receive and transmit the undulations of light and heat, and it is because the transmission of these radiations is not greatly altered when transparent bodies of measureable density are substituted for the so-called vacuum, that we are obliged to admit the undulations are those of an aetherial substance, and not of the gross matter, the presence of which merely modifies in some way the motion of the aether.

We have therefore some reason to believe, from the phenomena of light and heat, that there is an aethereal medium filling space and permeating bodies, capable of being set in motion and of transmitting that motion to gross matter so as to heat it and affect it in various ways.

We may therefore receive, as a datum derived from a branch of science independent of that with which we have to deal, the existence of a pervading medium, of small but real density, capable of being set in motion, and of transmitting motion from one part to another with great, but not infinite velocity.[14]

The nature of ether: empirical hypotheses

For nineteenth-century scientists the luminiferous (light-bearing) ether was an established theoretical entity and had the same status as atoms and molecules. Like the ether, these could not be directly observed and indeed diehard positivists rated them as nothing more than convenient notions for correlating observation, but most scientists took them to be as real as ordinary material objects such as tables and chairs and familiar media such as water and air. For this reason experiments were planned to discover more about their properties; scientists were particularly interested in the physical nature of the ether. For example Maxwell and his colleagues hoped to find explanations of optical phenomena and optical laws in terms of the mechanical properties of the ether.

It was clear that the ether was a very strange substance and difficult to study. It could not be extracted with the most powerful vacuum pump, for light was able to travel through the highest vacuum that could be obtained and it could only do this if the ether were present. Perhaps it was an elastic solid with the power of resisting permanent distortion of shape, but then why did it not offer resistance to the movements of the heavenly bodies? In answer to this question it was suggested that the ether might have properties similar to, but more pronounced than, a substance like pitch, which was rigid enough to suffer elastic vibrations yet sufficiently plastic to allow other bodies to pass through it. Some scientists surmised that the ether might be highly labile so that it was not displaced at all when solid bodies, such as the earth, passed through it.

It finally came to be agreed that comparisons with known materials were not helpful and towards the end of the nineteenth century it was generally recognized that it would be best to regard the ether as a unique substance, *sui generis*, which might not even be composed of any identifiable chemical elements. It was suggested that it might be more fundamental than matter and that perhaps matter ought to be explained in terms of ether rather than vice versa. In 1889 Oliver Heaviside (1850–1925) wrote to Joseph Larmor (1857–1942):

> It often occurs to me that we may all be wrong in thinking of the ether as a kind of matter (elastic solid for instance) accounting for its properties by those of the matter in bulk with which we are acquainted; and that the true way could we only see how to do it, is to explain matter in terms of the ether, going from the simpler to the more complex.[15]

and in the same year Heaviside wrote to Heinrich Hertz (1857–94):

> there is the vexed question of the motion of the ether. Does it move when 'bodies' pass through it, or does it remain at rest? We know that there is an ether; the question is therefore a legitimate physical question which must be answered.[16]

As far as these late-nineteenth century scientists were concerned there *had to be* an ether ('We know that there is an ether'). The existence of the ether was not a metaphysical presupposition but a direct consequence of an empirical theory, the wave theory of light. If there were no ether there would be no way of explaining the transmission of light rays; the nature of light would have to be fundamentally reassessed. At the time it seemed preferable to make fundamental changes to the concept of what could count as a material medium, so the view that the ether must be something other than merely a very unusual form of matter was seriously considered. Like Heaviside, Larmor thought that the ether might be more primitive and a more basic entity than matter; he called it 'Ur-aether'. In his book *Aether and Matter*, published in 1900, he said:

> An aether of the present type can hardly on any scheme be other than a medium, or mental construction if that term is preferred, prior to matter and therefore not expressible in terms of matter.[17]

He did not deny the value of attempting to describe the properties of ether in terms of a mechanical model, as Maxwell and Kelvin had done, but this was because he thought that such a description would permit extrapolation from the mathematics relating to a material model to something that might not be material. In an obituary on Kelvin he wrote:

It has come to pass that by making a model, with ordinary matter, of an elastic medium that has not the properties of ordinary matter, Lord Kelvin had vindicated to many minds ... the power and cogency of mathematical analysis which can reach without effort from the actual to the theoretically possible, and for example, make a mental picture of an aether which is not matter for the simple reason that it is something antecedent to matter.[18]

As we shall see in the next chapter, even the very accurate experiments of Michelson and Morley (carried out between 1883 and 1889) had failed to detect the ether; it appeared to have none of the properties of ordinary matter. For Larmor it had to be a dynamic medium, capable of elastic recoil and therefore capable of some movement, but Hendrik Antoon Lorentz (1853–1928) went further than Larmor and made the ether very little more than a frame of reference for electromagnetic equations. Even so Lorentz did not want to concede that the ether was *only* a mathematical postulate without any real existence. Even after he had considered Einstein's theory of relativity Lorentz wrote:

I cannot but regard the ether as endowed with a certain degree of substantiality, however different it may be from ordinary matter.[19]

Metaphysical speculations as to the nature of the ether

When we consider how the ether was coming to be treated in straight scientific debate – as a non-material medium which acted as the site of mathematical wave equations – it is understandable that further speculation did not seem to be beyond the bounds of legitimate empirical inquiry. As we have seen the very course of physics indicated that what had at first been postulated as a fluid 'exceeding rare' was a very remarkable and mysterious substance. It seemed that there was scientific justification for metaphysical and even theological speculation as to its nature and its functions. One of the less far-fetched surmises, made after the discovery of radio waves by Hertz, (see Chapter 9) was that the ether might be a medium for telepathic communication and that telepathy through the ether might be the ultimate form of wireless.[20] Some took the ether to be a third kind of substance which, although distinguished from mind and from matter, might explain how mind and matter interacted. Some believed that it could serve as a medium of communication for the spirits of the dead to those still living; others surmised that the ether might be the one *ultimate* substance and that both mind and matter were derived from the ether.

Spiritualism

Perhaps the spirits of the dead had ethereal bodies, or perhaps, though spirits were immaterial, they could reveal their thoughts and wishes to us with the help of the ether? The spiritualist movement began in America (New York) in 1848 and by the 1850s it was very popular in Britain, not only among the ill-informed and naïve but also with many scientists. For example Alfred Russell Wallace (1823–1913), a leading biologist, was convinced of the truth of spiritualism; he was the author of an article in *Chambers Encyclopaedia* of 1892 where he wrote:

> Its cardinal truth, imperishably established on the experiments and experiences of millions of sane men and women of all countries and creeds, is that of a world of spirits, and the continuity of existence of the individual spirit through the momentary eclipse of death; as it disappears on earth reappearing in that spiritual world, and becoming an inhabitant amid the ever-augmenting population of the spiritual universe.[21]

Wallace did not directly refer to the ether in this article but to evidence provided by witnesses 'of the highest character' and the investigations made by those 'of known integrity and ability'. In 1869 the committee of the London Dialectical Society (founded by Mill in 1866 for the discussion of 'advanced topics') decided to sponsor a scientific investigation of spiritualism and two years later the members of the investigating committee reported that they considered the matter to merit further careful study. Just before their report was submitted William Crookes (1832–91) began a series of experiments with a spiritualist medium; he said that he had originally thought that spiritualism rested on superstition and trickery but that he had become convinced of its truth. (Cynics held that he had been predisposed in favour of spiritualism from the start.) Crookes took the view that the ether was not a new kind of substance but a fourth state of matter,[22] more attenuated than the gaseous state. This implied that ordinary matter might undergo a change of state from gas to ether analogous to the change from liquid to gas. In 1871 he claimed to have established the existence of a Psychic Force flowing through the ether; he argued that this psychic force could be transmitted through the fourth state of matter (the ether).

Not all scientists thought that the ether was a medium for spirits and communication with spirits; Peter Guthrie Tait (1831–1901) and Balfour Stewart (1828–87) did not accept spiritualism. Tait was a mathematical physicist and Stewart was working on radiant heat; both helped to develop the notion of energy and the adoption of the Law of Conservation of Energy as a fundamental principle of physics. Their support for the law rested on overt appeal to God's constancy, immutability and rationality and, like Joule's, their arguments have a Cartesian ring. In their book, *The Unseen Universe*, published in 1875, Tait and Stewart invoked another principle, the Principle of Continuity, to justify their belief that there was no sharp divide between the observable (material) world and the non-observable (spiritual) world.

The Principle of Continuity had been formulated the year before by John Tyndall (1820–93) in his Presidential Address to the British Association for the Advancement of Science in Belfast. Tyndall was a materialist physicist and he had expounded the Principle of Continuity to support a materialist argument for the origins of life from inanimate matter. But he did not believe that his Principle could support a theory of gradual progression from material to spiritual. This was just what Tait and Stewart were suggesting. They thought that the ether might be the vehicle for the transmission of energy between the worlds of matter and spirit. They argued that since no energy could ever be destroyed, the energy dissipated in the material world might be absorbed into the spiritual world through the ether. They surmised that human thoughts, which they said produced energy in the form of thought waves, might be absorbed into the ether where they could be stored, ready for use in the immaterial world of the spirit after death. Though, as mentioned above, they did not think that there could be direct communication between the dead and the living.

By contrast Oliver Lodge (1851–1940) did take the ether to be a medium linking us to the world of spirits. Lodge was fully qualified to make a scientific assessment of the ether; he had worked with Maxwell, helping to show that light was an electromagnetic radiation and, like Maxwell, he believed that the ether transmitted electromagnetic waves. Along with Heaviside, Larmor and Lorentz, Lodge took the ether to be a new sort of entity and the fundamental basis of matter. Writing in *Nature* (1883), he said:

> Ether is often called a fluid, or a liquid, and again it has been likened to a jelly because of its rigidity; but none of these names are very much good; all these are molecular groupings, and therefore not like ether; let us think simply and solely of a continuous frictionless medium possessing inertia and the vagueness of the notion will be nothing more than is proper in the present state of our knowledge.
>
> We have to try and realise the idea of a perfectly continuous, subtle, incompressible substance pervading all space and pene-

trating between the molecules of ordinary matter, which are embedded in it, and connected with one another by its means. And we must regard it as the one universal medium by which all actions between bodies are carried on. This, then, is its function – to act as the transmitter of motion and of energy.[23]

and the conclusion of his paper was:

I have now endeavoured to introduce you to the simplest conception of the material universe which has yet occurred to man. The conception that is of one universal substance, perfectly homogeneous and continuous and simple in structure, extending to the furthest limit of space of which we have any knowledge, existing equally everywhere. Some portions are at rest or in simple rotational motion, in vortices that is, and differentiated permanently from the rest of the medium by reason of this motion.

These whirling portions constitute what we call matter; their motion gives them rigidity, and of them our bodies and all other material bodies with which we are acquainted are built up.

One continuous substance filling all space; which can vibrate as light; which can be sheared into positive and negative electricity; which in whirls constitutes matter; and which transmits by continuity, and not by impact, every action and reaction of which matter is capable. This is the modern view of the ether and its functions.[24]

The metaphysical presuppositions of late-nineteenth-century physics

1 The geometrical presuppositions of classical physics remained. Space was still three-dimensional and Euclidean; distances measured were held to be objectively established and completely independent of the position and velocity of the measurer and of other bodies.

2 It was accepted that any measurement of time depended on a regularity that might not be perfectly uniform and, influenced by positivism, many doubted that there was an absolute time independent of events. But time as measured by any chosen standard was held to be the same in all places.

3 Vitalism and nature-philosophy were not regarded as part of science. It was believed that all ultimate explanations, even of electromagnetic phenomena would have to be mechanical explanations so that fields of force and electromagnetic vibrations were ultimately to be described and explained in terms of the displacement of the ether.

Problems remaining at the end of the nineteenth century

All were agreed that there was an ether, but what was its nature? Some highly reputable scientists surmised that it might link body and spirit. Those more materialistically inclined disagreed but they conceded that the ether had mysterious properties and might be something other than ordinary matter.

9   Revolution

The problems of the second half of the nineteenth century were very different from those that had emerged in the late fifteenth century insofar as content was concerned but they were alike in that both produced revolutionary changes not only in the scientific but also in the common-sense view of the nature of the world. This was because they involved radical alterations of basic and previously unquestioned metaphysical assumptions.

At first the fifteenth-century problems had appeared to be little more than technical difficulties connected with obtaining more accurate predictions of the positions of the heavenly bodies – predictions that would give direct practical help to navigators and would also enable the Church to establish a more reliable religious calendar. Likewise nineteenth-century problems appeared at first to be of a technical nature, confined to reassessing relatively sophisticated scientific concepts and mathematical equations connected with the nature of the ether and with mathematical descriptions of electromagnetic waves. But it turned out that attempts to resolve both the earlier and the later problems showed the necessity for reassessing matters far beyond what had been thought to be the limits of those problems. Fundamental change was not proposed at the start: as we have seen, pre-Copernican philosophers did not question the Aristotelian and Ptolemaic cosmologies, and likewise pre-Einsteinian scientists did not question the Newtonian presuppositions, the presuppositions of classical physics. The first reformers offered marginal criticism and made peripheral adjustments but there was no suggestion of wholesale disruption beyond what were regarded as the boundaries of each set of problems.

It was not until 1905, and the publication by Albert Einstein (1879–1955) of his paper *On the Electrodynamics of Moving Bodies* that it started to become clear that twentieth-century physicists would need to reassess basic metaphysical assumptions about the nature of space and time and the relationship between mass and energy.

The Einsteinian revolution took place more quickly than the Copernican revolution. As we have seen Copernicus's book was published in 1543 but it was not until Galileo's new physics was accepted that it could be regarded as anything more than a calculating device to 'save the appearances' and it was not firmly established until Newton had achieved his grand synthesis; the process took some hundred and twenty-five years. Einstein's theory was established and accepted by most of his colleagues[1] within twenty-five years.

In this chapter we shall review the problems discussed in Chapter 8 and show how they developed to the point where Einstein saw the need to reject important presuppositions of both Newtonian physics and common sense.

Absolute and relative motion

Newton believed that his laws of motion would apply in precisely the same way to any system that was at rest or moving with constant velocity. For example, the Newtonian laws describing a coin rolling across a table and falling to the floor will be the same whether the event occurs in a room in a house or in a train moving at constant speed on a straight track. As was explained in Chapter 5, it is because bodies behave in the same way whether they are at rest or moving with constant velocity that it is impossible for people within a given inertial system to know whether their system is at rest or in motion. Of course people can tell whether their system is at rest or in motion relative to another system that they are able to observe but, even so, they are only aware of the relative motion of the two systems.

As we have seen, Newton fully appreciated this limitation, but he thought that God had established an absolute space which was at rest in an absolute sense. Any motion, as measured relative to absolute space, would be an absolute motion. Likewise he believed that God had established an absolute and perfectly regular flow of time and, in principle, all other measures calibrated against the absolute standard would give a true and absolute measure of the passage of time. In fact, as Newton well knew, human beings can only measure relative motion and can measure time only in terms of observed regularities but he held that their measurements gained significance from the implicit assumption that God would assess them against His absolute standards. Therefore it was meaningful to talk about absolute position and absolute rest even though it was impossible for any creature but God to know them. Newton did surmise that the fixed stars might provide the frame of absolute space but he could not demonstrate that this was so.

Such was the success of Newtonian physics, not only in explaining the behaviour of moving and stationary bodies on earth and in the heavens but also in many other fields (for example, the dispersion of light) that it came to be regarded as unassailable. Mention was made of the difficulty Young had, at least at first, in establishing the wave theory of light. In the nineteenth century, though views on the nature of light did change, Newtonian mechanics remained virtually sacrosanct, particularly since many data that first seemed to be incompatible with Newton's theories were ultimately shown to confirm them. It was believed that the few anomalies that remained, for example the unacountable 'wobble' observed in the orbit of the planet Mercury, would ultimately be explained by new evidence that would make them understandable in terms of Newtonian theory.

So firmly entrenched were Newton's laws that they were held to describe the way that human beings *had* to understand the behaviour of moving bodies. As we have seen, Kant,[2] who agreed with Hume that causal relations were not logically necessary affirmed that Newton's laws were among the *a priori* concepts whereby we constructed the phenomenal world; so that our concept of the world *had to be* that given by Newtonian physics. Implicit in the acceptance of those laws was a recognition of the possibility of there being an absolute space and time; explicit was the presupposition that the laws were the same in all inertial systems, an assumption that we may call *Newton's Principle of Relativity*. Though positivists such as Mach argued that postulates about the existence of absolute space were meaningless (because we had no way of showing, even in principle, whether a system was at rest or moving with respect to absolute space), they did accept Newton's Principle of Relativity. Moreover, along with everyone else, positivists did not question the assumption that measurements of time and space were independent of motion and remained the same in all systems, inertial and non-inertial.[3] They did not question the assumption that distances stayed constant and that clocks ran at the same rate in different systems. It was these assumptions that were questioned and undermined by Einstein.

Frames of reference

As we saw in Chapter 5, the position of any object can be described only by reference to other objects. If I ask 'Where am I standing?', the answer may be 'In this room'. Then 'Where is this room?'; 'In a house', 'Where is the house?', etc., etc. We shall end up with 'In the world' and, unless we are concerned with astronomical observations, the world will serve as an ultimate reference object. However, generally we appeal to much more localised objects; we may rely on ostensive definition, simply pointing to 'here' or to 'there'.

If we wish to describe the position and motion of objects to be studied in a laboratory it can be convenient to refer them to co-ordinate axes such as those used for graphs. The axes provide a frame of reference and the positions and motions of an object or a set of objects can be recorded as points and lines on a graph. If the whole system of objects is at rest or moving with constant velocity, the frame of reference is an *inertial frame of reference*. Since we shall be dealing solely with inertial frames of reference they will, from now on, be called simply 'frames of reference'.

Galileo had devised relatively simple mathematical rules whereby equations describing motion in one frame of reference could be modified so as to describe the same motion as viewed from another frame of reference; the rules are known as the *Galilean transformation equations*. In effect they represent in a formalized operation what is basically the procedure of intuitive common sense. For example, it is a matter of common-sense intuition, based on experience, that an object moving relative to a stationary observer will appear at rest to an observer who is moving along with the object. On the other hand, another observer, moving in the opposite direction to the first movement will see the object as travelling at a greater velocity than the stationary observer sees it. Thus if I am at the roadside and a car passes me at 50 m.p.h. all the passengers will appear to be travelling at 50 m.p.h. as far as I am concerned. But, within the car they will be at rest, relative to the car and to each other. On the other hand, to those in another car, approaching at 50 m.p.h. in the oppposite direction, the people in the first car will appear to be travelling at 100 m.p.h.. Clearly if the cars are not coming directly towards each other but approaching at an angle it is more complicated to estimate the relative velocity but the Galilean transformation equations enable this to be done. However, though they allot different values to velocities in different frames of reference, the basic laws, Newton's laws of motion, remain the same. We may say that the Galilean transformation equations embody, in mathematical form, Newton's Principle of Relativity.

Problems produced by electromagnetism

Between 1856 and 1873 Clerk Maxwell had studied the electromagnetic effects produced by the relative motion of electrically and magnetically charged bodies and by electric currents. He had come to the conclusion that electromagnetic forces produced mechanical disturbance in the all-pervading ether and in this way were able to travel through space. On the basis of his observations he formulated equations which, in mathematical form, described the waves in the ether. Unlike the Newtonian force of gravity, which was believed to be transmitted instantaneously, electromagnetic waves travelled with very high but finite velocity. Maxwell showed that this was the same as the velocity of light and he concluded that light itself was a mechanical disturbance of the ether which was set up by electromagnetic forces. Disturbances of the ether constituted what Maxwell called an electromagnetic field of force.

This hypothesis, that light was an electromagnetic disturbance of the ether, was published as a treatise in 1873. It offered a synthesis of three physical phenomena: light, electricity and magnetism, but it did not win immediate and widespread acceptance and it did not arouse any general interest in electromagnetic field theory. The significance of Maxwell's work became apparent some ten years after his (relatively early) death as more and more kinds of electromagnetic radiation (or electromagnetic waves) were discovered. For example, Heinrich Hertz (1857–94), using Maxwell's equations, showed that radio waves were also electromagnetic waves, travelling at the same speed as light but of longer wavelength. Soon a whole spectrum of these waves from very short wavelength cosmic and gamma rays, through X-rays, ultraviolet, visible light and infra-red (heat) and radio waves was revealed. Clearly electromagnetic phenomena permeated nature, and problems that had seemed restricted to a particular branch of physics in the 1870s had become of very general importance. Electromagnetic radiation began to attract a great deal of attention.

Attempts to detect the ether

The frame of reference in which Maxwell's equations were valid was generally assumed to be the frame in which the ether was at rest, though it might suffer transient disturbance by wave motion. This frame of reference had to be distinguished from other frames because the equations altered their form when subjected to the Galilean transformation rules. They appeared to show that the velocity of light *in different directions* would vary in frames of reference that were not at rest with respect to the ether. Maxwell suggested that electromagnetic waves of light might vary in velocity just as the velocity of water waves and sound waves could vary. Turbulence and pressure changes in the medium were known to affect these waves and turbulence in the ether might affect the velocity of light.

It was argued that there would be a variation of the velocity of light in different frames of reference which might be compared to the variation in the relative velocity of water waves in a swimming bath. The movement of the earth through the ether could be compared to the movement of a man swimming through water in a swimming bath: swimmer and water are moving with respect to each other and are in different frames of reference; likewise the earth and the ether are moving with respect to each other and are in different frames of reference. The ripples set up in a swimming bath, say by a vibrator, are analogous to light waves set up by an electromagnetic disturbance. The absolute velocity of the ripples can be taken as their velocity relative to the bath but their velocity relative to the swimmer will depend on whether he is swimming with the ripples, or in the opposite direction to them, or at an angle to them. Likewise the absolute velocity of light can be taken as its velocity relative to the static ether but its velocity relative to the earth will depend on whether the earth is moving in the direction of the light ray, or against it or at an angle to it. However, the difference in the apparent velocities will be very small, for light travels at about 300,000 kilometres a second and the earth at about 30 kilometres a second; very delicate instruments are required to detect a change of plus or minus 30 in 300,000.

The Michelson-Morley measurements

In the 1870s an American naval officer, Albert Abraham Michelson (1852–1931) devised various instruments for very accurate measurments and by 1880 he thought that there was a hope of being able to detect a difference between the velocity of light rays travelling parallel to the earth's motion and those travelling at right angles to that motion. He believed that he could be accurate to within 1 part in 100,000, an accuracy more than adequate to detect a change of 30 parts in 300,000. From 1883 to 1889 he carried out measurements with the chemist Edward William Morley (1838–1923); these were the famous Michelson-Morley experiments. However, even with their sensitive instruments, no significant variations in the velocity of light could be detected and so they obtained no evidence to show that the light passed as waves through the ether. But Michelson did not doubt that the ether existed and that light rays were disturbances, of some sort, in the ether. He thought that his experimental results showed that the earth was in the same frame of reference as the ether and therefore that the hypothesis that the ether was stationary was false. In other words the inference from his data was that the ether must move with the earth. To return to the swimming bath analogy: if the bulk of water moves bodily with the swimmer the velocity of the ripples relative to the swimmer will remain the same whatever direction he takes.

Michelson never abandoned the ether theory and as late as 1922 he was still attempting to measure the effect of the earth's rotation on the velocity of light and planning experiments to detect ether drift. To the end of his life he remained convinced that there must be an all-pervading ether, and this in spite of the achievements of relativity theory. This is especially ironic, for it cannot be denied that Einstein's theory would never have been accepted were it not for Michelson's measurements which showed, with such great accuracy, the constancy of the velocity of light.

Electromagnetism and the ether: Lorentz

The problem of the transmission of light (and of course it involved all electromagnetic radiations) was pursued by Lorentz. He thought that all electromagnetic radiation consisted of wave disturbances in the ether, but he suggested that the transmission had to be considered not only in terms of an etherial field of force, as Maxwell had said, but also in terms of small particles regarded as sources and recipients of electromagnetic energy. Because Maxwell based his theory on a mathematical analysis of waves in ether he had not discussed the physical nature of bodies carrying electric charges, referring to them as charged points. Lorentz, however, was much influenced by contemporary work on atomic structure (work published after Maxwell had died) and he suggested that the charged particles vibrating within atoms (electrons, for example) could be the source of light. He surmised that if this were the case then a strong magnetic field ought to have an effect on the wavelength of the light emitted, and his conjecture was confirmed when this effect was demonstrated by his own pupil Pieter Zeeman (1865–1943). The oscillating particles generated electromagnetic forces which were thought to be transmitted through the ether, thereby setting up an electromagnetic field. Lorentz assumed that the ether was the seat of the field and therefore, in his view, electromagnetic radiation involved two basic types of entity: particle and field.

But Lorentz's ether had ceased to be a material entity in the ordinary sense for it had no effective mechanical properties. Rosser says:

> To Lorentz, the ether was just an absolute system in which Maxwell's equations were valid; the ether was deprived of almost all its mechanical properties.[4]

Rosser quotes Silberstein, who was writing in 1914:

> Lorentz's ether is not deformed, it is subjected to strain, and does not, consequently, execute mechanical oscillations. And this being the case, it has, of course, no kind of elasticity, nor inertia or density. . . . One fails to see what properties, in fact, it still has left to it, besides that of being a colourless seat (we cannot even call it a substratum) of the electromagnetic vectors. . . . And although Lorentz himself continues to tell us, in 1909, that he "cannot but regard the ether as endowed with a certain degree of substantiality", yet for all the use he ever made of the ether, he might as well have called it . . . a purely geometric system of reference.[5]

Lorentz: a precursor of Einstein

Lorentz thought of himself as extending Maxwell's field theory, an extension which incorporated his own ideas about atomic structure and involved the activity of subatomic particles. He thought of himself as developing Maxwell's theory explaining the relationship between light, electricity and magnetism but, in fact, he had taken physical theory forward towards relativity. His equations were different from Maxwell's, though like Maxwell's they took different forms when subjected to the Galilean transformations; that is they altered when applied to different frames of reference. Since Lorentz's ether had no mechanical properties the alterations could not be explained, as Maxwell had explained his, by appeal to disturbance of the ether. Instead Lorentz developed new transformation equations, superseding those of Galileo. In order to achieve transformations that would keep his electromagnetic laws the same in different frames of reference he found that he had to make certain mathematical adjustments to the algebraic variables denoting time and distance. In 1895 (ten years before Einstein's paper appeared) he introduced the notion of 'local time', that is of different time rates at different places. In addition he allowed lengths of objects in motion to contract, that is the mathematical variables that denoted length in his equations decreased as the velocity variables increased. However, all the modifications of variables that occurred when his transformation equations were applied on changing frames of reference, had no theoretical backing. There was no explanation as to *why* they occurred; they were purely *ad hoc* adjustments and they were introduced solely in order to achieve the desired result, namely to maintain Newton's Principle of Relativity, the principle that the Newtonian laws of physics hold in all frames of reference. For Lorentz the alterations of his variables had absolutely no physical implications; he was sure that any particular body had only one *real length* and for all places there was one and the same *real time rate*. He also thought, though conceding that it could not be picked out, that there was one absolute frame of reference which was that of the non-mechanical (and mysterious) ether.

Elctromagnetism and the ether: Einstein

From letters written by Einstein to his fiancée between 1898 and 1902 it is clear that, at the time, and like everyone else, he had no doubt that the ether existed. By 1899 he knew of the Michelson-Morley experiments and, as we have seen, those experiments appeared to establish that the ether moved with the earth. Einstein had also re-read Hertz's papers and the work on Maxwell's electrodynamics. He wrote:

> I am more and more convinced that the electrodynamics of moving bodies . . . is not correct, and that it should be possible to present it in a simpler way. The introduction of the term 'ether' into theories of electricity leads to a notion of a medium of whose motion one can speak without, I believe, being able to associate any physical meaning with such a statement.[6]

We can see the influence of positivism here, with the implication that if the motion of the ether could not be detected, i.e. could not be associated with any physical observation, then a hypothesis appealing to such a motion was useless and otiose. But Einstein had not yet abandoned belief in the existence of an ether.

At this time he thought of himself as an experimentalist, not as a mathematical physicist, and he wanted to measure the earth's movement against the ether (what was called 'ether drift') but he was not able to construct the apparatus. As late as 1901 he was still writing to his fiancée about ether drift experiments, but he was also developing his ideas on electrodynamics (moving electric charges) and he was beginning to have doubts about the classical treatment of relative motion. By 1905 he had come to the conclusion that the concept of the ether was superfluous. It was superfluous because the ether had no detectable effects; Einstein's reasons for dismissing the notion of the ether are remarkably similar to Newton's (see quotation on p. 102).

Einstein's 1905 paper

When this paper was published Einstein was unaware of Lorentz's work and of the mathematical adjustments Lorentz had made to the variables in his equations. Einstein also wanted to preserve Newton's Principle of Relativity and in his paper he showed how this could be done. He began by drawing attention to certain asymmetries in Maxwell's equations; in virtue of those asymmetries and also in virtue of Michelson's and Morley's failure to detect motion of the earth relative to the ether, he suggested that the concept of an absolute frame of reference and the concepts of absolute rest and of absolute motion were redundant. In his paper he said:

> the unsuccessful attempts to discover any motion of the earth rela-
> tive to the 'light medium', suggests that the phenomena of electro-
> dynamics as well as of mechanics possess no properties
> corresponding to the concept of absolute rest. They lead one to
> conjecture that . . . the same laws of electrodynamics and optics will
> be valid for all frames of reference for which the equations of
> mechanics hold good. We will raise this conjecture (the purport of
> which will hereafter be called the 'Principle of Relativity') to the
> status of a postulate, and also introduce another postulate, which is
> only apparently irreconcilable with the former, namely that light is
> always propagated in empty space with a definite velocity c which is
> independent of the state of motion of the emitting body. These two
> postulates suffice for the attainment of a simple and consistent
> theory of electrodynamics of moving bodies. . . . The introduction
> of a 'luminiferous ether' will prove to be superfluous inasmuch as
> the view here to be developed will not require an 'absolutely
> stationary space' provided with special properties.[7]

Einstein extended Newton's Principle of Relativity, which had applied only to mechanics, to include electrodynamics. He pointed out that if physical laws were the same in all inertial frames of reference then there was no need to assume that there must be an absolute frame of reference or an absolute space; the notion of the ether was superflu-ous, not only as a carrier of light but also as providing an absolute frame of reference. He suggested that the velocity of light (and of all electromagnetic radiations) was a universal physical constant.

A new metaphysical principle

It might seem that the postulate that the velocity of light was constant in all frames of reference must violate the Relativity Principle for, as we have seen, the velocity of any given *body* as seen by observers in different frames of reference, will not be the same. However, light rays along with all electromagnetic radiations are not moving bodies, they are energy fields, fields of force. For Einstein the constancy of the velocity of light, the velocity of transmission of a field of force, was a metaphysical principle of physics analogous to the principle of inertia or to the principle of the conservation of energy. All these principles have some empirical justification in that they provide a basis for consistent explanations of what is observed but they are not empirical laws that can be falsified by experimental and observational data. A consequence of the postulate of constant velocity of light (and of all electromagnetic radiations) is that there is then need for a fundamental reassessment of other metaphysical assumptions that up to the time of the 1905 paper had been the unquestioned basis of much of the common-sense as well as the scientific view of the world.

A new view of time

Einstein did not jettison intuitive common sense; rather he invited his colleagues to reassess fundamental concepts *on the basis of a common-sense analysis of the significance of familiar and ordinary terms*. He began with a consideration of time. As we saw in Chapter 5, it had been acknowledged from the days of Aristotle that though the passage of time was appreciated as a subjective experience, it had to be *measured* by some objectively observable change; that change was almost in-variably some form of motion. Einstein pointed out that motion and time were interdependent concepts and that it was essential to under-stand what was signified by 'time'. He said that the crucial element in our notion of time was that of *simultaneity*, because any judgement we make of time, and the time of an event, must be a judgement of the simultaneity of that event with another event:

> If we wish to describe the motion of a material point, we give the value of its co-ordinates as functions of time. We must bear care-fully in mind that a mathematical description of this kind has no physical meaning unless we are quite clear as to what we understand by 'time'. We have to take account that all our judgements in which time plays a part are always judgements of *simultaneous events*. If, for instance, I say, 'That train arrives here at 7 o'clock', I mean

something like this: 'The pointing of the small hand of my watch to 7 and the arrival of the train are simultaneous events.'[8]

He continued:

It might appear possible to overcome all the difficulties attending the definition of 'time' by substituting 'the position of the small hand of my watch' for 'time'. And in fact such a definition is satisfactory when we are concerned with defining a time exclusively for the place where the watch is located; but it is no longer satisfactory when we have to connect in time series of events occurring at different places, or – what comes to the same thing – to evaluate the times of events occurring at places remote from the watch.[9]

Einstein was the first to point out that a finite time must be allowed for the message conveying the information as to the position of the watch hand to reach a site some distance from the watch. Thus if we are at site A and an event takes place at a distant site B, watches at the two sites must be calibrated so as to allow for the time taken for the light to travel from A to B or from B to A. Watches at other sites need to be analogously calibrated. It will be possible to do this if the sites are all in the same frame of reference and therefore, *within the same frame of reference*, observers in different places can agree as to the time of events.

However, because light travels at the *same* velocity for observers in different frames of reference, that is no adjustment to the velocity of light needs to be made when one observer moves relative to another, there can be no agreement about simultaneity between those observers. For example, an observer at the roadside seeing the reflection in the wing mirror of a passenger in a passing car could not agree with that same passenger as to when the reflection appeared. Of course as regards everyday observations the disagreement could not be noticed because the light travels thousands of times faster than any car, but a theoretical discrepancy is there. Hence it is impossible to synchronize clocks in different frames of reference; events that seem simultaneous to observers in one frame of reference will not seem simultaneous to those in another frame of reference.

A new view of size

Since the velocity of light is calculated from the distance travelled in a given time, Einstein was able to show that as the velocity of a frame of reference increased, relative to an observer outside the frame, so the lengths in the direction of motion of bodies within the moving frame of reference, would appear shorter, that is they would appear to contract and become thinner. This contraction had appeared in Lorentz's equations (see above) but for Lorentz it had been nothing more than a mathematical adjustment of an equation, not a physical description. Einstein was asserting that objects in a moving frame of reference would, when viewed from a stationary frame, actually appear to be flattened in the direction of motion, and, if the velocity of the frame of reference became equal to the velocity of light:

> moving objects – viewed from the 'stationary system' – would shrivel up into plane figures.[10]

For example, a sphere would become a disc, and finally a plane circle.

Of course observers in the moving system would see no change in the bodies in their system and to them it would be the objects in the 'stationary' frame of reference that would appear shrivelled. Einstein considered what would happen if the system moved faster than light, in relation to the 'stationary' frame, and said:

> For velocities greater than light our deliberations become meaningless; we shall, however, find in what follows, that the velocity of light in our theory plays the part physically, of an infinitely great velocity.[11]

A new view of mass

Einstein was able to show that mass would be affected by velocity in that observers from one frame of reference would be able to observe an increase in mass of an object moving relative to that frame of reference. Likewise observers in the moving frame would be able to detect a corresponding increase in the mass of objects in the 'stationary' frame of reference. As the relative velocity approached the velocity of light the apparent masses would approach infinity, so the notion of the constancy of mass, an assumption of classical physics, had to be abandoned. It was from further consideration of this effect that Einstein was able to show that mass was a form of energy, with consequences that we all know were literally earth-shaking.

Space-time

The theory of relativity developed in Einstein's 1905 paper was the Special Theory of Relativity, STR; it was later to be extended to a general Theory of Relativity, GTR, which treated of events in non-inertial frames of reference, but we shall not discuss this. For, from consideration of STR alone we can appreciate that the rejection of the postulate of absolute time (and along with it the Newtonian notion of a divinely ordered regular flow of time) and the rejection of the concept of absolute space (including dimensions as well as absolute position) introduce what seems to be an inevitable subjectivity dependent on the viewpoint and frame of reference of the observer. It would seem that this must affect all measurements of objects and events. Christensen says:

> The distance between two events (whether they are at the same place, or ten feet apart, or 500 light-years apart) and likewise the duration between them (whether they are simultaneous, or ten seconds apart, or 500 years apart) are taken to be dependent upon, or 'relative to', the observer who measures those quantities. And similarly, of course, for all quantities defined in terms of distance and duration (speed, acceleration, *etc.*), and others as well, such as mass: they are claimed to be not intrinsic to the objects or events that display them, but extrinsic, in this sense. They are relative to an observer – or better, perhaps, to the material 'observation frame' from which they are or might be observed or measured; the observer dependence involved here is not of the mentalistic sort ... the important point here is that in some way or other STR makes the observed inseparable from the observer; the former's very nature makes it dependent upon the latter.[12]

It must be stressed that this observer-dependence is not a matter of complete subjectivity, a matter of the response of different *individuals*, because, *for all observers in the same frame of reference* there can be objective and agreed measurement and values. As Christensen says, it would be less confusing to call the dependence 'observation-frame-dependence' but the term 'observer-dependence' is commonly used.

A way to establish independence of the frame of reference was proposed by Einstein's teacher Hermann Minkowski (1864–1909). In a lecture 'Space and Time' given in 1908 he suggested that events should be identified and described by their position and time in a four-dimensional frame of reference of space-time. This would allow objective measurements but it would entail making space and time interdependent because the 'time axis' would be as necessary for a description as the three 'space-axes'.

Unfortunately human beings find it very difficult to envisage events in four (as opposed to three) dimensions; it is too far removed from the common-sense metaphysical presuppositions whereby we structure our experiences. Minkowski's suggestion achieves objectivity by removing physical accounts of objects and events from common-sense intuition. Intuitively we take the positions of objects as being independent of time (time does not have to be stated); likewise we do not think that the time of an event depends, in the ordinary way, on where it occurred. As we saw in Chapter 5, Newton had asserted that space was always and that every moment of duration was *everywhere*. Minkowski rejected this and said that events could not be objectively described by direct appeal to common-sense assumptions. He pointed out that the feature of events that made them observer-independent was their 'space-time interval', an attribute that was a function of the distance and the time lapse between them. He said:

> Henceforth space by itself and time by itself, are doomed to fade away into mere shadows, and only a kind of union of the two will preserve an independent reality.[13]

Space-time is a new concept which can be regarded as providing a new metaphysical framework that could replace the two Newtonian concepts of absolute space and absolute time. We can think of our particular description of space position and time, *as given in our particular frame of reference*, as being projections of space-time; the projection is different for observers in different frames of reference just as the projection of a three-dimensional object on to a two-dimensional sheet of paper is different according to the point of view from which the projection is made:

> what determines how the world 'looks' to a given frame is its spatio-temporal *orientation*; ... that is to say, the world 'looks' different to *a* than it does to *b* (say, the distance and duration between two particular events are longer for *a* than for *b*) because they are oriented differently, relative to the things they are both observing.[14]

The concept of space-time allows facts that are observer-dependent to be explained in observer-independent terms:

> and it might be held that spatial and temporal properties and relations are mere appearances (in a broad sense of the term), somewhat like the illusory two-dimensional 'look' of a thing that is actually (it is supposed) three dimensional. Alternatively, it could be said that distance and duration do not, after all, even appear to be real, but represent a case of mistaken inference; accidental

features of our construction as knowers have led the human race to infer the existence of two separate continua, 'space' and 'time', in place of the four-dimensional continuum that is really there.[15]

However, in general, physicists have not adopted space-time descriptions; Einstein himself treated space and time as separate entities. For example his account of determining the time of a distant event in the same frame of reference was a method for determining the same times in different places; he did not suggest a way of measuring different times at the same place. It has come to be accepted that in different frames of reference measurements must be observer-dependent but even so the common-sense concepts of time and space and mass have had to be reassessed. The physical theories of the twentieth century are based on a new set of metaphysical presupppositions as to the nature of the world and they have had an impact similar to that brought about by the changed metaphysical presuppositions of sixteenth- and seventeenth-century natural philosophy.

Twentieth-century beliefs

1 There is no longer confidence that scientific inquiry can lead to a definitive and true account of the world.
2 It has come to be appreciated that any explanation must depend on metaphysical presuppositions which are to be accepted as the ones most appropriate for the solving of current problems rather than being seen as ultimate truths.
3 Although science is seen as a secular activity it is now acknowledged that the natural world, not only living things but also inanimate objects, cannot be adequately described, let alone explained, purely in terms of human sense experiences.

The position after Einstein

The order established by classical physics was no longer possible; Newtonian certainties had to be abandoned.

Nature and Nature's laws lay hid in night:
God said, *Let Newton be!* and all was light.[16]

It did not last: the Devil howling 'Ho!
Let Einstein be!' restored the status quo.[17]

10 Physics and metaphysics

The decline of metaphysics

The purpose of this book is to show that metaphysics plays an essential role in empirical inquiry and it is necessary to deal with the objection that, in the ordinary way, physics is sharply distinguished from metaphysics. Not only the 'plain man' but also many working scientists take physics to be a controlled discipline whereas they take metaphysics to be, at best a matter of speculation – the former concerned with facts, the latter with fancies. Today many would assert that metaphysical theorizing along with religous belief can only corrupt objective scientific thought and undermine scientific methodology. We have seen that though Renaissance and post-Renaissance philosophers (such as Copernicus and Descartes) undermined religious dogmas they did not dismiss religious faith; it gave essential support for their belief in Man's capacity to understand the world. The real separation of religion and metaphyhsics from science started with the Enlightenment and was made explicit by positivists. That positivist outlook is still influential today.

But positivism as developed by Mach is self-defeating. Far from leading to a triumph of fact over fancy, it leads to the primacy of personal sense experiences and collapses into solipsism or into a form of idealism that cannot help scientific inquiry. If metaphysics is overtly rejected either there must be complete scepticism as to knowledge of anything but personal sensations or else metaphysical beliefs will be covertly smuggled in to the purportedly metaphysics-free system. For, as our text has shown in relation to scientific concepts as broad as notions of time or as restricted as a notion of heat, we must make some assumptions that are not derived from experience. This is not to say that they may not be adjusted in the light of experience if they are found not to helpful – Newton's conjectures as to the existence of an absolute space and Einstein's arguments for a reassessment of that concept illustrate this. But we have no way of making sense of our experiences unless we make some assumptions that allow us to interpret them.

Metaphysical presuppositions

Thus it is not surprising that despite positivist influence there remained underlying metaphysical assumptions in nineteenth-century physics. We have seen that Maxwell, Hertz, Michelson and Lorentz followed the classical tradition and did not question metaphysical presuppositions as to the constancy of mass, the constancy of the dimensions of objects (whether at rest or in motion) and the assumption that time was independent of motion (and therefore the same in all frames of reference).

Study of natural philosophy and science as practised in the distant and in the recent past can help to show the essential role of metaphysical assumptions. As we have seen, until this century they were closely involved with religious beliefs. The warning in the Preface must be heeded for it is always dangerous to try to recapture the thoughts and ideas of the past, but we need to take this risk if we are to attempt to understand the *significance* of religion for the metaphysical assumptions of science. Because we have confined our attention to Western Europe we have been concerned solely with various forms of Christianity and any conclusions to be drawn from the cases considered can apply only to the interaction of Christian with other metaphysical beliefs. In respect of this limitation it should be clear that the nature of the religious beliefs of Copernicus, Kepler, Descartes, Newton, Joule and of many others was grounded in a mystical acceptance of a higher power rather than in Christian doctrine; all of them held opinions that were not or would not be acceptable to their Church. But underlying their heterodox and even heretical beliefs was the faith akin to the faith of the Schoolmen that human reason was the gift of a God concerned with human affairs and that it was adequate to the task of explaining events in the world.

Although today there is no direct appeal to religious faith we may see that something of such faith still survives. In the first part of this chapter we shall study Einstein's responses to positivism and his attitude to metaphysics and to religious beliefs. In 1949 he wrote:

A basic conceptual distinction, which is a necessary prerequisite of scientific and pre-scientific thinking, is the distinction between 'sense-impressions' (and the recollections of such) on the one hand and mere ideas on the other. ... one needs this distinction to overcome solipsism. ... We represent the sense-impressions as conditioned by an 'objective' and by a 'subjective' factor. For this conceptual distinction there also is no logical-philosophical justification. But if we reject it, we cannot escape solipsism. It is also the prerequisite of every kind of physical thinking.'[1]

Einstein's early views

In the late 1890s and in the early twentieth century, that is at the time he was writing his paper on the electrodynamics of moving bodies, Einstein was much influenced by Mach. Indeed until Mach's death in 1919, and possibly for some years after, Einstein thought of himself as one of Mach's disciples. Even after he had abandoned positivism Einstein said that Mach's influence had been so pervasive that even those who had opposed him had absorbed many of his ideas.

As we have seen Einstein approached the problems involved in the concept of the ether as a positivist, and in his youth mathematics and speculative conjecture played little overt part in his work. At that time he adopted what is called an *operationalist* view of physical concepts such as mass, length and time; that is he held that they were to be understood in terms of the operations whereby they were measured. The quotations from his 1905 paper, given in Chapter 9, show this. For example Einstein argued that time was to be understood exclusively in terms of simultaneity because to say that two events were at the same time was to say that they were simultaneous and to say that an event was at a certain time *meant* that its occurrence was simultaneous with some observable event on a selected clock. In this way the concept of time (potentially a subjective notion) was firmly bound to observation and measurement.

Yet this very operationalism had led him to put in question the *metaphysical* assumptions of nineteenth-century science and though his ideas were based on positivist (and therefore anti-metaphysical) principles he had not abandoned metaphysics; he had simply provided new assumptions. He laid down the Principle of Relativity and the constancy of the velocity of light as *postulates* to guide the interpretation of observations. Admittedly observers had been unable to detect any change or variation in the velocity of light but the move from 'The velocity of light has not been observed to vary' to 'The velocity of light never varies' cannot be justified by any positivist.

But Einstein went further for he wished to establish a theoretical framework that would unify a wide range of apparently disparate phenomena; he wanted to explain electromagnetic effects (which Lorentz had thought must involve particles as well as a field) in terms of a single basic entity. Initially he thought that particles were basic but later he returned to Maxwell's view that the field was fundamental. As early as 1901, before his paper on the electrodynamics of moving bodies, he wrote:

It is a wonderful feeling to recognize the unity of a complex of appearances which, to direct sense experience, seem to be separate things.[2]

Einstein's positivism

Despite these early signs of speculation and appeal to metaphysical postulates Einstein still regarded himself as a positivist. In 1918 he still seemed to rate observation much more highly than imaginative speculation. Writing of the development of relativity theory, he said:

a theory which wishes to deserve trust must be built upon generalizable facts.[3]

Yet his generalizable facts, his theories, do not support what he wrote. His letter continued:

Old examples: Chief postulates of thermodynamics [based] on impossibility of perpetuum mobile. Mechanics [based] on a grasped (*ertasten*) law of inertia. Kinetic gas theory [based] on equivalence of heat and mechanical energy (also historically). Special Relativity on the constancy of light and Maxwell's equation for the vacuum, which in turn rest on empirical foundations.[4]

It seems that he had persuaded himself that these theories were based on observation, and he concluded:

Never has a truly useful and deep-going theory really been founded purely speculatively.[5]

How soon this was to change!

Einstein's empiricism

Elsewhere[6] I have shown that facts are by no means simple and clear-cut entities and that our concept of *fact* is highly complex.

Einstein still gave facts priority but from his 1918 letter we can see that for him facts were much more than accounts of sense experiences, or even accounts of direct observations. The postulate of the constant velocity of light transcends the facts of experience and the same can be said of most of the other examples he gave: the law of inertia, the equivalence of heat and energy and relativity theory itself. He relied on metaphysics implicitly and cannot be regarded as a positivist, but he can still be regarded as an empiricist. In 1921 he reaffirmed that his relativity theory was suppported by experience and that his new concepts of space and time were an inevitable response to what was observed. In a lecture on his relativity theory in London he said:

> I am anxious to draw attention to the fact that this theory is not speculative in origin; it owes its invention entirely to the desire to make physical theory fit the observed fact as well as possible. We have here no revolutionary act, but the natural continuation of a line that can be traced through centuries. The abandonment of certain notions connected with space, time and motion, hitherto treated as fundamentals, must not be regarded as arbitrary, but only as conditioned by observed facts.[7]

Here there is a link with Copernicus for he too stressed that his theory had emerged as part of an older tradition (see Chapter 2, p. 28).

Einstein's imaginative rationalism

During the late 1920s Einstein began to lay less stress on observation for he came to appreciate the part played by pure reason and the fundamental importance of mathematics and mathematical speculation in physical science. He affirmed that the role of imaginative conjecture was not that of a potentially dangerous 'frill' but was an essential part of inquiry. He did not abandon his empiricism to become an out-and-out rationalist, for he did not think that reason could *replace* observation. There was, he thought, an interdependence so that rational speculation had to be related to experience; reason could not be of any help if it had no connection with what was observed. In his Herbert Spencer Memorial Lecture of 1933 Einstein said:

> Pure logical thinking can give us no knowledge whatsoever of the world of experience; all knowledge about reality begins with experience and terminates in it.
>
> Conclusions obtained by purely rational processes are, as far as Reality is concerned, entirely empty.[8]

but

> Reason gives the structure to the system; the data of experience and their mutual relations are to correspond exactly to consequences in the theory.[9]

and

> The basic concepts and laws which are not logically further reducible constitute the indispensable and not rationally deducible part of the theory.[10]

Yet these basic concepts and laws are imaginative conjectures, metaphysical speculations firming to metaphysical postulates. Einstein called them 'purely fictitious'[11] and he said that in the eighteenth and nineteenth centuries this had not been appreciated. However, in his view, their true character was coming to be realized 'because of the ever-widening logical gap between the basic concepts and laws on the one side and the consequences to be correlated with our experiences on the other'.[12]

He thought that as the number of logically independent conceptual elements in physics was reduced, by their being made interdependent, the gap between theory and fact must widen. For example his relativity theory entailed the interdependence of mass, time, length and position and so removed these concepts further from the observed 'facts' of common sense. Einstein pointed out that Newton had believed that all his basic concepts and laws could be grounded on appeal to commonsense experiences and that he was worried that he had not been able to demonstrate the existence of an absolute space and time; he had also been worried at having to postulate action at a distance for the force of gravity. But of course Newton did not think that his laws were human *inventions*; he thought that they were God's laws which humans had *discovered*. We may surmise that he underestimated his own imaginative genius; as I pointed out earlier his famous *hypotheses non fingo* indicates a dismissal of imaginative conjecture which he did not practise.

Einstein was aware that the fictitious character of theoretical principles was demonstrated by the fact that two sets of principles could exhibit two essentially different sets of assumptions and yet both might lead to predictions that were in agreement with what might be observed. It could then be argued that the so-called axioms at the base of physics were nothing more than convenient postulates, free inventions, and that it was futile to seek for *correct* explanations of events. However, he was now so far away from positivism that he dared to suggest that this was not the case and that there were correct explanations that mirrored an objective reality rather than being merely a base for predictions. For Einstein, as for classical physicists and for the Ancient Greeks, this was intimately involved with a belief in mathematical elegance and simplicity. He said:

Nature is the realization of the simplest conceivable mathematical ideas. I am convinced that we can discover, by means of purely mathematical constructions, those concepts and those lawful connections between them which furnish the key to the understanding of natural phenomena. Experience may suggest the appropriate mathematical concepts, but they most certainly cannot be deduced from it. Experience remains, of course, the sole criterion of physical utility of a mathematical construction. But the creative principle resides in mathematics. In a certain sense, therefore I hold it true that pure thought can grasp reality, as the ancients dreamed.[13]

Einstein's affirmation reflects a belief in the possibility of success for the human search for understanding and a belief in the descriptive powers of mathematics which was a feature of classical physics. It is worth remembering that Newton was convinced that God, the designer and master of the cosmos, was a mathematician.

Like earlier natural philosophers Einstein, though more conscious that theory must relate to experience, did not think that an explanation should be rejected because current observations (and current interpretations of those observations) were incompatible with it. It might be necessary to reassess the significance of the observations, to reconsider their relevance, and to check their accuracy, before dismissing an explanation. Copernican theory had not been compatible with the physical theory accepted in his time although later he had been shown to be broadly correct and contemporary physics hopelessly wrong. Likewise a modern theory, superficially unacceptable, might be supported if it were believed that other, currently accepted laws, ought to be modified. Holton writes:

only a few months after Einstein had written in his fourth letter to Mach that the solar eclipse experiment will decide 'whether the basic and fundamental assumption of the equivalence of the acceleration of the reference field and of the gravitational field really holds', Einstein writes to Besso in a very different vein (in March 1914), before the first, ill-fated eclipse expedition was scheduled to test the conclusions of the preliminary version of the general relativity theory: 'Now I am fully satisfied, and I do not doubt any more the correctness of the whole system, may the observation of the eclipse succeed or not. The sense of the thing (*die Vernunft der Sache*) is too evident.'[14]

and Holton also quotes from the reminiscences of one of Einstein's students, Ilse Rosenthal-Schneider:

'Once when I was with Einstein in order to read with him a work that contained many objections against his theory . . . he suddenly interrupted the discussion of the book, reached for a telegram that was lying on the windowsill, and handed it to me with the words, "Here, this will perhaps interest you." It was Eddington's cable with the results of measurement of the eclipse expedition (1919). When I was giving expression to my joy that the results coincided with his calculation, he said quite unmoved, "But I knew the theory is correct"; and when I asked if there had been no confirmation of his prediction, he countered: "Then I would have been sorry for the dear Lord – the theory *is* correct.'[15]

Clearly Einstein had finally come to rate explanatory theory higher than observation – it was theory which provided a conceptual scheme that made experience so significant.

We may note here a certain arrogance, an arrogance that will remind us of Descartes and his confidence that by reason all would be explained. Perhaps the scientists who make discoveries need this confidence in the power of reason and need something of Cartesian arrogance. Certainly they seem to accept that their own metaphysical postulates must be the correct ones and it is interesting that with Einstein, as well as Descartes, there is more than a metaphorical reference to God. Descartes thought that God guaranteed the uniformity of events and had given mankind the power to discover the laws of nature; Newton thought also of a uniform process of events, overseen by God, a God who supplied the physical framework of an absolute space and time. Einstein referred to 'the dear Lord' as ultimate master of the cosmos.

In his book *A Brief History of Time* Stephen Hawking shows the need to appeal to some power transcending human capacities to account for the existence of the universe though he also shows that perhaps essential arrogance and confidence in the understanding of nature. He appreciates that the problems have to be tackled piecemeal but he affirms that the *ultimate* goal of science is to provide a single theory that describes the whole universe.[16] In the chapter significantly called 'The origin and fate of the universe' he reveals a Cartesian concept of laws of nature and though he does not insist that they are divine decrees he does entertain this notion:

> Science seems to have uncovered a set of laws that . . . tell us how the universe will develop with time, if we know its state at any one time. These laws may have originally been decreed by God, but it appears that he has since left the universe to evolve according to them and does not now intervene in it.[17]

Insofar as God does not intervene in the world Hawking's God is a Cartesian as opposed to a Newtonian God but, unlike Descartes Hawking does not accept the necessity for God's existence. He implies that whether or not there *is* a God depends on the nature of the universe:

> The idea that space and time may form a closed surface without boundary also has profound implications for the role of God in the affairs of the universe. With the success of scientific theories in describing events, most people have come to believe that God allows the universe to evolve according to a set of laws and does not intervene in the universe to break these laws. However, the laws do not tell us what the universe should have looked like when it started – it would still be up to God to wind up the clockwork and choose how to start it. So long as the universe had a beginning, we could suppose it had a creator. But if the universe is really completely self-contained, having no boundary or edge, it would have neither beginning nor end: it would simply be. What place, then, for a creator?[18]

Can we ever hope to arrive at an ultimate explanation? Hawking is well aware that scientists in the past have triumphantly but erroneously proclaimed that they had at last found the secrets of nature and were fast approaching an ultimate explanation, 'we have had false dawns before',[19] but he has some confidence that at last science really is approaching its goal:

> I still believe there are grounds for cautious optimism that we may now be near the end of the search for the ultimate laws of nature.[20]

The quantum mechanics of modern physical theory introduces the notion of statistical predictions but Hawking dismisses the suggestion that natural events occur in a random manner as one which would undermine the whole purpose of science – we *have to* assume there are laws of nature. This leaves him with two alternatives: either there is a complete unified theory that we might be able to discover or there is no *ultimate* theory but an infinite sequence of theories that describe the universe more and more accurately.[21] He concedes that the second alternative 'is in agreement with all experience so far'[22] but, as we have seen, he believes that in fact the sequence not only is coming to an end but that we are now very close to that end, and to a final and true account.

> Thus it does seem that the sequence of more and more refined theories should have some limit. . . . I think that there is a good chance that the study of the early universe and the requirements of mathematical consistency will lead us to a complete unified theory within the lifetime of some of us who are around today.[23]

He appreciates that we could not be *certain* that we had achieved our goal:

> But if the theory was mathematically consistent and always gave predictions that agreed with observations, we could be reasonably confident that it was the right one. It would bring to an end a long and glorious chapter in the history of humanity's intellectual struggle to understand the universe.[24]

I fear that Hawking's confidence is misplaced; not only because the evidence of the past gives greater grounds for pessimism than he is prepared to acknowledge but also because it still remains an open question as to whether the laws of nature are or are not *human* constructions which we must make in order to make sense of our experiences and to establish ourselves in the world. But what he does clearly reveal is the necessity for metaphysics and possibly religious belief for science to be possible. His exposition shows that the basic metaphysical assumptions of Aristotle, the medieval Schoolmen, the founders of classical science (Descartes and Newton) and the founder of modern science (Einstein) are still with us. The assumption is that there is an objective order, perhaps an order divinely ordained, and that humanity is capable of *discovering* that order and of arriving at ultimate truth.

My arguments to support the view that there is an esssential metaphysical underpinning for science have been based on appeal to the practices and ideas of natural philosophers and scientists, but we may also find support from a philosophical consideration of the role of art as well as science in helping us to understand the world. In his book *The Element of Fire* Anthony O'Hear contends that the arts contribute to our understanding in a most important way and that our non-scientific response to sense perception is not necessarily misleading and certainly not false:

> something which belongs, and necessarily belongs, to the way in which certain sentient beings perceive some physical reality, surely has for that very reason a perfectly good title to be thought of as part of what the world is really like.[25]

He claims that the objective viewpoint of science:

> in which reference to human perspectives, types of perception and concern is intentionally eliminated[26]

is itself an abstract conception, and indeed rather more abstract and removed from 'reality' than the common-sense appearances of things. We can sympathize with this view if we reflect on our own reactions to the account of the 'reality' offered by the modern (post-Einsteinian) scientists such as Hawking. Thus O'Hear says:

> We are fast coming to the conclusion that the scientific image of the world is not an image at all; it is not something that a perceiving consciousness such as ours could experience, or even imagine, if by imagine one means construct a visual image of; this thought is reinforced further if we include as part of the scientific image, as many would, the idea that the passing of time itself is simply an aspect of the observer's experience, and that if we looked at the world with total scientific objectivity, we would see it as a four-dimensional block, a relativistic space-time manifold, with temporal relationships as dependent on spatial ones, and we ourselves as space-time worms embedded in it like fossils.[27]

O'Hear argues that a full picture of what the world is like must take into account the way we see it and the very secondary qualities and subjective experiences that science has sought to eliminate. He refers to Schiller's view that the role of art is to find form in the formlessness of nature[28] and he suggests that art, unlike science, 'is intimately involved in our sense of the value of things'.[29]

He thinks that, despite its tendency to present an objective account of the world and an objective explanation of events, science must inevitably be constrained by the fact that it is a human endeavour:

> But science itself is a human practice, one practice among others. Examination of its theories and methods does not support the view that scientific knowledge is specially privileged or free from unprovable and mythological elements.[30]

Although I do not think that scientific inquiry will ever attain knowledge of ultimate truths, even truths that are necessarily restricted by the human condition, I do not argue that science is based on myth in the sense of superstition – though it does not of course follow that individual scientists are not inevitably affected by non-rational beliefs. For though science itself is practised by human beings it is fair to say that there is at least the intention of eliminating personal superstitions. But I do agree with O'Hear that there are and must be unprovable elements in science, though I would call these 'metaphysical' rather than 'mythological'. I do not think that religious belief is itself an essential feature of scientific inquiry and there are good grounds for believing that various branches of the Christian Church have interfered with progress. However, insofar as belief in order in nature and in the human capacity to have knowledge of the world is linked to religion, religion may be said to have played an important part in our search for understanding and the possibility that it is necessary to scientific inquiry cannot be dismissed out of hand.

Notes

Preface: what is metaphysics?

1 Karl R. Popper, *Conjectures and Refutations*, Routledge & Kegan Paul, London, 1969, p. 256.
2 ibid., p. 115.
3 See p. 32.
4 See p. 95.
5 Bertrand Russell, *The Problems of Philosophy*, Oxford University Press, Oxford, 1978, p. 11.
6 See p. 173.
7 William Whewell, quoted in *Theories of Scientific Method*, ed. E. H. Madden, University of Washington Press, London and Seattle, 1966, pp. 185–6.
8 ibid., p. 188.
9 This is based on Kant's exposition of the role of *a priori* concepts. 'Experience rests on a synthesis according to the concepts of an object of appearances in general. Apart from such a synthesis it would not be knowledge but a rhapsody of perceptions.' *Critique of Pure Reason*, ed. and trans. N. Kemp Smith, Macmillan, London, 1929, p. 193. See also p. 122 of this volume.
10 David Hume, *Enquiries Concerning the Human Understanding and Concerning the Principals of Morals*, ed. L. A. Selby-Bigge, Clarendon Press, Oxford, 1970, section XII, part III, p. 165.
11 L. P. Hartley, *The Go-Between*, Penguin Books, Harmondsworth, 1958, Prologue, p. 7.

1 The ordered cosmos

1 Quoted by David C. Lindberg, 'Science and the early Church', in *God and Nature*, ed. D. C. Lindberg and R. L. Numbers, University of California Press, Berkeley, Los Angeles, London, 1986, p. 34.
2 ibid., p. 31
3 Edward Grant, 'Science and theology in the Middle Ages', in Lindberg and Numbers, p. 50.
4 Amos Funkenstein, *Theology and the Scientific Imagination*, Princeton University Press, Princeton, 1986, p. 358.
5 Lindberg, op. cit., p. 21

6 Quoted by G. Holton and D. Roller in *The Foundations of Modern Physical Science*, Addison-Wesley, Reading, Mass., 1958, p. 160.
7 Quoted by S. F. Mason, in *A History of Science*, Routledge & Kegan Paul, London, 1953, p. 174.
8 Lindberg, op. cit., p. 36
9 The coin falls faster than the feather through air; but a familiar school demonstration shows that they fall at the same rate in an evacuated tube. Neither Aristotle nor the Schoolmen were able to observe this for there were no vacuum pumps until the seventeeth century.
10 In fact Aristotle's cosmology is very different from that of Genesis but the Church had conceded that the earth was spherical rather than flat; this Biblical description was not taken literally.
11 John Dryden, 'A Song for Saint Cecilia's Day', 1687.
12 William Shakespeare, *The Merchant of Venice*, Act V, sc. i.
13 Most modern Christian Fundamentalists are not scientists but there are a few who claim to be, and who take the Genesis story of the origins of Man as factual and as providing a scientific explanation of our presence on earth.
14 In the future our present theories of matter and energy may seem as bizarre and vague as Aristotle's account of matter and form seems to us now.
15 Dante Alighieri, *The Divine Comedy*, 'Paradiso', Canto 29, trans. Kenneth Mackenzie.
16 There was confidence 'that a personal, rational, and provident Being, absolute and eternal, is the ultimate source of intelligibility insofar as he is the Creator of all things visible and invisible. Conviction it was and not merely an intellectual fashion.'
17 Stanley L. Jaki, *The Road of Science and the Ways to God*, Scottish Academic Press, Edinburgh and University of Chicago Press, Chicago, 1978, p. 34.

2 Old beliefs and new ideas

1 Amos Funkenstein, *Theology and the Scientific Imagination*, Princeton University Press, Princeton, New Jersey, 1986, p. 170.
2 ibid., p. 62. See also Newton's account of absolute space on p. 99.
3 ibid., footnote 18.
4 The Church also had little patience with those who made use of astrology to avoid duties. Writing to the Duke of Modena in 1459, Aeneas Sylvius (Pope Pius II) rebuked him for his excuse in failing to respond to a papal summons to a Congress at Mantua. In the quotation below Pius II refers to himself as the pope:

> When however he was actually summoned, he wrote that *he would come in a few days. When summoned yet again he had changed his mind and refused, giving as an excuse the evidence of astrologers, who said that the stars foretold his death if he went to Mantua. The Pope rebuked him for heeding pagan nonsense and for saying that he could know the future by inspection of the stars and he accused him of inventing all this to avoid coming to the Congress.*
> Aeneas Sylvius, *Secret Memoirs of a Renaissance Pope*, ed, L. C. Gabel, trans. F. A. Gragg, Folio Society, London, 1988, p. 126.

5 William Shakespeare, *Julius Caesar*, Act II, sc. ii.

In *King Lear*, (1606) the villain, Edmund, is portrayed as *not* believing in astrology, whereas his father the Earl of Gloucester does:

> *Glouc.* These late eclipses in the sun and moon portend no good to us: though the wisdom of nature can reason it thus and thus, yet nature finds itself scourged by the sequent effects: . . .
> *Edm.* This is the excellent foppery of the world, that when we are sick in fortune – often the surfeit of our own behaviour – we make guilty of our disasters the sun, the moon and the stars: . . . My father compounded with my mother under the dragon's tail and my nativity was under Ursa major; so that it follows I am rough and lecherous. Tut, I should have been that I am, had the maidenliest star in the firmament twinkled on my bastardizing.

> *King Lear*, Act I, sc. ii

6 See Ben Jonson's *The Alchemist*, published in 1610.
7 The new calendar was introduced by Pope Gregory XIII (1502–85) in 1582.
8 For example, earlier in this century it was held that electrons were confined to certain orbits round an atomic nucleus, and yet the explanation of the occurrence of spectral lines appealed to electrons passing from one orbit to another through the 'forbidden' zones.
9 Quoted by Robert S. Westman, 'The Copernicans and the Churches', in *God and Nature*, ed. D. C. Lindberg and R. L. Numbers, University of California Press, Berkeley, Los Angeles, London, 1986, p. 83.
10 ibid., p. 88.
11 ibid., p. 89.
12 Quoted by W. C. Dampier, *A History of Science and Its Relations with Philosophy and Religion*, Cambridge University Press, Cambridge, 1974, p. 120.
13 Quoted by S. F. Mason, *A History of the Sciences*, Routledge & Kegan Paul, London, 1953, p. 102.
14 Guillaume de Bartas, quoted by M. Boas, *The Scientific Renaissance 1450–1630*, Collins, London, 1962, p. 102.
15 There were no telescopes in the sixteenth century but parallax could not be observed with seventeenth- or eighteenth-century telescopes; it was not detected until 1838.
16 Quoted by R. Hooykaas, *The Conflict Thesis and Cosmology*, AMST 283, Units 1–3, Open University Press, Milton Keynes, 1974, p. 61.
17 By most astronomers at the time; see p. 25, and note 9.
18 Quoted by M. Boas, op. cit., p. 126.
19 See reference to Reinhold, p. 25, and also Westman, op. cit., pp. 87–9.

3 Chaos

1 In fact they were the work of several authors who had lived in the second and third centuries AD.
2 Frances Yates suggests that this was because Cosimo de Medici was anxious to read the *Corpus Hermeticum* before his death. (He could not read the original Greek.) Ficino started work in 1463 and completed the translation in a few months. See Frances A. Yates, *Giordano Bruno and the Hermetic Tradition*, Routledge & Kegan Paul, London, 1964, p. 13.

3 It will be remembered that the Bible story (Exodus, Chapter 2) tells of Pharaoh's daughter finding the infant Moses.

4 See p. 20.

5 *Encyclopaedia Britannica*, 15th edn, Micropaedia, vol. I, William Benton, Chicago, London, etc., 1943–73, p. 223.

6 Quoted by Yates, op. cit., p. 36 from *Corpus Hermeticum*, vol. II, ed. A. D. Nock, trans. A.-J. Festigière, Paris, 1945 and 1954, p. 319.

7 Quoted by Marie Boas in *The Scientific Renaissance 1450–1630*, Collins, London, 1962, p. 81, from *On the Revolutions of the Celestial Orbs*, ed. J. F. Dobson and Selig Brodetsky, *Occasional Notes*, Royal Astronomical Society, no. 10, 1947.

8 Quoted by Yates, op. cit., p. 236, from Giordano Bruno, *Dialoghi Italiani*, 3rd edn, Florence, 1957, p. 28.

9 Yates, op. cit., p. 208.

10 ibid., p. 356.

11 ibid., p. 415.

12 ibid., p. 450.

13 ibid., p. 361.

14 ibid., p. 451.

15 A pupil of Dee's, and the son of Leonard Digges (see pp. 21–2). See also 'A Perfect Description of the Celestial Orbs', in M. B. Hall (formerly Marie Boas), *Nature and Nature's Laws*, Macmillan, London, 1970, pp. 20–34.

16 Quoted by Boas, op. cit., p. 108.

17 ibid.

18 For Tycho Brahe's own account see Hall, op. cit., pp. 58–66.

19 Yates, op. cit., p. 151.

20 ibid., p. 442.

21 Johannes Kepler, *Mysterium Cosmographicum* (Tübingen, 1596), from Werner Heisenberg, *The Physicist's Conception of Nature*, trans. A. J. Pomerans, London, 1958, pp. 73–4. (This and the following extracts are also reprinted in *Science and Religious Belief 1600–1900*, ed. D. C. Goodman, Open University Press, Milton Keynes, 1973.)

22 ibid., p. 79.

23 ibid., p. 83.

24 R. S. Westfall, 'The rise of science and the decline of orthodox christianity: a study of Kepler, Descartes and Newton', in *God and Nature*, ed. D. C. Lindberg and R. L. Numbers, University of California Press, Berkeley, Los Angeles, London, 1986, p. 221.

25 ibid., pp. 223–4.

26 Johannes Kepler, *Gesammelte Werke*, 1616, trans. W. Paulin, *The Interpretation of Nature and the Psyche*, quoted by Westfall, op. cit., p. 223.

27 Westfall, op. cit., p. 221.

28 Of course Galileo did not think that the sun had a circular orbit but he did believe that it rotated on its own axis.

29 William R. Shea, 'Galileo and the Church', in *God and Nature*, p. 123.

30 Galileo Galilei, *Dialogue Concerning the Two Chief World Systems*, trans. Stillman Drake, University of California Press, Berkeley, 1970, pp. 18–19.

31 ibid., p. 19.

32 ibid., p. 20.

33 ibid., p. 21.

34 Quoted by Arthur Koestler in *The Sleepwalkers: A History of Man's Changing Vision of the Universe*, Hutchinson, London, 1961, p. 356.
35 *Discoveries and Opinions of Galileo*, ed. Stillman Drake, Doubleday, New York, 1957, pp. 276–7.
36 ibid.
37 ibid., pp. 255–6.
38 ibid., p. 197.
39 Edwin Arthur Burtt, *The Metaphysical Foundations of Modern Physical Science*, Routledge & Kegan Paul, London, 1949, p. 77.
40 It was not detected until the nineteenth century, see Chapter 2, note 15.
41 *Discoveries and Opinions of Galileo*, pp. 182–3.
42 ibid., p. 186.
43 R. S. Westman, 'The Copernicans and the Churches', in *God and Nature*, p. 101.
44 ibid., p. 89.
45 Richard Rorty, *Philosophy and the Mirror of Nature*, Blackwell, Oxford, 1980, pp. 330–1.
46 Alexander Koyré, *Metaphysics and Measurements*, Chapman and Hall, London, 1968, pp. 19–20.
47 John Donne (1573–1632), 'The First Anniversary', lines 205–19.

4 The search for a new order

1 Developments in the twentieth century have led to some modification of this view for we have begun to appreciate that the relatively simple mechanical models of classical physics are inadequate. There will be discussion in Chapters 9 and 10. However it still remains the case that even in modern science explanations are sought in terms of physical laws.
2 Edwin A. Burtt, *The Metaphysical Foundations of Modern Physical Science*, Routledge & Kegan Paul, 1949, p. 83.
3 ibid., p. 85.
4 With some notable exceptions; for example Spinoza and Leibniz both thought that human actions were determined.
5 Burtt, op. cit., p. 96.
6 ibid., pp. 92–3.
7 Not for Newton; see p. 101.
8 Étienne Gilson, *Études sur le rôle de la pensée médiévale dans la formation du Système Cartésien*, Paris, Librairie Philosophique J. Vrin, 1951, p. 9.
9 ibid., pp. 105–7.
10 ibid., p. 107.
11 ibid., p. 126.
12 Richard H. Popkin, *The History of Scepticism from Erasmus to Spinoza*, University of California Press, Berkeley, Los Angeles, London, 1979, especially Chapter 9.
13 Francis A. Yates, *Giordano Bruno and the Hermetic Tradition*, Routledge & Kegan Paul, London, 1964, p. 452.
14 *Descartes: Œuvres Philosophiques*, ed. Ferdinand Alquie, Garnier Frères, Paris, 1963, pp. 52–9. (Précis in English; Marie-Therèse Crowle and Jennifer Trusted.)

15 René Descartes, *Philosophical Writings*, ed. E. Anscombe and P. Geach, Nelson, London, 1970, p. 4.
16 ibid., p. 21.
17 ibid., p. 199.
18 Burtt, op. cit., p. 101.
19 Anscombe and Geach, op. cit., p. 75.
20 *The Essential Descartes*, ed. M. D. Wilson, Meridian, New American Library, New York, 1983, p. 232.
21 Anscombe and Geach, op. cit., p. 221.
22 Gilson, op. cit., p. 179.
23 Ralph M. Blake, 'The role of experience in Descartes' theory of method', in *Theories of Scientific Method*, ed. R. M. Blake, C. J. Ducasse and E. H. Madden, University of Washington Press, Seattle and London, 1966, pp. 79–89.
24 Amos Funkenstein, *Theology and the Scientific Imagination*, Princeton University Press, Princeton, New Jersey, 1986, p. 75.
25 Wilson, op, cit., p. 345.
26 Gerd Buchdahl, *Metaphysics and the Philosophy of Science*, Blackwell, Oxford, 1969, pp. 89–90.
27 Wilson, op. cit., p. 325.
28 Anscombe and Geach, op, cit., p. 69.
29 ibid., p. 39.
30 Stanley L. Jaki, *The Road of Science and the Ways to God*, Scottish Academic Press, Edinburgh, and University of Chicago Press, 1978, pp. 69–70.
31 Francis Bacon, *The Advancement of Learning and New Atlantis*, Oxford University Press, London, 1966, pp. 93, 121, 123.
32 Francis Bacon, *Novum Organum*, ed. T. Fowler, Clarendon Press, Oxford, 1889, vol. II, p. 40.
33 Bacon, *Advancement*, pp. 31–2.
34 ibid., p. 37.
35 ibid., pp. 117–18.
36 ibid., p. 119.
37 Bacon, *Novum Organum*, vol. I, p. 41.
38 ibid., p. 53.
39 ibid., p. 60.
40 ibid., p. 61.
41 ibid., p. 105.
42 *Novum Organum*, vol. II, p. 10.
43 ibid., p. 24.
44 ibid., p. 23.
45 ibid., p. 25.
46 ibid., p. 36.
47 ibid., p. 27.
48 ibid.
49 Bacon did not put the final 's' on 'physic' nor on 'metaphysic'; he also acknowledged that he used the term 'metaphysic' in a different sense from the commonly received one. See *Advancement*, pp. 106–7.
50 *Advancement*, p. 113.
51 ibid., p. 110.

52 ibid., p. 111.
53 ibid., p. 116.
54 ibid., p. 11.
55 ibid.
56 Jaki, op. cit., p. 53.
57 ibid., p. 54.
59 Bacon, *Advancement*, p. 42–3.

5 The grand design

1 We shall see that the empiricist Locke used the term 'scientific knowledge' in the same way. For all seventeenth-century philosophers scientific knowledge had to be indubitable knowledge.
2 Descartes's view was closer to that of Plato.
3 See below, p. 93.
4 John Locke, *An Essay Concerning Human Understanding*, IV, 12, 9.
5 ibid.
6 ibid., IV, 11, 9.
7 ibid., IV, 11, 10.
8 ibid., IV, 12, 10.
9 The corpuscles were held to be responsible for the primary and secondary qualities of macro-objects and materials (see quotations on p. 94) but this was a causal relation, not one of logic and therefore not logically deducible.
10 Many philosophers, for example Robert Boyle, thought that we could know something of God's purposes; Boyle explicitly rejected the Cartesian view. The Argument from Design, very common from the mid-seventeenth century into the nineteenth century, presupposes that there is at least partial knowledge of God's intentions.
11 However, many philosophers, and in particular Newton, believed that God not only could but did intervene.
12 It is true that Locke gives a 'nod' in this direction, op. cit., IV, 18, 4, but he rates the certainty of our 'clear and distinct perception of the agreement and disagreement of our *ideas*' as higher than what might be conveyed by '*traditional revelation*'.
13 In fact all material bodies have weight on earth, but bodies less dense than air tend to rise and in mid-seventeenth century they were thought of not as having weight (gravity) but as possessing a negative weight (levity).
14 R. Descartes, 'Principles of Philosophy, Part II', 26, in *Philosophical Writings*, ed. E. Anscombe and P. Geach, Nelson, London, 1971, p. 209.
15 ibid., p. 210.
16 ibid., 27, p. 210.
17 ibid., 36, p. 214.
18 ibid., 37, p. 216.
19 ibid., 39, p. 217.
20 ibid., 40, p. 218.
21 ibid., 43, p. 219.
22 G. W. Leibniz, 'Discourse on Metaphysics', in *Philosophical Writings*, ed. M. Morris and G. H. R. Parkinson, Dent, London, 1984, p. 30.
23 Quantity of motion, what we call 'momentum' is the product of mass and velocity. For Leibniz it was the product of weight and velocity.

24 Leibniz, op. cit., p. 31.
25 All Monads were able to perceive in the sense that they all passively reflected the world from their point of view, but apperception was a conscious perception and only some Monads had this capacity. See also note 28 below.
26 Leibniz, op. cit., p. 27.
27 ibid.
28 ibid., p. 26. To refer to 'outside us' when writing of the ultimate metaphysical and non-corporeal reality is inconsistent. In his book *A Critical Exposition of the Philosophy of Leibniz*, Allen & Unwin, London, 1975, Bertrand Russell argues (see especially Chapter X) that Leibniz's account of the Monads, their perceptions and apperceptions, illegitimately implies positions in space and spatial order. This is illegitimate since Leibniz denied the ultimate reality of space.
29 Leibniz, 'Correspondence with Clarke', op. cit., p. 211.
30 ibid., p. 212.
31 ibid., p. 211.
32 ibid., p. 212.
33 Leibniz, 'New System, and Explanation of the New System', op. cit., p. 124.
34 Leibniz, op. cit., p. 122.
35 Leibniz, 'Correspondence with Clarke', op. cit., pp. 205–6.
36 Amos Funkenstein, *Theology and the Scientific Imagination*, Princeton University Press, Princeton, New Jersey, 1986, p. 201.
37 Leibniz, 'New System and Explanation of the New System', op. cit., p. 116.
38 Leibniz called this primitive force 'first entelechy' and it was in some respects analogous to soul. He made no dynamical use of it but it underlay his concept of force (energy) that is central to the physics of his phenomenal world.
39 It is possible that Newton did not formulate his laws as early as he claimed. See Stephen F. Mason, *A History of the Sciences*, Routledge & Kegan Paul, London, 1953, p. 157.
40 That is, the attractive force *decreases* as the square of the distance *increases*. For example, if the distance is doubled the attractive force is quartered.
41 'Classical physics' is perhaps a better term to use today.
42 Locke, op, cit., II, 8, 9.
43 ibid.
44 The corpuscles were not indivisible in principle; the seventeenth-century corpuscular theory was not an atomic theory. Their corpuscles were closer to the modern conception of molecules. See also note 9.
45 Funkenstein, op. cit., p. 91.
46 Here 'acceleration' signifies change of velocity, that is an increase in speed, a decrease in speed, and/or a change from the straight-line path.
47 For accurate calculations allowance must be made for the fact that the attractive force on a falling body increases as it approaches the earth since the distance between it and the centre of the earth steadily becomes less. There are occasions when this can have important implications outside science. For example when the Olympic Games were played at Mexico City (higher than most sites and therefore further from the centre of the

earth), the attractive force was less than at sea level and so all competing athletes would weigh less than at other venues. Hence less effort was needed to run and jump and it was easier to break earlier Olympic records established elsewhere.

48 Not quite of course; see note 47.
49 Units have been chosen so as to eliminate the constant of proportionality.
50 Alexander Koyré, *Metaphysics and Measurement*, trans. R. E. W. Madison, Chapman and Hall, London, 1968, p. 96.
51 Alexander Koyré, *Newtonian Studies*, Chapman and Hall, London, 1965, p. 105; quotation from Newton's *Scholium* etc., p. 6.
52 ibid., p. 106; quotation from Newton's *Principia* (1687), p. 7.
53 ibid., p. 103; quotation from Newton's *Principia* (1687), *Scholium to Definitiones*, p. 5.
54 ibid., p. 104; quotation from *Scholium* etc., p. 7.
55 Funkenstein, op. cit., pp. 96–7.
56 Koyré, *Newtonian Studies*, p. 108; quotation from Newton's *Optice* (1706), p. 310.
57 ibid.; quotation from Newton's *Optice*, p. 313.
58 ibid., pp. 93–4; quotation from Newton's unpublished scientific papers.
59 Gary B. Dawson, 'Reformation theology and the mechanistic conception of nature', in *God and Nature*, ed. D. C. Lindberg and R. L. Numbers, University of California Press, Berkeley, Los Angeles, London, 1986, p. 187.
60 Funkenstein, op. cit., p. 116.
61 Had he lived in the sixteenth century Newton would have been thought as great a heretic as Bruno.
62 See quotation on pp. 105–6.
63 Funkenstein, op. cit., p. 191.
64 I. Newton, letter to Richard Bentley, December, 1692; see *Science and Religious Belief*, ed. D. C. Goodman, Open University Press, Milton Keynes, 1973, p. 134.
65 cf. Leibniz's view; as the first quotation on p. 91 shows, Leibniz thought that Newton underrated God.
66 R. S. Westfall, 'The rise of science and the decline of orthodox Christianity: a study of Kepler, Descartes and Newton', in *God and Nature*, p. 232.
67 ibid., p. 235.
68 Edwin A. Burtt, *The Metaphysical Foundations of Modern Physical Science*, London, Routledge & Kegan Paul, 1949, pp. 236–7.
69 Joseph Addison, 'Ode', 1712; the poem is an adaptation of the first part of Psalm 19.

6 The age of reason

1 The 'test' required by the Test Acts was to receive Holy Communion according to the rites of the Church of England. The first Act (1661) applied to those seeking to be members of a town corporation; the second Act (1663) required compliance by those wishing to go to university or seeking to hold any public office.
2 Robert K. Merton, 'Puritanism, pietism and science', *Social Theory and*

Social Structure, New York, Free Press of Glencoe, 1957, pp. 574–606. First published in *Sociological Review*, January, 1936.

3 R. Hooykaas, *Religion and the Rise of Modern Science*, Scottish Academic Press, Edinburgh and London, 1973, p. 143.
4 Thomas Paine, *The Age of Reason*, Pioneer Press, London, 1937, p. 20.
5 ibid., pp. 21–2.
6 ibid., p. 23.
7 ibid.
8 John Locke, *An Essay Concerning Human Understanding*, IV, 18, 9.
9 John Kempthorn (1775–1838), *Hymns of Praise*, 1796.
10 Stephen Mason, *A History of the Sciences*, Routledge & Kegan Paul, London, 1953, p. 235.
11 Spinoza used the personal pronoun and I have therefore kept to this, though it would have been more compatible with his exposition of the nature of God to have referred to 'it', 'its' and 'itself'.
12 Benedict Spinoza, *The Ethics*, part I, Definition I.
13 ibid., Definition III.
14 ibid., Proposition XXV, Corollary.
15 ibid., part II, Proposition VII and Corollary.
16 In the light of Hume's analysis (see later this chapter) Spinoza's account can be disputed; but there is little doubt that Spinoza regarded causal laws as embodying *necessary* connections. We cannot surmise what he would have concluded had he lived 100 years later and had read Hume.
17 Spinoza, op. cit., part I, Proposition XXXII, Corollary II, and Proposition XXXIII and Note I.
18 Thus, like Descartes, Spinoza thought that we could *know* that we knew, see *Ethics*, part II, Proposition XLIII and the exposition on grades of knowledge in *On the Improvement of the Understanding*.
19 E. A. Gellner, 'French eighteenth-century materialism', in *A Critical History of Western Philosophy*, ed. D. J. O'Connor, Free Press, Macmillan, New York, and Collier-Macmillan, London, 1964, p. 279.
20 ibid., p. 285.
21 Paul Heinrich Dietrich von Holbach, *The System of Nature*, trans. Samuel Wilkinson, London, 1820–1, vol. i, p. 20.
22 ibid., p. 23.
23 ibid., p. 25.
24 ibid., p. 21.
25 ibid., pp. 30–1.
26 ibid., pp. 23–4.
27 ibid., p. 27.
28 Gellner, op. cit., p. 286.
29 ibid.
30 ibid., p. 285.
31 Locke, op. cit., II, 13, 16.
32 Julien Offray de la Mettrie, *Man a Machine*, trans. Gertrude C. Bussey *et al.*, Open Court, La Salle, Ill., 1912, p. 93.
33 ibid., p. 94.
34 ibid., p. 95
35 ibid., p. 122.
36 See fourth quotation on p. 82.

37 George Berkeley, 'Of the Principles of Human Knowledge', XXXI, pp. 127–8, from *A New Theory of Vision and Other Writings*, Dent, London, 1969.
38 Lewis Carroll makes gentle fun of logical possibilities in Alice's encounter with the White Knight in Chapter 8 of *Through the Looking Glass*. For example:
   'I was wondering what the mouse trap was for,' said Alice. 'It isn't very likely there would be any mice on a horse's back.'
   'Not very likely, perhaps,' said the Knight; 'but if they *do* come, I don't choose to have them running all about.'
39 David Hume, *Enquiries Concerning the Human Understanding and Concerning the Principles of Morals*, ed. L. A. Selby-Bigge, Clarendon Press Oxford, 2nd edn, 1970, section IV, part I, pp. 25–6.
40 For example, Joseph Priestley, the eminent chemist who discovered oxygen. See *Letters to a Philosophical Unbeliever*, Bath, 1780, pp. 105–25.
41 Hume, op. cit., section XII, part III, p. 165.
42 Immanuel Kant, *Critique of Pure Reason*, ed. and trans. N. Kemp-Smith, Macmillan, London, 1929, p. 193.
43 See Jennifer Trusted, *Inquiry and Understanding*, Macmillan, London, 1987, pp. 16–18.
44 Kant, op. cit., p. 22
45 Kant, *Prolegomena*, trans. P. G. Lucas, Manchester University Press, Manchester, 1971, pp. 77–8.
46 Kant, *Critique*, p. 93.
47 Kant, *Prolegomena*, p. 31.
48 Geoffrey J. Warnock, 'Kant', in *A Critical History of Western Philosophy*, p. 301.
49 William Wordsworth, *The Prelude*, Book xiv, lines 190–3.
50 William Blake, 'Auguries of Innocence', lines 1–4.

7 The age of experience

1 John Locke, *An Essay Concerning Human Understanding*, IV, 12, 10; see also p. 82 and quotations.
2 Watts, *Logic*, II, ii, para. 9, cited in *The Compact Oxford English Dictionary*, Oxford University Press, Oxford, 1971, p. 2668.
3 W. G. Ward, *Dublin Review*, April, 255, note, cited in *The Compact Oxford English Dictionary*, ibid.
4 William Whewell, *The Philosophy of the Inductive Sciences*, vol. I, John Parker, London, 1840, Aphorisms II and III, p. xvii.
5 ibid., Aphorism VII, p. xviii.
6 See p. 122.
7 Whewell, op. cit., pp. 158–9.
8 ibid., p. 159.
9 ibid., p. 390.
10 Whewell, op. cit., vol. II, p. 215.
11 ibid., pp. 217–19.
12 John Stuart Mill, *A System of Logic*, 9th edn, Longmans, Green, Reader, & Dyer, London, 1875, vol. I, p. 348.
13 ibid., p. 374.

14 ibid.
15 ibid., p. 377.
16 ibid., pp. 377–8.
17 See p. 76.
18 Mill op. cit., vol. II, p. 117.
19 ibid., p. 122.
20 Auguste Comte, *A General View of Positivism*, trans. J. H. Bridges, Robert Speller & Sons, New York, 1957, p. 64.
21 ibid., p. 3.
22 John Stuart Mill, *Auguste Comte and Positivism*, Trubner, London, 1865, p. 9.
23 Comte op. cit., pp. 11–12.
24 ibid., pp. 35–6.
25 ibid., pp. 37–8.
26 David Hume, *Enquiries Concerning the Human Understanding and Concerning the Principles of Morals*, ed. L. A. Selby-Bigge, Clarendon Press, Oxford, 2nd edn, 1970, section XII, part III, p. 165; see also Chapter 6, p. 121 and quotation.
27 Comte, op. cit., p. 50
28 Mill, *Comte*, pp. 57–8.
29 Comte, op. cit., p. 120.
30 ibid., p. 364.
31 ibid., p. 365.
32 ibid., p. 367.
33 ibid., p. 368.
34 Maurice Mandelbaum, 'Philosophic movements in the nineteenth century', in *Darwin to Einstein, Historical Studies on Science and Belief*, ed. C. Chant and J. Fauvel, Open University Press, Milton Keynes, 1980, pp. 8–9. Taken from Maurice Mandelbaum, *History, Man and Reason: A Study in Nineteenth-Century Thought*, Baltimore, Johns Hopkins Press, 1971, Chapter 1.
35 op. cit., p. 10.
36 See p. 94 and quotations.
37 Locke, op. cit., II, 23, 2.
38 See quotation on pp. 129–30.
39 John Stuart Mill, *Philosophy of Scientific Method*, ed. E. Nagel, Hafner, New York, 1950, p. 45.
40 ibid.
41 ibid., pp. 371–2.
42 Ernst Mach, 'The Economical Nature of Physical Inquiry', trans. T. J. McCormack, in *The Philosophy of Science*, ed. J. J. Kockelmans, Free Press, New York, Collier-Macmillan, London, 1968, p. 181.
43 A. J. Ayer, *Language, Truth and Logic*, Gollancz, London, 1970, p. 42.
44 A. J. Ayer, *The Problem of Knowledge*, Penguin Books, Harmondsworth, 1956, p. 119.
45 ibid., p. 129.
46 Mandelbaum, op. cit., p. 13.
47 ibid., p. 13–14.
48 Mach, op. cit., p. 182.
49 ibid., p. 185.

50 ibid., p. 177.
51 ibid., p. 178.
52 Mandelbaum, op. cit., pp. 16–17.

8 Problems: energy and ether

1 Newton also believed that heat was a form of motion but, surprisingly perhaps (considering that his views on the nature of light predominated) his opinion was disregarded.
2 J. P. Joule, 'On the calorific effects of magneto-electricity, and on the mechanical value of heat', *Philosophical Magazine*, 3rd series, 1843, vol. 23, pp. 263–76.
3 J. P. Joule, 'On matter, living force and heat', lecture 147, in *The Scientific Papers of James Prescott Joule*, London, 1884, p. 268.
4 This was his final figure. Kelvin made several estimates as to the age of the earth and used calculations based on the retardation of the diurnal rotation by the tides as well as considering heat loss.
5 Quoted by A. Koyré, *Newtonian Studies*, Chapman and Hall, London, 1965, p. 103, from Newton's *Principia* (1687), *Scholium to Definitiones*, p. 5. See also Chapter 5 of this volume.
6 Quoted by S. Mason, *A History of Science*, Routledge & Kegan Paul, London, 1953, p. 162.
7 Koyré, op. cit., p. 108. See also Chapter 5 of this volume.
8 J. W. von Goethe, *Theory of Colours*, trans. C. L. Eastlake, MIT Press, Cambridge, Mass., 1970. This is taken from Eastlake's translation published by John Murray, London, 1870.
9 See Chapter 3.
10 See Chapter 2.
11 Quoted by Mason, op cit., p. 288.
12 Quoted by E. Whittaker, *A History of the Theories of Aether and Electricity*, Nelson, London, 1951, p. 194.
13 See also Chapter 9.
14 Quoted by K. F. Schaffner, *Nineteenth Century Aether Theories*, Pergamon Press, New York, 1972, p. 81.
15 Quoted by Schaffner, op. cit., p. 90.
16 Quoted by Schaffner, op. cit., p. 101.
17 Quoted by Schaffner, op. cit., p. 94.
18 ibid.
19 Quoted by Schaffner, op. cit., p.115.
20 James R. Moore, 'Communication', in *Science, Technology and Everyday Life 1870–1950*, ed. Colin Chant, Routledge, London and New York, 1989, p. 233.
21 A. R. Wallace, 'Spiritualism', *Chambers Encyclopaedia*, 1892, p. 645.
22 Matter can exist in three states: solid, liquid and gas; for example ice, water and steam. The state depends on the proximity of the constituent molecules: closely packed in solids, less so in liquids and relatively far apart in gases. Those who took the ether to be a fourth state of matter envisaged an even greater separation of the molecules.
23 O. Lodge, 'The ether and its functions', *Nature*, XXVII, 1883, p. 304.
24 ibid., p. 330.

9 Revolution

1 There were important exceptions among the older generation; Poincaré, Lorentz, Planck and Michelson all had reservations. (See later this chapter, *re* Michelson and Lorentz.)
2 See p. 124
3 The velocity of a non-inertial system is not constant.
4 W. G. V. Rosser, *An Introduction to the Theory of Relativity*, Butterworth, London, 1964, p. 69.
5 ibid. See third quotation on p. 157.
6 J. Stachel, 'Einstein and ether drift experiments', *Physics Today*, May 1987, p. 45.
7 Gerald Holton, 'A student's guide to Einstein's paper "On the Electrodynamics of Moving Bodies" (1905)', unpublished.
8 ibid., p. 45–6.
9 ibid., p. 47.
10 ibid., p. 92.
11 ibid., p. 93.
12 Ferrel Christensen, 'Special relativity and space-like time', *The British Journal for the Philosophy of Science*, 32, 1, 1981, p. 39.
13 ibid., p. 41.
14 ibid., p. 41–2.
15 ibid., p. 42–3.
16 Alexander Pope, 'Epitaph. Intended for Sir Isaac Newton'.
17 Sir John Collings Squire, 'Answer to Pope's epitaph for Sir Isaac Newton'.

10 Physics and metaphysics

1 A. Einstein, 'Remarks concerning the essays brought together in this co-operative volume', in *Albert Einstein: philosopher-scientist*, ed. P. A. Schilpp, Evanston, Ill., Library of Living Philosophers, 1949, p. 671.
2 A. Einstein – letter to Besso, 28 August 1918. Quoted by Gerald Holton in *Thematic Origins of Scientific Thought, Kepler to Einstein*, Harvard University Press, Cambridge, Mass., 1973, p. 220.
3 ibid., p. 229.
4 ibid.
5 ibid.
6 Jennifer Trusted, *Inquiry and Understanding*, Macmillan, London, 1987, Chapter 4.
7 Holton, ibid., p. 233
8 A. Einstein, *On the Method of Theoretical Physics*, The Herbert Spencer Memorial Lecture, 1933; also in *Darwin to Einstein, Primary Sources on Science & Belief*, ed. N. Coley and V. M. D. Hall, Longman, with the Open University Press, Harlow and Milton Keynes, 1980, p. 144.
9 ibid., p. 145
10 ibid.
11 ibid.
12 ibid.
13 Holton, ibid., p. 234
14 ibid., p. 236.
15 ibid., p. 236–7.

16 Stephen W. Hawking, *A Brief History of Time*, Bantam Press, London, New York, Toronto, Sydney, Auckland, 1988, p. 10.
17 op. cit., p. 122.
18 ibid., pp. 140–1.
19 ibid., p. 156.
20 ibid.
21 ibid., p. 166.
22 ibid.
23 ibid., p. 167.
24 ibid.
25 Anthony O'Hear, *The Element of Fire*, Routledge, London, 1988, p. 9.
26 ibid., p. 8.
27 ibid., p. 12.
28 ibid., p. 150.
29 ibid., p. 162.
30 ibid.

Index